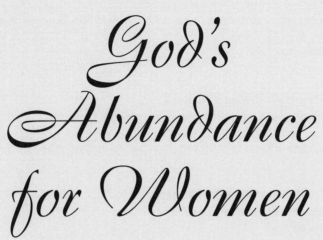

God's Abundance for Women

Devotions for a More Meaningful Life

EDITED BY

Kathy Collard Miller

STARBURST PUBLISHERS

P.O. Box 4123, Lancaster, Pennsylvania 17604

To schedule author appearances, write: Author Appearances, Starburst Promotions, P.O. Box 4123, Lancaster, Pennsylvania 17604 or call (717) 293-0939. Website: www.starburstpublishers.com.

CREDITS:
Cover design by Richmond & Williams
Text design and composition by John Reinhardt Book Design

All scripture was taken from the New International Version unless otherwise indicated.

GOD'S ABUNDANCE FOR WOMEN

First Printing, August, 1999

ISBN 1-892016-15-X
Library of Congress Catalog Number: 99-63788
Printed in the United States of America

To Carolyn Phillips, my writing mentor.

Contents

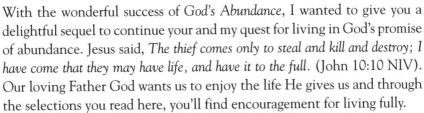

Introduction

With the wonderful success of *God's Abundance*, I wanted to give you a delightful sequel to continue your and my quest for living in God's promise of abundance. Jesus said, *The thief comes only to steal and kill and destroy; I have come that they may have life, and have it to the full.* (John 10:10 NIV). Our loving Father God wants us to enjoy the life He gives us and through the selections you read here, you'll find encouragement for living fully.

Through each piece in this book, you'll be inspired to love your family more heartily, notice God's little gifts in daily life, seek your Lord with greater passion, and develop your character with more contentment, self-lessness and self control. With each day's thought-provoking quote, motivating tip and God-breathed Scripture, you'll begin or end your day with thoughts of God for energized living.

I know you'll enjoy every page because I was thoroughly blessed by the selections as I read them. At times, I laughed. Other times, I cried. But always I was reminded that God loves us and wants to be included in each and every part of our lives, whether it's parenting, marriage, friendships, the holidays, or work or play. Every area of life is full of His touch if we'll but let Him be Lord and Master.

If you enjoyed *God's Abundance*, you'll find a slightly different format for arranging the selections in *God's Abundance for Women*. There are four sections based on the four seasons of the year. Although every selection in each season won't refer to that season, you'll find many that do. Also, I put the selections about the Christmas holidays into the Fall section, so that you can find them toward the end of the book.

Whether you read one selection each day or can't get enough and read more, I know your heart will be drawn closer to our wonderful God.

It's a delight for me to make this available to you. Enjoy!

Kathy Collard Miller

Spring

pring is famous for its message of fresh life as we watch the flowers bloom and unthaw from a long Winter. As Winter's cold blast ends, and the green earth is restored, each of us can enjoy God's abundance, knowing His love never ends.

Just as the bulbs, which have lain silent, again burst into blossom, you and I can be ever confident of God's work in our lives, even after a season of quiet. God may be silent at times, but He never stops working. We are truly and abundantly blessed when, by faith, we trust that God is working everything for our good.

Beauty And Courage
In Unexpected Places

FREDA FULLERTON

Courage is one white flower in a fire-swept land.

Helen Frazer Brown

I love black-eyed susans for the beauty they spread in unexpected places. You may find them in a vacant lot that has trash scattered about. You may find them in a ditch beside a road, growing among other nameless weeds. I smile when I see them, thinking of the courage it takes to spread beauty in such a hostile environment.

You may have seen small flowers like black-eyed susans growing up through ashes in a fire-ravaged forest or tender green shoots springing up amid the devastation of a lava flow. Such flowers demonstrate beauty and courage in unexpected places. That's why I wrote the following poem to celebrate such qualities.

BLACK-EYED SUSAN

> *I'd rather be a black-eyed susan*
> *Growing wild and free*
> *Than to be a hybrid rose,*
> *With palace walls surrounding me.*
>
> *I'd rather grow out in a meadow*
> *Where God's nature doth abound,*
> *Than to be all pruned and pampered*
> *In a city or a town.*
>
> *I'd choose wide open spaces,*
> *With blue skies overhead,*

Sunshine in the morning
And soft clover for a bed.

I'd never grace a crystal vase
On a table fair,
But I would brighten up the day
For the weary traveler.

When I drive out in the country
I'd surely like to see,
Those lovely black-eyed susans,
The flower I'd like to be.

The courage of black-eyed susans also reminds me of Jesus' death. Golgotha was a place of shame, a garbage dump outside the city of Jerusalem. Two-thousand years ago, Roman soldiers crucified a nobody, a trouble maker in their eyes. He had no distinguishable characteristics to let them know that they were participants of the greatest event in the history of the world! Jesus had beauty and courage in an unexpected place.

Will you look today for beauty and courage in unexpected places?

. . . He had no beauty or majesty to attract us to him . . .
Isaiah 53:2b

Make a copy of the important pages of your purse calendar,
so that if it's lost, you can have that information.

Know Your Heavenly Father's Nature

MARILYN WILLETT HEAVILIN

Communion with God is the one need of the soul beyond all other needs; prayer is the beginning of that communion.

George Macdonald

If you have a poor relationship with your parents, or if you have been victimized by the father-figure in your life, you may have difficulty relating to God as Father. On a journal page, start your prayer with a different name for God than you have ever used before and build a setting around that name. One of the names I have enjoyed using is "O King, O Sovereign King." In Scripture David said many times, "My King and my Lord." In Deuteronomy He is referred to as "Our Sovereign Lord." When I think "king," I think of myself entering the royal palace, walking in, and bowing before my king. Then I see myself able to tell Him the things that I need because He has summoned me to come into His presence.

This kind of exercise can refresh our prayer life and add some excitement to it that we may not have had in quite a while. Choose a name or names that appeal to you which will cause you to worship and glorify God. Write your prayer to God using these new names. Picture yourself in each new setting and share your thoughts with God.

In the same way your Father in heaven is not willing
that any of these little ones should be lost.

Matthew 18:14

Put plastic dishes in the cupboard
where children can reach them to set the table themselves.

All Manner Of Hospitality

GAYLE CLOUD

Preach the gospel—but use words only when you have to!
Unknown

Not so long ago, I was homebound with many small children—four under five, in fact. Obviously, it was difficult for me to get out to get groceries, let alone to socialize. When my husband and I did manage a break, we had to hire two baby sitters to watch all those kidlets. Needless to say, our breaks were few and far between. And I desperately wanted fellowship.

So I got creative. Since I was home nearly all the time, I thought about inviting folks into our home for dinner or dessert. I could manage to bake a dessert or a casserole once in a while in the midst of our daily chaos. As more babies came, we managed to keep the invitations going. We often invited older folks whose children were grown. They seemed to enjoy our brood. Through the years, we've been visited by missionaries, pastors, retired folks, young families, single folk, and while they got the invitation, the blessing was always ours.

As our older children reached school age, they attended the nearby public elementary school. And I still had younger children to keep me housebound. So I began to ask their teachers over for lunch. What a blessing! Not only did I get to know their teachers in a relaxed setting and to offer them an hour's break from the classroom, I got the blessing of fellowship. Several of the teachers became lifelong friends who had the opportunity of watching their future students grow up. And a few, I discovered, were fellow believers who encouraged my children in virtuous behavior at school.

God created us with a desire, even a command, to fellowship with one another. As I gave that desire to the Lord, He gave me a creative, exciting way to be obedient.

Even if you are housebound for whatever reason, still consider sharing your home with others. You don't have to serve an extravagant meal or decorate elegantly to be a blessing to others.

> . . . *Practice hospitality.*
> Romans 12:13

Read *Friends for the Journey* (Vine Books)
by Madeleine L'Engle and Luci Shaw.

Find Something To Laugh About
CHARLES R. SWINDOLL

Man is distinguished from all other creatures by the faculty of laughter.
Joseph Addison

Even though pain or difficult circumstances (Paul the apostle had both on a daily basis) may be our faithful companions, we encounter something each day that can prompt a chuckle or, for that matter, a hearty burst of laughter. And besides, it's healthy!

Experts tell us that laughter not only makes our serious lives lighter, but laughter also helps control pain in at least four ways: (1) by distracting our attention, (2) by reducing the tension we are living with, (3) by changing our expectations, and (4) by increasing the production of endorphins, the body's natural painkillers. Laughter, strange as it may seem, turns our minds from our seriousness and pain and actually creates a degree of anesthesia. By diverting our attention from our situation, laughter enables us to take a brief excursion away from the pain.

Sometimes it is not literal pain but a too-serious mind-set. When our world begins to get too serious, we need momentary interruptions of just plain fun. A surprising day off, a long walk in the woods, a movie, an enjoyable evening relaxing with a friend over a bowl of popcorn, a game of racquetball or golf—these diversions can make all the difference in our ability to cope with life's crushing demands. We need to give ourselves permission to enjoy various moments in life even though all of life is not in perfect order. This takes practice, but it's worth the effort.

She is clothed with strength and dignity; she can laugh at the days to come.
Proverbs 31:25

Make a tape of yourself laughing
and then play it when you feel sad.

Heal A Relationship ✓
MURIEL LARSON

Peace is such a precious jewel that I would give anything
for it but truth.
Matthew Henry

"All my life I longed for my dad's approval," Cheryl told me, "and I never felt I had it. He never hugged or kissed me or told me he loved me. Often I hoped for a word of commendation when I did something good, but I never received one."

Cheryl was in her thirties when she wrote a letter to her father telling him how she felt. "What do I have to do to get your approval?" was the most important question she asked in the lengthy letter she had prayerfully and lovingly composed. After reading it over, she dropped it off at her parents' home.

About an hour later, she heard the doorbell chime in her apartment. When she went to answer, she found her father standing there. For the first time in his life, he hugged his daughter tightly and kissed her. "I do love you, honey," he said shakily. "I really do love you!"

According to Cheryl, that was the beginning of a new life, not only for her and her father, but for her mother, brother, and sister as well.

How many parents and children are estranged because they don't understand one another? Unfortunately, many people seem unable to express their feelings and may be misunderstood by those closest to them. As a result, an artificial barrier can stand between family members for years.

If you have a similar problem, perhaps you can accomplish the same thing as Cheryl in your family by writing a letter expressing sorrow over a rift and asking forgiveness for anything you might have contributed to the breach.

Here are some suggestions for writing a reconciliation letter:

Pray first. When we have been hurting for years because of an estranged relationship, we may get bogged down in self-pity. We definitely need the Lord's guidance in writing a letter like this. Pray that the Lord will lead you in what you may leave unsaid. Pray the Lord will work in the recipient's heart for His purpose and glory.

Write in love. If necessary, be explicit about some things, but prayerfully write in a spirit of love and humility, willing to confess where you may have erred.

After writing the letter, put it aside for the night and prayerfully read it over the next day. If anything you have written troubles you, consider whether you really want to include it. Remember, you don't want to hurt; you want to heal.

Edit the letter—and then send it. Procrastination often robs us of the peace and joy we might have through forgiveness and reconciliation. If we have done all we can to repair a relationship, then we can rest in the peace that passes all understanding—God's promise to those who trust Him and seek to do His will.

Turn from evil and do good; seek peace and pursue it.
Psalm 34:14

When measuring for a home project, make sure to
measure twice and cut once. It'll save you from mistakes.

Welcome, New Day! ✓
PATSY CLAIRMONT

Those who bring sunshine to the lives of others
cannot keep it from themselves.
James M. Barrie

The ritual of opening my house to a new day allows me to invite in the
wonder of a fresh beginning. It also gives me a visual check on my world—
the weather, the garden, the bird feeders, my neighbor's welfare, and the
newspaper's arrival. In dayspring's light I amble through my home, lifting
shades, drawing back curtains, and parting shutters. I feel as if I'm awaken-
ing each room, offering it yet another chance to afford cheer, comfort, and
refuge to its daytime visitors.

Because my tendency has been to enter into the morning drowsily, I have
had to set my mind toward praise. We didn't create day and we can't uncreate
day, but we can purpose to join the daylight hours with an uplifted heart.
Praise boosts my lagging spirit and causes me to be grateful for the moments
allotted to me. Besides, I find it inspiring to take morning by the hand and
guide her through my home.

I remember when I was a child, my mom would softly call my name until
I awoke or would gently jostle my shoulder until my sleepy eyes would focus.

That's how I encourage my home into a day. Instead of calling the rooms by name, I whisper prayers throughout. . . .

"Dear Lord, when individuals enter my home today, I want them to feel a sense of acceptance and safety. May they, even for a brief interval, be uplifted. For life can be worrisome and at times lonely. So whether it is a deliveryman, a family member, or my dearest friend, may all feel welcomed and valued. Amen."

This is the day the LORD has made; let us rejoice and be glad in it.
Psalm 118:24

Hang bread baskets on the kitchen wall
so that they are easy to use.

Easter Tree ✓

CHRISTINE R. DAVIS

Our Lord has written the promise of resurrection,
not in books alone but in every leaf of springtime.
Martin Luther

Springtime heralds a new beginning for every creation on earth. It's a season of rebirth and renewal. A time to start over. For centuries, the egg has been a symbol of birth and resurrection.

Each year during the Easter season, I set up an Easter egg tree in my home. The tree is a daily reminder of new beginnings, hope, and the blessings our Heavenly Father has promised us. The tree is simple. It's made of a dry tree branch secured in a clay flowerpot and covered with brightly colored and decorated, blown-out eggs suspended from ribbon or fishing line.

Children of all ages enjoy blowing out the egg contents, then coloring and decorating the eggshells.

To make your own Easter egg tree, you'll need to gather the following items: a dry tree branch; a heavy pot (i.e., clay flowerpot); plaster of paris or gravel; a small piece of aluminum foil; large chicken eggs; a small nail; table knife; bowl; egg dyes; stickers; markers; ribbon or fishing line; hot glue and glue gun, or fast-drying glue.

To pot your tree, secure the branch in a large, heavy pot filled with gravel. Or you can mix plaster of paris according to the package directions. Be sure to cover the drainage hole in the pot with a piece of aluminum foil; then pour the mixture into the pot. Place the branch in the center of the plaster and allow it to dry.

To prepare the eggs, begin by holding the egg vertically with the smaller end up, then take a small nail and with the end of a table knife, gently tap a small hole in the egg. Turning the egg over, tap a slightly larger hole in the bottom end of the egg. Over a bowl, hold the egg gently in both hands and blow the egg's contents out through the larger hole. Rinse eggshells out with warm water and allow to drain. When thoroughly dry, dye them with color tablets and decorate with markers, paints, or stickers. Attach a ribbon or fishing line with glue to the eggshells and hang them on your tree. The trees can also be decorated with candy, cards, and miniature white or pastel-colored lights.

Stored properly, your tree will last for years and the eggshells you and your children design will become treasured heirlooms you can display year after year during this beautiful season.

Forget the former things; do not dwell on the past.
See, I am doing a new thing! . . .
Isaiah 43:18,19a

Make a small Easter egg tree for a friend, shut-in, or nursing home resident to enjoy this Spring.

Parents Need To Change, Too!

EVELYN CHRISTENSON

He who is good at making excuses is seldom good at anything else.
Benjamin Franklin

When our first child turned eighteen, and became of legal age in Illinois, she announced at the dinner table one night that she never wanted to hear Mother's philosophy of life again. She had always been an independent child, and since she was about to enter college she decided she wanted to find out about the world for herself; to find her own way in life.

But the clincher came when she said, "Mother, do you know you actually change the tone of your voice when you give us your philosophy of life?" That really horrified me. I flew upstairs and threw myself on the bed. I sobbed and cried and prayed, "Lord, I already have promised You that I'll be the wife You want me to be. Now do I have to be the mother You want me to be, too?"

The answer from God was yes. After that I went underground with the Lord, so to speak, for fourteen months. I threw myself into the Word and let God show me the mother He wanted me to be. In doing so, I applied the principle of I Peter 3:1-2 (a wife winning her unbelieving husband by her chaste and reverent behavior) to my relationship with my daughter. I began to realize that my daughter was becoming an adult and I had to release her from my authority; I had to cut the apron strings. This hurt me more than it hurt her, but as I read the Word and prayed, I discovered that I had replaced motherhood with smotherhood and I needed to change that.

An amazing thing happened as I kept quiet with Jan. A few months after she told me she had had enough of my philosophy, I overheard her telling a friend, "Mother says this" and "Mother says that." I could hardly believe that my daughter, who hadn't wanted to hear my views on life, was now sharing them with someone else.

Had I fought with her instead of withdrawing, I think that to this day she might be trying to find herself. Fortunately, I did the changing and allowed her to discover her own character. As a result she was able to develop confidence that I wasn't going to superimpose my will on her forever. When she realized this, she came back as my friend, closer than before. And because I learned my lesson, my two other children didn't rebel in a similar fashion. They could rest assured that I didn't try to run Jan's life and I wouldn't try to run theirs either.

A man finds joy in giving an apt reply—and how good is a timely word!
Proverbs 15:23

Remember to throw away medications
which are past their expiration date.

Waiting In The Race

EVA MARIE EVERSON

Let us, then, be up and doing,
With a heart for any fate;
Still achieving, still pursuing,
Learn to labor and to wait.

Henry Wadsworth Longfellow

"A fifth grader running on the varsity track team?" I questioned.

My ten-year-old daughter nodded excitedly from the passenger's seat of my car. "The coach saw me running in P.E. He says my timing is so good, I can be on the high school team."

That evening, Coach Danuser confirmed my daughter's report. "Even though your daughter is young, her timing will put her on the team. She's an incredible runner and I think her strength lies in long-distance running."

Coach Danuser was correct. Jessica had been running 5K's—three-point-two miles—with her father for about three years. She had a shelf full of plaques and trophies. I knew she had the discipline to be on the team, but I worried about her running against the more seasoned high schoolers.

A few weeks later my husband and I stood on the sidelines near Jessica's coach as she competed in a one-mile race. As she neared her third lap of the field's track, she was several feet behind the last-place high school runner. I felt panicky. Jessica would come in last place in her first varsity competition. She would be devastated. *Would she want to quit?* I wondered. *Would I allow her to, or would I remind her of her commitment to the team?*

As she began her fourth lap she neared the three of us. Her pace was steady and her eyes were focused straight ahead. She seemed perfectly at ease with where she was: last place! Just as she neared Coach Danuser, he leaned over and yelled, "Now, Jessica!"

I cannot tell you the thrill that went through me as she picked up speed and began passing the entanglement of runners ahead of her. By the last half of the fourth lap, she was several yards ahead of everyone else. As she neared the finish line, her coach, her father, and I began to cheer in anticipation. My baby was going to win!

As soon as Jessica composed herself, I asked, "What were you waiting for? You nearly gave me a heart attack!"

"I did what my coach told me to do," she explained. "You have to wait, wait till the time is right. The ones who were ahead in the beginning were exhausting themselves, trying to get it right away."

How like our spiritual lives! God shows us what He has in mind for us and we begin working furiously to get it right away. But when we wait on Him, the victory comes easier, swifter, and so much sweeter. Jessica listened and trusted her coach, and that led to victory. When we listen and trust our Heavenly Coach, we can be assured of the same.

I wait for the LORD, my soul waits, and in His word, I put my hope.
Psalm 130:5

For organizational helps, ask for the catalogue from
"Get Organized!" (800) 803-9400.

Singleness—A Plus Or A Problem? ✓
LOIS A. WITMER

A mind content both crown and kingdom is.
Greene

As a single, I have struggled with the unfilled desire for a spouse, home, and family. Yet Psalms 84:11b (NIV) promises: *No good thing does He (God) withhold from those whose walk is blameless.*

I know many godly singles who are living purposeful lives. So it appears that marriage is not the only good thing for children of the King. A single person's life can be satisfying in spite of an unrealized dream. Consider the following:

- Try to work in a job where you are in contact with both men and women. This can help keep a social balance.
- Spend time with God. Develop your relationship with Christ. He loves you more than anyone else. He cares about your total being. Become a part of a small-group Bible study where you are comfortable expressing your needs.
- Accept leadership positions when asked to serve. Expand your faith through these experiences. Be helpful where the church needs you.
- Develop hobbies and interests. Don't live your life "on hold." Work at fulfilling personal dreams and life goals. Experience growth through reading, seminars, adult education courses, and travel.
- Enjoy the "grass" where you are. Believing the "grass is greener on the other side" will get you nowhere. God has placed you where you are for a real purpose.

- Rejoice in God's leading. Do not allow resentment to grow when you think of the things you have missed (spouse, children, grandchildren). Thank God for the abundance of blessings He has given you. Remember, there are things you can accomplish that as a married person you could not do.

Here are suggestions for married people in ministering to the singles around you:

- Include singles in your times of fellowship. Singles need the balance that a mixed group can bring. Don't assume a single is "out to get a spouse."
- Help assume responsibility for aging parents. Do not expect the single one in the family to be sole care-giver. Relieve him/her occasionally so he/she can know the refreshment of a retreat, a trip, or some other way to relax and grow.
- Be careful and tactful in overt public displays of affection for each other when in a group.

Suggestions for the church:

- Recognize talents and abilities in all your church members. Use the gifts of both men and women. Be open, and affirm the gifts God has given each believer.
- Organize programs so the entire church feels involved, not overloading your program with family events only. Invite singles to participate. Many stop coming to Sunday School because they don't fit in. Don't tie them to teaching a children's class because you don't know in which adult class to place them.
- Try a time for "ladies night out" instead of having mother/daughter banquets. Instead of father/son events, think of a way to include the single man.

Above all, remember that Jesus was a single. Treat others as you would treat Him.

. . . those who seek the LORD lack no good thing.
Psalm 34:10b

Put a magnetized packet of paper on the refrigerator
for making note of items needed on next shopping trip.

HMD Labels ✓

MARTHA BOLTON

*A man is rich in proportion to the number of things
which he can afford to let alone.*
Henry David Thoreau

When I was growing up, HMD was the major label (Hand Me Down). It was a different kind of Guess clothing. Everyone had to *guess* whose outfit it used to be. And just like the ad promised, I outgrew all my Carters before they wore out. But I *still* had to wear them. One T-shirt was so snug, my arms swelled up like Popeye's every time I put it on. I was wearing miniskirts long before they were in style, and when a blouse didn't fit, my mother would try to convince me that the cuffs were made to stop at the elbow. The very first words I ever spoke were, "Are we expecting a flood—or is it just these pants?"

Don't get me wrong. I'm not saying there's anything wrong with designer wear. I've bought my share of it, too. But babies look cute in *anything*—whether it's an HMD or an outfit direct from Rodeo Drive. Why worry about whether or not their clothes are flattering to their figure, or whether the color is in their "season," or if another baby is going to show up at pre-school wearing the exact same outfit? Who they are is far more important than who they wear.

Do not conform any longer to the pattern of this world, but be transformed by the renewing of your mind. Then you will be able to test and approve what God's will is—His good, pleasing and perfect will.

Romans 12:2

Soap will not melt as fast if it is left unwrapped
for a while before being used.

Cutting The Pain In Two

Jeri Chrysong

"Cookie say effen de pain git too bad, jes' you put a knife unner Miss Melly's bed an' it cut de pain in two."

Prissy in *Gone With The Wind* by Margaret Mitchell

I've found that you have to advertise your pain. I rarely suffer in silence. If I'm in misery, I tend to bring others along with me. It's one of my more endearing qualities. However, in so doing, I generally cut the pain in half because sharing my mishap with others often results in laughter . . . like when I slammed my little toe into the bedpost while rushing out the bedroom door. The sound my little toe made could have been likened to the Civil War's "shot heard around the world." The crack also sent me into a dancing frenzy the likes of which my kids will never forget. And did I mention I was wearing sandals at the time?

Amazing how the human body works. Injured toe signals brain which activates voice to scream and body limbs to lurch and jerk uncontrollably which alerts others to a major toe event, all in split-second timing. And the uninhibited showing of pain usually elicits genuine sympathy from empathetic onlookers.

The Body of Christ reacts to pain the same way the human body does. God knew what He was doing when He compared the two. I was recently reminded of this Biblical principle when two young brothers in our community were critically injured in a car accident. The prognosis looked grim for both boys as their little bodies struggled to overcome comas, paralysis, and what seemed probable brain damage. The agony their parents endured required a different kind of healing, as well.

When believers heard about the dire need for prayer for this family, prayer chains in congregations and parishes all over southern California and beyond were activated. Why? Because a part of our "body" was hurting and it was up to us healthy members to rush to the aid of our suffering members to pray for healing, as our most effective tool is prayer. Indeed, the din of our prayers on behalf of this family would have deafened a lesser god! But not our magnificent God! When combined, the loving vigil of the boys' parents, the diligent prayers of the Body, and the skill and compassion of the medical professionals snatched these children literally away from death's door. Their recovery has been miraculous!

Those of us who witnessed this miracle have been blessed, not only by seeing the children back at play, or hearing about their progress from afar, but by being part of something really powerful, even unexplainable. I have also been blessed to witness firsthand the power of prayer chains, and to see how strangers united in prayer worked silently behind the scenes toward the common goal of restoring health to these precious little boys. Although the parents' burden was so very heavy, sharing it with others made it a little bit lighter. As our human bodies are remarkable, so too is the body of believers. It's miraculous how God knew to compare the two.

When was the last time you took advantage of the benefits of the Body of Christ? You don't have to be in a crisis to do so, just call upon your brothers and sisters in Christ for whatever needs you have.

But God has combined the members of the body . . . so that there should be no division in the body, but that its parts should have equal concern for each other. If one part suffers, every part suffers with it; if one part is honored, every part rejoices with it.

I Corinthians 12:24b–26

Have a list of people you can call in the event
of an emergency close to your phone,
and become familiar with your church's prayer chain.

Six Everyday Ways To Say I Love You

JILL L. FERGUSON

Love is enough . . .

William Morris

My husband, Darren, and I made a promise to each other before we were married. We would work on loving each other with God's love, even on days when we did not really like each other. Through this promise, we have developed six principles in our lives.

1. We pray together every morning, even if we're not in the same cities, as is often the case with the traveling we do for our jobs. We thank God for each other, pray for protection, and ask to be a blessing and in turn to be blessed.
2. We telephone at least once a workday, even when we are in the same town. Just to say, "I love you."
3. We make every meal together a candlelight one, including those with take-out or leftovers. The candlelight adds an ambience of romance and helps relax us after a tense day.

4. We have devotions together every evening. Before we go to bed we commune with God.
5. We cuddle. Touch is one of the five basic needs of humankind. Cuddling brings an intimacy that even sex doesn't. If we are physically apart, we talk about cuddling by phone, until we can do the real thing.
6. We say the words "I love you." I remind my husband that I really do love him, even when we fight or are discouraged with one another.

Darren and I practice these six easy steps daily and are often surprised about how much value they have brought into our marriage, making it truly a treasure from God.

Which principles will you commit to, even if your husband doesn't value it? You can make a choice to bless and love even without his knowledge, and if you can work together, so much the better!

. . . Give thanks to the LORD, for he is good; his love endures forever.
Psalm 106:1b

> Think about and write down ways you and your spouse
> could say "I love you" every day; then share them
> and practice them.

Hearing The Shepherd's Voice

CINDY BAILEY

We need to find God, and He cannot be found in noise and restlessness.
Mother Teresa

Every time my husband, two daughters, and I visit my father-in-law's sheep farm, we get a chuckle out of the big ol' Merino buck that comes running when I call out, "Hey, Lamby Pie! Where are you?"

"Lamby Pie" was once a sick, rejected lamb twin which arrived unexpect-edly on my doorstep to be bottle-fed and nursed back to health. My husband brought him home late one night in a big cardboard box. He was the tiniest lamb I'd ever seen, too weak to stand, and too much for Pap to take care of.

Taken aback as I was (I'm not the agricultural type), the girls and I quickly grew attached to the waif-ling, tenderly caring for him, and giving him the nickname that still makes my father-in-law smile. Of course, I spent the most time with him in those early days, fussing with him at first to get him to eat, and later wrestling him to the ground to get the empty bottle out of his mouth! I suppose that's why he still knows my voice.

Soon, his size and appetite outgrew our house. The three of us cried as we watched my husband drive off with that lamb in the back of the pick-up one late summer afternoon. Yet it was good for him to return to the farm, and Pap gave our pet extra special care.

It's been nearly five years now, and we still enjoy returning to the farm and saying hello to Lamby Pie. Big as he is, when I brush the wool back from his face, I see his beseeching eyes and recognize the little lamb I once held in my arms. And he still checks our pockets for his favorite fig bars.

Lamby Pie's story is one of those great illustrations from real life that helps me to cling to a promise from our own Good Shepherd. Jesus said we would always know His voice, just as the sheep of the fields know the voice of the one who tends them. What peace there is in knowing that no matter how cacophonous our lives become, if only we'll stop and listen, the sweet voice of Jesus rises above it all. Always, He stands ready to share whatever we need, abundant wisdom and guidance, but mostly grace that is sufficient even for these hectic times.

And no matter how much life has changed or scarred us, He can brush away the pain or anger or bitterness, and see in us the lambs He sought fit to die for two millenniums ago.

"My sheep listen to My voice; I know them and they follow me."

John 10:27

> Ask yourself if you really need to turn the radio on
> every time you get in the car. Maybe God has more to
> tell you than the disc jockey.

Unexpected Gifts ✓

CATHY S. CLARK

Have a heart that never hardens, a temper that never tires,
and a touch that never hurts.

Charles Dickens

My four-year-old daughter sat in the middle of the living room eager to open the large Christmas present from her favorite friends. She tore the paper revealing the long-awaited contents. She pulled a huge mapbook out of the paper bundle on her lap. One look at the gift and she cried, "This is not what I expected!" A book of maps made perfect sense to the giver, but brought tears to my daughter.

Thinking back on that scene, I realize I have behaved just like that—allowing expectations to keep me from enjoying precious gifts: my children. During my pregnancies I anticipated the unveiling of those gifts. Soon I learned that life consists of tough, as well as tender, moments. What happened to the fluttery feelings? Instead I'm on my knees begging the Lord for wisdom and help. And at times I cry, "This is not what I expected!"

During one of those times, the Lord gave me a simple, yet abundant, Scripture. *You too, be patient and stand firm, because the Lord's coming is near* (James 5:8). Although James did not write this verse to a mother struggling with a new teenager, it ministered to me exactly as if he had.

Be patient. An apple seed needs favorable conditions and plenty of time to grow into a fruit-bearing tree. My children need time and proper instruction to develop into godly grownups. It doesn't happen overnight—it takes time. Sometimes I forget this truth and expect my adolescent children to respond and behave like adults, causing nothing but frustration. Many factors play into how young people feel about themselves: appearance, friendships, school, peers, and changing hormones. A little patience can go a long way, not to mention the example it is of true love (I Corinthians 13:4).

Stand firm. In this present culture with the shifting sand of the world's standards, I must be devoted to standing firm in the Lord. Some days it is more difficult than I expected. Another version of this scripture says, *strengthen your heart.* I like that. As I seek the Lord and study His Word, I find that He strengthens my heart to do the right thing (Psalm 31:24).

The Lord's coming is near. It is easy to get caught up in the trivialities of today and not see beyond. The only way to discern the important from the unimportant is to view life through an eternal perspective. During days brimming with interruptions, frustrations, and unrealistic expectations, I need to ask myself: What will be important five years from now? Or even ten years from now? What will be significant for eternity? That puts things into proper focus (Revelation 22:12).

In time, my daughter grew to appreciate that mapbook and learned a lot of geography along the way. As I embrace the unexpected moments in motherhood, I find I'm learning a whole lot more than geography!

. . . you did awesome things that we did not expect . . .
Isaiah 64:3a

A great way to read aloud as a family is to listen
to audio books while traveling in the car.

S·P·R·I·N·G

Exceedingly Abundantly

LINDA HARMAN

The Lord be praised for this precious encouragement,
which has still further quickened me for prayer!

George Muller

My doorbell rang early one Saturday morning. I wondered who it was at 8:00
A.M. There in the doorway was my friend, Janet. She stood there with a
large bottle of Clinque Clarifying Lotion. I was a little surprised and curious.
She asked me if I wanted it. I was amazed because just the night before, I had
stopped at a drugstore to pick up some items. While in the store, I could only
afford the bare necessities and astringent wasn't one of them. As I stood in
the middle of the store, I simply talked to the Lord. "It would be nice to have
some astringent but that's a luxury item right now. I'd really like some, Lord,
but if you don't think I need it, it's okay."

With no one around to listen to this conversation, I paid the cashier and
left the store. I went on home and read a book.

Then my doorbell rang the next morning and there was the love of God
wrapped up in a simple bottle of Clinique and my girlfriend, Janet. She explained that the Lord had impressed upon her the idea of bringing me the
astringent.

Not only was He concerned about my every need, but He was concerned
with the desires of my heart. He wanted to demonstrate to me that He heard
my cry. He showed me He is intimately involved with the smallest of details
of my life.

What is the desire of your heart today? Is it your finances? Is it your family? Is it your career? He longs to demonstrate exceedingly abundantly His
love for you. He knows the cares of your heart. Not only does He care for
your needs, He wants to answer the desires of your heart. Reach out to Him.
Look to Him. He desires to have such intimacy with you.

And just maybe you will hear your doorbell ring . . . .

Now to Him who is able to do immeasurably more than all we ask or imagine,
according to His power that is at work within us.

Ephesians 3:20

> Each day after dinner, set your alarm clock for
> fifteen minutes. Each member of your family is to do
> a household chore until the alarm sounds.

The Value Of Truth

PAULINE RAEL JARAMILLO

"While God waits for His temple to be built of love—
men bring stones."

Tagore

A HOUSE, A TEMPLE

Driven by our desire to possess
we grab at lies and build a house.
We lay a foundation of greed,
erect walls of illusions
and bind them with a roof of false security
in order to hide from Truth.

We name our abode Happiness
and hire Selfishness, Jealousy and Doubt
to secure our dwelling.

We give them the keys and
clothe ourselves in blindness.

Selfishness takes what it wants.
Jealousy destroys what it can't have.
Doubt mocks what remains.

The foundation cracks.
The walls crumble.
The roof caves in.
Doom fills our house.
Driven by our desire to give,
we reach for Truth and build a temple.
We construct a foundation of generosity,
erect walls of transparency
and bind them with a roof of faith
in order to make Truth known.

We name our sanctuary the House of God
and invite Love, Peace and Joy
to welcome all who come.
We give the keys to Christ
and clothe ourselves in humility.

Love accepts without judging,
Peace restores harmony,
Joy renews hope.

The foundation stays firm.
The walls remain strong.
The roof holds fast.
God fills His Temple.

*Don't you know that you yourselves are God's temple
and that God's Spirit lives in you?*

I Corinthians 3:16

Post inspirational sayings at various places in your home
or office and read them throughout the day.

"Your Roses Are Lovely"

MARILYN JASKULKE

The fragrance always remains in the hand that gives the rose.

Gandhi

"Your roses are lovely," my daughter-in-law, Debi, said to the woman in the International Airport Terminal.

"Would you like one?" she quickly asked. From her bouquet she removed not one, but two perfect pink roses and handed them to us. Of the original six roses in her bouquet, only four remained. In a moment the woman disappeared from our sight. We were thrilled, not only by the beauty of the roses, but by the unselfish gesture.

For several minutes our conversation buzzed. "Wouldn't it be nice to give someone a rose?" Debi exclaimed.

"If more people were so gracious, what a pleasant world this would be," I replied.

We carried the beautiful roses in our hands as we walked through the terminal. To treasure the occasion, Debi and I decided to press and save one of the roses. We would give away the other pink rose.

We both saw the girl at the same time. She shifted from one foot to the other and appeared to be anxiously waiting for someone. Limp brown hair framed a worry-filled face. Lifting her arm to check her watch, she nervously looked up at the time schedule on the wall.

Together we approached the girl slowly. "Would you like a rose?" Debi asked. Lines of concern began to melt from the girl's face.

"You should keep it for yourself," she said.

"We are leaving the country soon. Would you like it?"

With a half-smile she said, "Yes. Have a nice trip."

In a few moments, Debi and I stepped onto the ascending escalator. We glanced back at the girl. Her friend had arrived, and they stood with their arms around each other. With their eyes fully focused in our direction and their beaming smiles, they followed us up the escalator that carried us to the next floor. We waved and smiled back at the blissful couple holding one pink rose.

Now, years later, the pressed rose reminds us of the excessive joy we received by sharing one of our pink roses.

One man gives freely, yet gains even more...
Proverbs 11:24a

Buy six roses in a busy place.
Offer the roses to people, one by one.

The Tarnished Truck

VICKIE JENKINS

Our deeds are seeds of fate, sown here on earth, but bringing forth their harvest in eternity.
George Dana Boardman

A friend of my husband's had given him a truck. It wasn't an ordinary truck. It was a 1963 Chevy that had been deserted and mistreated. Most of the paint consisted of three shades of green, along with gray primer that dotted the bare spots. It had some rust peeking through, and patches of dents here and there. With broken tail-lights and windows missing, it wasn't much for looks. But, it had a great personality. It had four tires and ran great. It was reliable when we needed to use it for hauling different things.

One particular Saturday, one of the hottest days of the summer, we had just finished having a garage sale. There were several large boxes full of toys, clothes, and miscellaneous items that didn't sell. We decided that we would load up the back of the truck and donate them to the Jesus House, a shelter for less fortunate families.

With the truck loaded to the max, my husband and I, and our two small children, climbed into the front. The hot air blew in as the four of us seemed to cling to one another from the stickiness. Adhering to the torn upholstery of the seats, our bodies had nowhere to move.

Finally, we arrived, hot and thirsty! Just inside the gated area, we saw Sister Ruth. She came over to us, holding a clipboard and pen. There she stood, looking at the four of us, peering at the tied-down boxes. Summing up the situation, with a friendly smile on her face, she said, "Come on in out of the heat, and then we'll see about getting you checked in. You're just in time for supper."

"Oh, no, we are not here to check in," my husband said, as his face turned a brighter shade of red. "We have some donations for you." With a hand over her mouth and a gasp, Sister Ruth realized that she had misunderstood. She pointed us in the right direction.

As we unloaded boxes of clothes, several children ran over to us and began admiring each piece. "Ohh . . . Ahh . . . look at this one," we heard them sigh. Their faces lit up as we saw excitement in their eyes. One little boy spotted a blue T-shirt sporting a baseball logo. "Momma, momma, look what I found!" he shouted, as he ran off, waving it in the air. A little girl ran to a doll that seemed to be peeking over the edge of the box. She cradled the doll in her arms, rocking back and forth.

That night, I thought about our mistaken identity. Sister Ruth was there for us, inviting us into her humble home. She had looked past the old tarnished truck, seeing a chance to share God's love with us. She had succeeded. We all received many blessings that day.

Isn't that what God wants us to do? To see past the tarnished trucks that cross our pathways?

. . . It is more blessed to give than to receive.
Acts 20:35c

When staying in a hotel, agree to allowing your bed
to be remade without washing the sheets. This is a part of
the American Hotel and Motel Association's
"Good Earth Keeping Campaign."
As a result, water and energy will be saved.

One Week At A Time
VEDA BOYD JONES

How can there be so much difference between a day off and an off day?
Larson

For years I daily experienced the four-thirty panic. What's for supper? Sure, I could grab some chicken or hamburger out of the freezer, thaw it in the microwave, and cook it in a different fashion than how I'd fixed it the day before. I could open a can of green beans or corn or peas and quickly bake some potatoes. But the meal looked as thrown together as it was.

One Christmas I received a dry-erase marker board, which I affixed to the refrigerator door. I decided to try menu planning. It was no new bright idea, but it was something new for me.

I listed each day of the week, then I put what events we had scheduled underneath that day. Next I planned what I'd serve for supper. It was really easy. If we had early activities, I'd plan something simple like hamburgers or tacos. If we were free, I planned a nice meal. A great load was lifted from my shoulders.

Planning ahead! What a unique idea. It took less than five minutes a week to schedule events and meals. Now each weekend, I erase the board and plan the new week. It has made a big difference in my life. If you try it, maybe you'll find it as significant as I did.

> *That everyone may eat and drink, and find satisfaction*
> *in all his toil—this is the gift of God.*
> Ecclesiastes 3:13

> Try a new recipe from a cookbook tonight
> to add variety to your meal.

Scrubbing Power ✓
HELEN LUECKE

Cleanliness is next to Godliness
Unknown

Last Monday was not a good day. Minutes before time to leave for work, I dropped a jar of sweet pickles. The container shattered on the kitchen floor. I grabbed some paper towels and mopped up the best I could.

When I returned home that night, my shoes literally stuck to the floor. I kicked them off, filled a pail with hot, soapy water, and swabbed the kitchen.

The next morning as I made coffee, my stocking feet felt like Velcro fasteners as they clung to the tile. I again filled the pail with hot water and added a generous amount of cleaning agent with ammonia. After two scrubbings and a rinsing, I could walk, even slide my feet with ease.

Sin is much like that sticky pickle juice. It enters our lives and tries to cover us. It bogs us down. Its stain sinks deeper and spreads out wider. Is it too late for the scrubbing team?

God needs no mop, water, or cleanser to remove our sins. If we trust in Him, He can change us in a moment. Then with the Holy Spirit in our heart, sin can not find a place to hide—or make further sin stick.

"Come now, let us reason together," says the LORD. "Though your sins are like scarlet, they shall be as white as snow; though they be red like crimson, they shall be like wool."

Isaiah 1:18

The next time you have a chore to do, whistle, hum, or sing.
Time will fly by.

Resurrection Rolls

KATHY COLLARD MILLER

The stone at the tomb of Jesus was a pebble to the
Rock of Ages inside.

Fred Beck

I recently found a wonderful visual aid for preparing our hearts for Good Friday and Easter. I hope that you'll share it with the people in your life, especially children. Each ingredient represents how Jesus' body was prepared for burial.

Ingredients:

Large Marshmallows
Melted Butter
Sugar/Cinnamon Mixture
Cans of Crescent Rolls
Directions:

1. Open the can of crescent rolls and separate into triangles. The rolls represent the linen wrapping used in covering the dead.
2. Dip and roll one marshmallow, representing Jesus' body, into melted butter. The butter represents the oils used in anointing the dead body.
3. Roll the marshmallow in the sugar/cinnamon mixture. The mixture represents the spices used in burials.
4. Place the marshmallow in the center of the crescent triangle. Fold and pinch the edges tight. Put each crescent-wrapped marshmallow on a slightly greased cookie sheet.
5. Bake the rolls as directed on he package. The oven represents the tomb.

When cooked, the marshmallow melts leaving only the puffed crescent roll. This demonstrates how Jesus rose from the dead. All that remained in the tomb were the linen wrappings.

If we have been united with Him like this in His death,
we will certainly also be united with Him in His resurrection.
Romans 6:5

To include regular page-width information (like your son's baseball schedule) in your smaller purse calendar or time organizer, use a copy machine's ability to reduce its size to fit your organizer.

The Crystal Goblets

DELORES ELAINE BIUS

*On money and possessions, it all depends on whether
you have things or they have you.*

Robert A. Cook

"Sterling and crystal have I none," used to be my doleful lament. Although not poverty-stricken, neither were we affluent. Our dinner table was not spread with china dishes, crystal goblets, and sterling silver flatware. Instead we had stoneware dishes, juice glasses that formerly contained jelly or cheese spread, and silverplated flatware.

On the whole, I was satisfied with what I had. But there were times when I saw beautifully appointed dining room tables in magazine pictures and wondered if the meals tasted better when served so luxuriously.

Then the supermarket where I shopped had a special offer, as they had done in the past. Over the years I had obtained not only our dishes and silverware this way but also a collection of reproductions of great paintings.

My husband marveled at how I obtained such things free by saving cash register tapes from my grocery purchases each week. He could not share my enthusiasm for the latest "free with each $200 in cash register tapes" offer, though. It featured crystal goblets.

For weeks I hoarded my receipts until I had enough for eight goblets. When I brought them home, I put them up on one of the topmost kitchen shelves in order to save them for extra special occasions.

Then one day I came in the house from shopping to discover my husband drinking iced tea from one of the goblets. "You are right," he remarked. "These glasses are nice."

Raising my eyebrows, I cautioned, "Yes, dear, but do be careful. I really meant to use those just for special occasions. They cost five dollars each, you know."

"What?" my husband gasped. "I thought you said they were free with cash register tapes."

"They were," I explained, "but the offer is over now and to buy them without receipts, they would cost five dollars each."

Later that evening I reflected on the Gershwin folk opera, *Porgy and Bess*. In it the hero explains that when you are poor you don't have to worry about things breaking or being stolen, since you have nothing of great value to lose anyway.

There is a contemporary painting that portrays the marriage supper of the Lamb in Heaven. The table rivals any in *Better Homes and Gardens*. Now, every time we use our crystal goblets, I think of that grand occasion. I am grateful for the opportunity to acquire my crystal goblets, and I enjoy them and thank the Lord for them. But they really remind me to lay up my treasure in Heaven and set my sights there more than on the things of this world.

The abundant life enjoys every treasure while knowing our earthly treasures will be destroyed. Are you laying something aside for a special time to use them? Enjoy them now and also reflect about the spiritual treasures that are being stored up for you in heaven.

Do not store up for yourselves treasures on earth, where moth and rust destroy, and where thieves break in and steal.

Matthew 6:19

Set the table with crystal and china dishes tonight—even for just the family. Enjoy what God has generously provided.

A Good Steward

RONICA STROMBERG

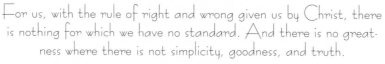

For us, with the rule of right and wrong given us by Christ, there
is nothing for which we have no standard. And there is no greatness where there is not simplicity, goodness, and truth.

Leo Nikolaevich Tolstoi

When I was growing up in Iowa, a source of constant agitation for my family
was people who drove by our house in the country and threw pop and beer
cans into our yard. Sunday afternoons would typically find us in the yard,
slinging cans into bags and grousing about litterbugs.

One day, our attitudes changed and we began to appreciate the litterbugs.
That was the day the Iowa five-cent refund law went into effect. Under this
law, each can gained us five cents when we turned it in at the grocery store for
recycling. On a "good Sunday," we might reap fifty cents just by strolling around
our front yard.

That was my introduction to *recycling*, and it was only a short time before
I began taking part in the similar practices of reducing and reusing. A person
who *reduces* waste buys in quantity, pays less for packaging, or makes do
without altogether. The person who *reuses* finds alternative uses for packaging and products that would have otherwise gone into the trash and, from
there, to landfills. All three practices—recycling, reducing, and reusing—
save money (sometimes even make money!) and exercise good stewardship
of the earth's riches.

In what ways can you do more recycling, reducing, and reusing?

Then God said, "Let us make man in our image, in our likeness, and let them
rule over the fish of the sea and the birds of the air, over the livestock, over all
the earth, and over all the creatures that move along the ground."

Genesis 1:26

To determine if a plastic container is recyclable, look at the bottom of it. You should see three arrows drawn together to form a triangle with a number in it. If the number in the triangle is a one or a two, the plastic is recyclable. If the number is higher than that, the plastic is usually non-recyclable.

Persevere To Abundance ✓

A. JEANNE MOTT

Opposition is a powerful instrument to develop our relationship with God. It moves us closer to Him and makes us more susceptible to His shaping.

David Roper

It was only about ¼ inch in diameter, yet I couldn't take my eyes off it. The tiny spider was between the window and storm window. For perhaps an hour I sat watching, marveling at the perseverance of this little insect as he spun webbing around a centipede four times larger than himself. The spider proceeded step by step—beginning with the back legs and rear body of the centipede. It was a dangerous and difficult task for the little spider but he never gave up. The centipede struggled and fought desperately, so the spider knew he had to keep working. Periodically the wee worker would distance himself from his prey and rest a few minutes, renewing himself for this arduous task.

Not having time to watch continuously, I periodically checked on the progress, to see if the centipede or spider would prevail. The spider worked nearly the entire day to completely enshroud the centipede. In spite of the larger insect's struggles, the spider's persistence gave him the victory. Then he began to leisurely enjoy the conquest by dining on his prey.

Oftentimes life's problems appear so much bigger than us. So we run from the trouble, in which case we are never rid of it because it follows us. Or we just succumb to the problem, and let it bury us—leaving us in deep depression. Neither is God's choice for our lives. Rather, the plan is for us to have lives of joy and abundance.

Admittedly, life presents us with many problems we cannot overcome on our own. But we are not on our own. God is constantly with us, and He is our resource for triumphing over trials. If the Creator of the universe provides a tiny spider with means to conquer a seemingly undefeatable enemy, how much more will He equip us (whom He created in His own image, and for whom He died) to surmount our troubles?

As the spider conquered step by step, so we can overcome if we seek God's direction day by day. God can use the hardship to fine-tune our character and mold us more into His image. What a wonderful witness for others to see the Lord glorified through our perseverance in life.

Consider it pure joy, my brothers, whenever you face trials of many kinds, because you know that the testing of your faith develops perseverance.
James 1:2–3

Take everything out of your purse and re-evaluate whether it's necessary.

Making Space
Biswita Chaudhuri Mozumdar

A wise man will make more opportunities than he finds.
Francis Bacon

I wanted a piano at home. I could afford to buy one, but I did not have the space for a huge musical instrument. I lived in a small apartment with a living room, a bedroom with a tiny closet, a kitchen, and a bathroom. There wasn't a place for all my clothes, let alone a piano. I groaned and grumbled about the space constraints, and my husband, tired of my complaining, suggested that we rent a larger apartment next year. The rents would be higher, but it seemed that there was no way out.

The decision made, we marched to the rental office to make inquiries about the availability of two-bedroom and three-bedroom apartments. We'd have to wait till the expiration of our lease period before we could move, but the manager promised to find what we wanted, provided we were willing to pay more rent—$100 a month.

A few days later I was glancing casually at a flyer from the rental office. On it was a small column about available storage space. We made a second trip to the rental office, and managed to get hold of the last of the storage spaces, for the nominal amount of $20 per month.

On returning home, I looked around and I realized that the apartment was not as small as it appeared. There was simply too much stuff, mostly useless stuff. I made a mental list of the things I seldom or never used, but which I could never part with, and I was soon making a very long list which included:

• *Books and magazines.* I seldom open any paperback from my vast book collection. I subscribe to a number of magazines, but flip through the pages only once. I decided that I could do without the stacks of books and bundles of magazines, and piled them into a suitcase.

• *Clothes.* This was another common culprit, and most of us have too many of them. If I couldn't resist the temptation to expand the wardrobe, the next best alternative was to sort through my clothes, putting my summer outfits into suitcases when it's winter and vice versa. I also set aside old garments to be given to the Salvation Army.

• *Shoes.* Along with clothes, they can make you feel as if your closets are miniscule, when in fact they're not. I own at least half a dozen pairs, which I could not bring myself to throw away but rarely wore. I kept my sneakers, a pair of formal shoes, and slippers, and packed up the rest into boxes. I was careful to make separate suitcases for the books, clothes, etc., so I didn't have to hunt when I'd try to find something.

- *Miscellaneous.* I looked at the junk mail cluttering up several tables and shoved it into a separate wastepaper basket along with other outdated correspondence, without trying to sort it. Then every two months, I emptied it into the permanent trash can so that I had time to retrieve any valuable documents which inadvertently might have been put there.

After the suitcases had been put into storage, I could finally squeeze in a piano. I played to my heart's content. I found I could easily do without the stuff that was now lying in the storeroom, although I occasionally retrieved some things from it. I realized we didn't need room for ourselves, but for all our possessions.

Look at your home. Are there things that could be put into storage? You'll find your house is less cluttered and you'll have a greater sense of abundance without as many things around.

> *The way of the sluggard is blocked with thorns,*
> *but the path of the upright is a highway.*
> Proverbs 15:19

Look at your possessions with a fresh eye. Ask yourself,
"Is this something I really need?"

Tea Or Something

ELAINE F. NAVARRO

We need time to dream, time to remember,
and time to reach the infinite. Time to be.

Gladys Tabor

Not long ago I dropped in on my daughter and found her working at top speed.

She had washed the kitchen floor and vacuumed the whole house. The baby needed food and it was nearly time to pick up her oldest child from school.

When I told her to slow down a bit, she said, "I don't have time." I then reminded her, from my own experience, just how important it was to do "little somethings" for herself. I'm sure she'd heard my story before, but now was the time for her to put my ideas into practice. Here are some suggestions I gave her:

1. Take a few minutes to read a chapter in a favorite book. My interest is in mysteries, so I read just enough to be able to set about solving the crime. That keeps my mind busy while I wash, dust, and clean my house. In no time I've completed my work.
2. Take time out for a cup of tea, a soft drink, or coffee. When my children were napping, I would make tea in a small yellow ceramic teapot, set out Scottish butter cookies, and enjoy my refreshments for a precious few minutes before the children awoke.
3. Drop a bit of scented oil in a tub, grab a magazine, and soak for whatever time you can allow yourself. Even ten minutes will refresh you. Afterwards you will perform household or family tasks with greater ease.
4. Dream of things that make life good for you. I plan a train trip when I'm too involved in my busy life. I plan what I will wear, where I will go, or what I will eat. I see myself staring out of a coach window, enjoying the scenery as it races past, stimulating my thoughts and imagination.

It is amazing how one can re-light the pilot of one's soul with these simple rest and relaxation techniques. By doing so we get a greater feel of the abundance of the Lord. And after all, isn't that what life on God's earth is all about?

Take my yoke upon you and learn from Me, for I am gentle and humble in heart, and you will find rest for your souls. For My yoke is easy and My burden is light.
Matthew 11:29–30

Take a ride to the country, seashore, or mountains
for a day of rest and relaxation.

Prayer Plan ✓

AMBERLY NEESE

I must often be glad that certain past prayers of my own
were not granted

C. S. Lewis

Often my desire for meaningful prayer is thwarted by a cumbersome prayer list. I love to pray, but the magnitude of needs in my life and those of others can become overwhelming. Although I never feel limited to adhere to the day's theme, a friend and I devised a daily prayer program, alliterating the days of the week as a guide. The program is as follows:

Monday—**M**issionaries and church leaders, both from my church and others.

Tuesday—**T**hose troubled in health or spirit. Often, I will hear of these people from church prayer chains.

Wednesday—**W**ashington D.C. and society leaders. I pray for God's will and humility to be developed within our governing offices, law enforcement, and educational programs.

Thursday—**T**hanksgiving. I concentrate on who God is and all that He does. As a result, I take time to thank Him.

Friday—**F**riends and Family. This is often the longest and most difficult list, and where I see the most improvement firsthand.

Saturday—**S**alvation. I pray for those who have not come to a saving knowledge of Jesus.

Sunday—**S**elf-improvement. I listen to what the Lord has to share about areas of needed growth in my life.

I always include studying the Bible and a time of silence before the Lord during my prayer time. By using this guide, it has helped me alleviate feeling overburdened and it has helped me to focus my prayer time. Could you also use it as a helpful guide?

Devote yourselves to prayer, being watchful and thankful.
Colossians 4:2

Follow successful big business practices in your personal life by adhering to the "1/3" rule in meeting deadlines; add 1/3 of time to the projected completion time to save yourself stress and heartache. If you think it will take three hours to do something, give yourself an additional hour for unexpected delays and/or interruptions.

Get Rid Of That Chaff

LLOYD JOHN OGILVIE

The true way to be humble is not to stoop until you are smaller than yourself, but to stand at your real height against some higher nature that will show you what the real smallness of your greatness is.

Phillips Brooks

Recently I passed through a very difficult and painful period of seeing myself realistically through the eyes of a couple of people I love very

much. They pointed out a developing pattern which could cause ineffec-
tiveness in my relationship with them, possibly others. The only place I
could go with the data was to prayer. The Spirit was firm and yet gentle.
He confirmed aspects of the criticism and helped me see the insecurity
which prompted the pattern. Then He gave me power to do something
about it. The amazing thing was that just before this need for change was
brought to my attention, I had been feeling very secure and at peace, as if
my growing in Christ had finally reached a quiet maturity. Not so! Chaff
I hadn't realized was there had to be burned away. And it will be like this
for as many years as I have to live on earth. Under the fire of the Spirit
the dross will surface and have to be skimmed off to make the metal pure.

. . . Do not be proud, but be willing to associate with people
of low position . . .
Romans 12:16b

Any shoes that you like but don't use because of the color,
have them dyed a dark, basic color like black, brown, or navy.
You may be able to use them more.

When God Hears

FAYE LANDRUM

The gospel must be the bad news of the conviction of sin before it
can be the good news of redemption.
Charles Colson

For a few weeks that summer my husband was particularly "hard to live with."
Bob was excessively critical of me; nothing I did pleased him. He was ex-

tremely irritable with the children, and this produced a mounting tide of resentment in both them and me.

This was just before vacation. I knew Bob was tired from unsolved problems nagging him at work, but knowing this didn't ease the domestic tension that hung over our house like a threatening storm cloud.

One night I went to bed feeling that I couldn't stand it any longer. I retreated into a cocoon of self-pity and sobbed silently. Bob's heavy breathing next to me told me he was asleep and my little orgy would go undetected. "Lord," I prayed, "You know all the ways Bob has hurt me lately. He is so moody and irritable. Maybe I would have been better off if I had stayed single."

In the darkness, I continued praying, asking that God would help me to tolerate my misery. For quite some time I prayed for the courage, strength and grace I needed. I also prayed that God would bring about some sort of change in Bob.

Then suddenly, I was overcome with a feeling of guilt. My sin of self-pity seemed almost unbearable. My tears flowed even more freely and I prayed that God would forgive me for my selfish martyrdom, my lack of understanding, and my inability to help my husband when he undoubtedly needed me the most.

I went to sleep with that prayer in my heart.

A few hours later I was awakened by one of the children needing attention. I was groggy, but as I walked to the bathroom I was aware of a great inward levity. I felt as if a heavy burden had been lifted. I knew God had forgiven me, and I was changed.

The next morning, I was still conscious of the exhilaration I had felt during the night. But more wonderful than that was the change in Bob. He talked freely and pleasantly with all of us. The dark cloud of tension lifted. Even the children noticed the difference.

That was my first experience with the eternal truth that God cannot be reached through a veil of sin. It is only when we bring ourselves to Him and are cleansed by seeking His forgiveness for our own transgressions, that we are able to pray for ourselves and others.

If the sin of wanting to control others while being unwilling to see your own weaknesses is veiling your mind from seeking God in true humility, be honest and willing to allow God to make the changes He wants in *your* heart. Although there are no guarantees, you may just find that changes are made in others as well.

If I had cherished sin in my heart, the Lord would not have listened; but God has surely listened and heard my voice in prayer.
Psalm 66:18–19

To organize magazines, make a photocopy of the Table of Contents of each one and put that copy into a notebook. Now you'll only have to look through the notebook to find an article you want rather than all the magazines.

Single Serving

SYLVIA DUNCAN

Necessity is the mother of invention.
Anonymous Latin saying

Alone for lunch? Do you get bored eating the same things, yet want something easy and quick? One rainy day, I craved something different, something warm, smooth, and nutritious. The cupboard was almost bare. I found one can of tuna, a potato, and the mayonnaise. I invented this tasty tuna dish and have shared it with single friends. When a friend was recovering from surgery, this was something he could eat easily. Canned salmon may be substituted for the tuna.

Tuna Smoothie for One

Preparation time: 12 minutes; Total cost: Approx. $1.50.
1 medium potato, cubed, boiled, and drained.
One 3-oz. can white tuna.
Mayonnaise to mix. (The amount depends on how much mayonnaise
you allow yourself to eat.)

Mix all ingredients while the potato is still hot. Sprinkle with white pepper and eat immediately. A small can of peas, green beans, or stewed tomatoes makes a good side dish.

LORD, You have assigned me my portion and my cup:
You have made my lot secure.
Psalm 16:5

Buy a beautiful old soup bowl in a thrift shop. Use it when you eat alone. Remember, it was once part of a cherished set.

Learning From Young And Old
JOAN CLAYTON

Happiness is where God is.
Joan Clayton

One of the happiest people I have ever met is a 93-years-young, wonderful soul in a rest home. She held me close the day I entered my two aunts in the nursing home where she resides. My tears were falling on her feet as she reassured me that she would befriend them. "Miss Bea" never failed to give me a report in the weeks and months that followed. She took note of how my aunts were eating, how they were sleeping, and how they were enjoying the activities.

Miss Bea is everyone's favorite. She hugs the nurses and is always cheerful and positive. I will never forget something she told me. "Honey, someone can have everything in the world, but without God, they are miserable. Take me! The Lord has blessed me so much. I have a wonderful place to stay, good food to eat, and people to take care of me. Yes, Jesus is in my heart. That's why I'm so happy!"

Kallie, our youngest granddaughter, was hugging herself later that day. I asked her what she was doing.

"I'm hugging Jesus. He's in there you know. He's in my heart. That's why I'm so happy!"

What a simple yet profound lesson I learned from them both. I am rich . . . rich in family, friends, health, and in all spiritual blessings. That makes me a millionaire!

Miss Bea, age 93, and Kallie, age 7, have a lot in common. Happiness is where God is!

A cheerful heart is good medicine, but a crushed spirit dries up the bones.
Proverbs 17:22

Prevent stress by planning a daily round of errands in geographic order—and have the order written down so you won't forget.

Burning Bushes

WENDY DUNHAM

What we believe about God is the most important thing about us.
A. W. Tozer

Several days ago, as I was looking through my hope chest, I came across a letter I'd written as a child. It was tucked inside a yellowed envelope and on the front was written, "To God." As I read it, I was overwhelmed by God's graciousness to me. Twenty-four years after writing that letter, I still have the child-like faith that burned in my heart when I wrote it:

Dear God,
I'm so confused. I don't know what to do about my dad, he doesn't believe in you. I'm sorry, I wish he did. He says the stories in the Bible aren't true, and that there's no way they could have happened. Remember Jonah and the whale? He said that's a fable because no one could survive in a whale for three days. He said Moses never separated the Red Sea, because the laws of physics make it impossible. He heard about the burning bush, but he says that if it was on fire, it would have burned up, and that I should know bushes don't talk! What should I do? I love you, God, and I believe the Bible is true. But what about my dad? I thought he knew everything, but now I'm not so sure.
Love, Wendy

After I'd written the letter, I hid it in my dresser. My mother must have found it while doing laundry, because I later found she'd written a response. At the time, my mother was a "silent" believer and rarely voiced her love for God. Because of my dad's disbelief, she felt "being quiet" about her faith would keep peace in our home. How thankful I was for her response:

Dear Wendy,
I found your letter and couldn't help but read it; please forgive me. I'm sorry about your dad, I wish he'd believe too. I know how confusing it must be for you. Try to understand; sometimes grown-ups reason too much with their mind, and not enough with their hearts. Your dad reasons with his mind. He has chosen his disbelief, but don't let that change you. Be strong in your faith. Continue to seek God. You've been saved by faith, a gift God has given you.
    And yes, Wendy, burning bushes do talk!
Love, Mom

In the later years of his life, my dad has come to know the Lord with child-like faith. Bible "fables" have become facts. Jonah is no longer a fictitious character, but a real man whom God used. The Red Sea no longer represents the laws of physics, but a miraculous passageway for the Israelites. God is still a God of miracles!

I always thank God for you because of His grace given you in Christ Jesus.
I Corinthians 1:4

> If you've started to give up praying for someone you love who still doesn't believe, make a fresh commitment to pray for his or her salvation.

The Coupon Bank ✓

MARIE ASNER

Take care of the pence and the pounds will take care of themselves.
William Lowndes

My husband and I were newly married and on a shoestring budget. He was making car payments on his latest acquisition and I was making dental payments on mine. We wanted to tithe ten percent of our income but didn't know how to do it. Every penny, it seemed, was being used.

One day, while diligently going through the newspaper for food coupons, I hit upon the idea of using the coupon savings as our tithe money. At first, I was ashamed at this idea, but then, I reasoned, "The coupons are there regardless, so why not use them?"

So, each shopping trip from that day, I carefully took the "saved money" and put it in an envelope for the Lord—my "coupon bank." At first, it didn't seem like much, but gradually, I became "savvy" about looking for coupons in unexpected places, like newspapers I usually didn't read or junk mail. The savings began to add up and by the end of our first year of marriage, I was able to give the Lord $500 or ten percent of our income for 1968.

This continued for five years until we had a steady income and were able to actively tithe ten percent on a regular basis. But I have still continued to use coupon savings in many different ways. As a result, we were able to afford pets and give them the best care because this was "their money." Our family also had celebration parties for special events and our budget remained untouched because the "coupon bank" was open. Many times, we were able to financially assist someone in need because of "our bank."

Now that my husband is retired, the "coupon bank" is his responsibility and he has become adept at "clipping his coupons."

Then you will understand what is right and just and fair—every good path.
Proverbs 2:9

Begin tithing today in whatever way you can.

Playday On The Boss's Time

Esther M. Bailey

The best prize that life offers is the chance to work hard at work worth doing.
Theodore Roosevelt

Do you fight boredom on the job by watching the clock or dreaming of a vacation? How would you like to turn the ordinary workday into a play day and get a payday besides? If that sounds like cheating, Scripture gives you permission to play the following games on company time:

Promote Other Players to Stardom. One woman I know was rebuked by a co-worker and instead of taking offense, she decided to give him the VIP treatment. Imagine her delight when her boss reported that that co-worker had paid her a compliment. My friend had allowed her co-worker to be the star, but she herself received the applause.

This kind of game is described in Philippians 2:3.

Make Your Turn to Serve Count. In tennis or volleyball, you make points while serving. On the job, you have even greater opportunity to score because your turn to serve never ends.

As a sales representative, one woman learned the importance of service. The crankier the customer, the harder she worked to solve the problem. "If the competition writes off a difficult customer, that gives me an edge to make them a loyal client," she said.

If serving isn't your idea of fun, check out Matthew 20:26.

Increase Your Batting Average. As a billing clerk, one woman thought her job was a drag until she began to challenge herself to produce more invoices each day than she had the day before. Shouldn't it be as much fun to increase production as it is to increase your batting average? It can be. It's up to you and your willingness to play ball.

You may not receive an audience with a king as suggested in Proverbs 22:29, but would you settle for a pay raise?

Play Golf. When counting mistakes, make it a game of golf. Mistakes cost money. Instead of later taking hours to correct a mistake, double-check your work in a minute in the beginning. Make it a goal to keep the score on mistakes below par. Why not go for a birdie? Then better it. A week or a month without mistakes qualifies for a hole-in-one.

The person who fails to check mistakes is described in Proverbs 18:9.

When you discover how to play on company time, a whole new world will open up. You may even forget about vacation. But don't worry, when the time comes, you'll enjoy time off as much as if you'd spent all year dreaming about it. Maybe more!

A man can do nothing better than to . . . find satisfaction in his work . . .
Ecclesiastes 2:24

Try to create your own game of play at work that will
make you a better employee or boss.

Untangling The Knots

JOAN RAWLINS BIGGAR

The worst sorrows in life are not in its losses
and misfortunes but in its fears.

A. C. Benson

With the edging tool, I sliced the outline of my new flower bed through the
grass. Then I pried up chunks of sod and shook out the loose dirt. Fat crane-
fly larvae, beetles, scuttling earwigs, earthworms, and cutworms tumbled out
of the grass roots, but I only half-noticed. Worries chased each other round
and round in my head, tangling my thoughts in a hopeless snarl. Financial
disasters and health problems had wiped out nearly all we'd gained in twenty-
five years of marriage. Our marriage itself was in trouble. My dreams seemed
crushed.

I picked up another chunk of sod. A pinkish-brown ball dropped onto my
knee and bounced into the dirt. A lumpy marble? A knot of roots? No, it was
soft, pulsating . . . an earthworm, with a problem he'd never solve by himself! Tied up like a knot in a shoelace, his body contracted, then bulged as he
tried to crawl out of his predicament. The knot only tightened. Somebody
would have to help him.

I ran for a couple of cotton swabs and probed gently. I saw how the three-
inch creature had twisted himself into a double loop. Next, he'd somehow

threaded one end through both loops and tried to pull his body after it.

I freed what I assumed was his head. For a moment, the little fellow lay coiled in two loop-the-loops. Slowly as an arthritic old man, he straightened. I could almost hear his drawn-out "Ahhh!" of relief. Then, never knowing what had extricated him from his difficulty, he tunneled back into the dirt.

I knelt in my soon-to-be flower bed, my heart suddenly lighter. I'm sure God smiled as He reminded me that I too have an unseen power to untangle my knotty problems. The earthworm had to wait for me to find him, but I don't have to wait for God to find me. I might have to wait for His solutions, but God is beside me all the time. And He has the answers to all my problems—and yours!

Since ancient times no one has heard, no ear has perceived, no eye has seen any God besides You, who acts on behalf of those who wait for Him.
Isaiah 64:4

On your family's calendar, use different colored pens to indicate different family member's activities.

Turn A How-To Idea Into A Friendship Gift

INA MAE BROOKS

For a unique hostess gift, give a pretty spray bottle filled with homemade glass cleaner.
Anita Noel

Share a gift with friends that is fun and easy. Homemade glass cleaner in a plastic spray bottle makes a simple, yet practical, token gift. Affix a label with the cleaner's formula and make it more valuable.

HOMEMADE GLASS CLEANER RECIPE

Step 1. Combine in a large container:
   1 gallon distilled water
   1 pint rubbing alcohol
   ¼ cup Prell brand shampoo.

Step 2. Pour mixture into plastic spray bottles. Store unused product.

Step 3. Prepare a label which lists the ingredients and its uses.

Step 4. Add a bow and a gift tag.

I received the glass cleaner in a pint plastic spray bottle along with the formula. It was called homemade window glass cleaner. It worked nicely on windows, mirrors, and other glass, including eyeglasses. Using eight-ounce plastic spray bottles, I called the product homemade eyeglass cleaner as I shared it with others.

The label was prepared on a word processor, but it could have been typed or handwritten. The ingredients came from the local grocery store. The plastic spray bottles were found in the cosmetics department of the local discount store. During the growing season, a good selection of these inexpensive bottles can be found in the yard and garden section.

Efficient cleaning products need not be expensive nor harmful to our environment. Mixtures of typical household products work just as well. And friends will appreciate this thoughtful, practical gift. In addition, you share information for how to make, use, and pass on a gift which brightens the world.

But whoever lives by the truth comes into the light, so that it may be seen plainly that what he has done has been done through God.

John 3:21

Consider whether an organizing product called "EZ Pocket" might fit your family's needs. It hangs on the back of a door and has pockets available for holding different items. Request information at (800) 681-8681 or stationery stores.

Groceries And Grace

Max Lucado

We make a living by what we get, but we make a life by what we give.

Winston S. Churchill

This story made its way to me from a friend who heard it from a friend who heard it from who knows who. Chances are it has suffered through each of the generations—but even if there is only a splinter of fact in what I heard, it's worth retelling.

Seems a fellow is doing some shopping at a commissary on a military base. Doesn't need much, just some coffee and a loaf of bread. He is standing in line at the checkout stand. Behind him is a woman with a full cart. Her basket overflows with groceries, clothing, and a VCR.

At his turn he steps up to the register. The clerk invites him to draw a piece of paper out of a fishbowl. "If you pull out the correct slip, then all your groceries are free," the clerk explains.

"How many 'correct slips' are there?" asks the buyer.

"Only one."

The bowl is full so the chances are slim, but the fellow tries anyway, and wouldn't you know it, he gets the winning ticket! What a surprise. But then he realizes he is only buying coffee and bread. What a waste.

But this fellow is quick. He turns to the lady behind him—the one with the mountain of stuff—and proclaims, "Well, what do you know, Honey? We won! We don't have to pay a penny."

She stares at him. He winks at her. And somehow she has the wherewithal to play along. She steps up beside him. Puts her arm in his and smiles. And for a moment they stand side-by-side, wedded by good fortune. In the parking lot she consummates the temporary union with a kiss and a hug and goes on her way with a grand story to tell her friends.

I know, I know. What they did was a bit shady. He shouldn't have lied and she shouldn't have pretended. But that taken into account, it's still a nice story.

A story not too distant from our own. We, too, have been graced with a surprise. Even more than that of the lady. For though her debt was high, she could pay it. We can't begin to pay ours.

We, like the woman, have been given a gift. Not just at the checkout stand, but at the judgment seat.

And we, too, have become a bride. Not just for a moment, but for eternity. And not just for groceries, but for the feast.

Don't we have a grand story to tell our friends?

> *. . . are justified freely by His grace through the redemption*
> *that came by Christ Jesus.*
>
> Romans 3:24

Replace your dictionary if it's over ten years old.

Baskets Of Memories

Cindy Bailey

Time for a little something.

A. A. MILNE

In the spring before we were married, my then husband-to-be surprised me one afternoon with a large, handmade picnic basket, complete with a red-and-white checked tablecloth. I soon added plates, fancy water goblets, and red cloth napkins—all purchased from yard sales. That way, all I had to do was pack a couple of sandwiches and brownies, toss in a jug of lemonade, and we were on our way. Those early days together, sharing snacks and dreams in the sun, have become some of my fondest memories. Of course, through the years, we added first one, then two Sippee cups, along with a couple of cartoon plates for our little girls. The basket also came in handy for transporting hot dishes to church dinners or meals to shut-ins. In later years, the basket was like taking a familiar friend along when I put jars of broth in it for my mother-in-law during the final days of her life.

Today when I look at that basket, with it's still-cheery checked tablecloth, I think of all the times it nourished our family and friends in both body and soul. Then I feel blessed. These days, I often present spring and summer brides with a similar basket of their own so they too can begin a family tradition.

I buy a large, sturdy basket at a discount store and fill it with service for two, including unique plates and beverage glasses, as well as vintage tablecloths and napkins that I have found for just a few dollars at yard sales or second-hand shops. Non-perishable food items, such as gourmet tea biscuits, crackers and cheeses, along with a bottle of non-alcoholic champagne, are also a nice touch. I then tie a big bow on the handle and attach the following poem:

This basket is already packed
With napkins, cups, and plates,
In hopes that God will give you
Some time for picnic dates.
May this basket come to symbolize
Days of love and care,
And may the Lord always provide you
With food enough to share.

*Praise the LORD, O my soul, and forget not His benefits . . . who satisfies
your desires with good things so that your youth is renewed like the eagle's.*
Psalm 103:2, 5

Fill a new or vintage picnic basket with service for the
bride and groom in your life, and watch the memories begin.

The River

DENISE E. YOUNG

Bitterness is when you swallow the poison and wait for the other person to die.
Unknown

A river rafting trip! At first it had sounded exhilarating and exciting. However,
following seven years of drought in the San Joaquin Valley, we had a blockbuster
winter. The rivers were higher, faster, and more dangerous than ever before.
Warnings were posted in local newspapers about the danger of strong currents in
the Kings River.

Just to reassure myself, I went to our soon-to-be guide, who had years of
experience on the river. I was confident he would calm my fears.

"Ron," I said, "there's talk of the river being dangerous. Even people that are good swimmers have been known to drown. I don't understand it. With a life-jacket and common sense, how can that happen?"

"You're right," he said, "it shouldn't happen, but it does. You see, the river is very forgiving. If you fall in and go with the flow of the water, you will float to the top, to safety. But if you fight it in a panic and don't let go, it will pull you down and drag you under."

"Ron, I think I'm ready to go on that rafting trip now."

"I think you are too, Denise. You'll be fine. Just remember that if you go under, be ready to let go and you'll come out on top!"

Later, I realized how Ron's comment also applies to forgiveness. Forgiveness is about letting go. When we forgive, we are telling God that whether that person was right or wrong in what they did, we will not be the judge. Only God can do that. We are letting go.

Our physical bodies, as well as our spirits, are not designed to bear the stress that unforgiveness causes in our lives. How many times have I refused to give in to the flow of forgiveness only to find that bitterness was pulling me down and threatening my own life and peace of mind? The times I felt justified in wearing that chip on my shoulder only meant more weight to carry around and pull me down.

But how could I forgive when I hurt so much? How could I forgive when I did nothing to deserve the wrong that was done to me? As a Christian, I forgive by faith, because God says so. I may not feel like it, and the pain may be just as real after I forgive as it was before. I believe that God is a far better judge than I, and by forgiving, I am leaving it in His hands. My feelings will get in line later. By an act of my will, I am letting go.

Peter asked Jesus how often he should forgive his brother if he should sin against him. Jesus answered, "seventy times seven." In other words, to forgive as many times as someone sins against you. Numbers don't count when we're not keeping score. Our job, if we truly wish to obey God, is to forgive. That means letting go so that bitterness doesn't drag us under, just like on a river rafting trip.

Then Peter came to Jesus and asked, "Lord, how many times shall I forgive
my brother when he sins against me? Up to seven times?" Jesus answered,
"I tell you, not seven times, but seventy-seven times."

Matthew 18:21–22

> If you have some bitterness toward someone, write it
> down and then burn the piece of paper in a ceremony
> of letting it go and letting God take care of it.

Never-Ending Gratitude

KAREN JOHNSON ZURHEIDE

For those of us who live with young children, the opportunities
for discovery and reawakening are without limit, if only we open
our senses, minds and spirits.

Karen Johnson Zurheide

I do believe that the very best pray-ers in the world are children. They can
be so honest, so uninhibited, so fresh and new. Without intending it, they
are downright funny and often incredibly insightful.

We adults take time to teach our children how to pray, saying, "Fold your
hands, bow your head, close your eyes, talk like this, say 'In Jesus' name,
Amen.'" But I think we have things backwards. Really, we are the ones who
should be studying the children. We have so much to learn from overhear-
ing young ones talk to God, if we only will really listen.

When she was a preschooler, my daughter was a very eager pray-er, especially at meals. One Sunday we were about to have lunch at home with
guests. By the time we had made it back from church and gotten the food on

the table, it was late and we were all hungry. Our daughter asked to pray. How can one say no to such a request?

She began, very slowly and carefully, as only a nearly-four-year-old can. "Thank you, God, for the lettuce, and the carrots, and the celery, and the tomatoes, and the cucumbers, and the croutons, and the onions." She was obviously praying with her eyes open, studying the salad set before us.

She continued, with painstaking slowness, "Thank you for the avocados, and the olives . . ."

There were yet half a dozen salad ingredients to go, not to mention a main course consisting of many elements, plus bread and butter, beverages (with ice) and dessert. We were in for a long one, while cold foods were getting warm and hot foods were cooling off, and we were all getting hungrier.

Unable to wait any longer, my daughter's little friend piped up, in obvious exasperation, "Aaaaaaaall right, Molly!"

We were all grateful for the interruption. With a quick, corporate "Amen!" we raised our forks at last.

While we chuckled at this exceptionally detailed liturgy of thanks, it made me think. How often do I truly enumerate the good things I enjoy in this life? How often do I take the time to think of all the little blessings that make up my world? How much more of an attitude of gratitude would I have if I did stop to count my blessings once in a while?

It's not too late to start. Today would be a good time. Right now, as I write, I am thankful for electricity, my computer, e-mail, quiet, special memories, children and spouse, this spot, God's Spirit, clean clothes (make that pajamas), hot tea and honey—and so much more.

By a child's very long prayer, I am reminded of all I have, of the abundance of good things that are mine to enjoy. You and I need to remember that lesson. May we more often stop, look, listen, and give thanks.

And he said, "I tell you the truth, unless you change and become like little children, you will never enter the kingdom of heaven."

Matthew 18:3

Today, let's make a detailed list of our blessings.
But let's be ready to take a little time, for the list may be
longer than we expect.

A Basil Bush

JANE TOD JIMENEZ

God who gives the wound gives the salve.

Miguel de Cervantes

Today I bought a small pot of basil. Unfortunately, it was a terrible specimen. I might have once considered it beautiful, but an unexpected garden lesson taught me the truth.

Twenty years ago I grabbed my first packet of basil seed in an urgent determination to grow an herb garden. Never mind that I didn't recognize the names of half the packages in my hand. I would learn.

My first wonder at planting all those herb seeds was in how very tiny they were. They showed up like heavy dust at the bottom of each packet.

Once planted, their potential lives were impossible, if not miraculous. Buried under too much soil, they had no hope of growing tall enough to reach sunshine. The birds didn't mind, their bird eyes were able to find a miniscule basil seed under half an inch of soil.

Imagine my shouts of joy two weeks later, as here and there, I found lucky herb sprouts around the garden. One stubborn basil sprout grew tall and proud at the corner post closest to the path. I loved to check its progress every morning. What joy I felt as it reached eight inches tall!

And what despair I knew the next day when I discovered it broken off just above the bottom leaves! It was more than I could bear. I quit looking to the corner of the garden in the mornings.

Weeks later, poking and prodding under and around plants checking for ripe squash and tomatoes, I came upon a lovely small bush in the corner where my broken basil had been. It spread out three large branches close to the ground in brilliant emerald green, and it smelled delicious. It smelled Italian! Basil!!

I broke off the ends of the stems and ran into the house to find a recipe for my first herb harvest. Over the weeks, I continued to break off the ends of the basil limbs for new recipes. Undeterred, the basil bush grew and grew. Visitors to my garden commented, "I've never seen such a beautiful basil bush!"

Succeeding gardens taught me the secret of my basil plant. It must be pruned early and continuously. At every juncture where a sprig of basil is broken and harvested, two or more new branches will grow.

I've also learned this is God's secret with me. While I would like to have my life grow untamed and free from pain, God knows the power of pruning. Carefully, He pinches off a life option here, but He opens two doors for me there. Firmly, He breaks off my prideful branches and waits for humility to grow in their place. And the more I turn to His Word, the more He teaches me about the pruning I have come to expect.

The basil plant I bought yesterday is tall and stringy, eight inches tall in one strong stem. But I know how to fix it. I know it has the makings of a beautiful bush.

He cuts off every branch in me that bears no fruit, while every branch that does bear fruit He prunes so that it will be even more fruitful.
John 15:2

Think back to a major disappointment of your childhood, and think of two blessings that enriched your life from it. Tell these to a close friend.

Joy's "Simple" House D.I.E.T.

Joy L. Newswanger

Dieters are people who get up in the morning and the first thing they say is, "Mirror, mirror, on the dresser— do I look a little lesser."

Robert Orben

"I've lost over two hundred pounds in the past two years. In fact, just yesterday I lost another twenty pounds."

Most people are intrigued by promises of instant cures to weight woes. In fact, right now you are probably on a diet or know someone who is. But the fact is—diets don't work.

So what do you do? What do you do when you and your house struggle with weight? What do you do when the biggest abundance you see is not God's provision but the amount of stuff cluttering your house? My house wouldn't fit on a set of scales. Still I knew it was overweight.

How did I know my house's obesity was a problem? 1) No space. When I had to go outside to see open space I knew there was too much stuff. 2) Family resemblance. My house was starting to look like my mother's. My mother has had forty-two more years to accumulate stuff but my stockpiles were rivaling hers. 3) Body breakdown. My house's closet shelves and cupboards were literally breaking from carrying too much weight. 4) Activity limitations. My house's stuff took so much time and energy to maintain that I couldn't do much else.

What to do? I knew diets didn't work, but I tried them repeatedly. One diet was "Cold Turkey." I tried to stop shopping. I tried to discard stuff. But I'd soon "reward" myself for my decluttering progress with a shopping binge. My house would not just gain back what it had lost but add more.

Still, my house has lost over two hundred pounds in the past two years. Quick diets didn't work but my own simple house D.I.E.T. *is* working. In-

stead of instantaneous results I am seeing consistent progress. I actually can tell you the color of all the walls in my house now! So here goes. Here's Joy's Simple House D.I.E.T.

D. = DECIDE. Decide what your priorities are, what's important to you. Narrow the list to five or less of your absolute non-negotiables. You'll be amazed at how much extra stuff there is taking up space, time, and energy.

I. = INVEST. Invest your energy, time, and resources in what's important and valuable to you. Investment implies that there are few guaranteed or immediate results. Still, the investment process itself will bring joy.

E. = ENLIST. Enlist support. Get cheerleaders. Find friends who will cheer about even your simplest decluttering choice.

T. = TODAY. Today is the day to do this. Don't endlessly relive the past trying to figure out how you got to this point. Don't obsess about the future. Perseverance is a critical factor in success and it happens one day at a time.

So DECIDE, INVEST, ENLIST, TODAY. Sometimes to see God's abundance we need to get rid of the stuff that is blocking our view. Besides this weight loss is inspiring. A garbage bag can weigh ten or more pounds. A box of books . . . need I say more?

> . . . *let us throw off everything that hinders and the sin that so easily*
> *entangles, and let us run with perseverance the race marked out for us.*
> *Let us fix our eyes on Jesus . . .*
> Hebrews 12:1b–12a

Take the time to make a list of your non-negotiables,
the things most important to you. Narrow the list down to
five or less. Then keep these things in view
when you make your schedule and purchases.

Accepting Others

LEE EZELL

Love is a deep, continuous, growing, and ever-renewing activity of
the will, superintended by the Holy Spirit.

Mike Mason

Most of us sincerely desire to fulfill Christ's command to love one another but need to examine the "as I have loved you" portion of that concept. Somewhere, before the foundations of the earth were laid, God made a decision to love and accept you and me. *God so loved the world that He gave His only begotten Son. . . .* (John 3:16) was determined way before He saw whether we deserved it or not. Because He set the example first, God can tell us to love one another in the same abandoned, unconditional way. As God accepts me, He expects me to accept others and myself. Believers should gladly follow suit, loving prickly people whether we think they deserve love or not. How else is God going to be able to show His unconditional love to the world if not through us? He has chosen us to be His hands, His feet, His eyes, His lips, and His heart of compassion.

Think of all the embarrassing things God has accepted about you and me: our stubbornness, unfaithfulness, quick tempers, lack of discipline, ingratitude. Once you've taken that little inventory, don't you want to thank Him for the way He has blessed you, warts and all? Doesn't that make it easier for you to thank Him for your porcupine people? After thanking God for putting that specially challenging person in your life, try this: ask God to help arrange a time and an appropriate way for you to tell that person that you accept them just as they are—no changes necessary.

If you love those who love you, what reward will you get? Are not even the tax collectors doing that? And if you greet only your brothers, what are you doing more than others? Do not even pagans do that? Be perfect, therefore, as your heavenly Father is perfect.

Matthew 5:46–48

When checking into a hotel, check to see that everything is working correctly—*before* the bellman leaves.

Summer

With the lazy, hazy days of summer, we take time to relax and vacation, knowing that God has determined that leisure and festivities should be as much a part of our lives as work. For many, the children are out of school, and life may not be quite as structured. For there can be more stress from added work as co-workers go on vacation.

Regardless, God is there for us, wanting us to live abundantly in His power. He calls to us, "Come aside and focus on me. I love you too much for us not to have intimate conversation."

With the readings in this Summer section, remember God's complete and unconditional rejoicing over you and relax in His ability to help you with every situation . . . wherever you are.

Dream Big

CHARLES SWINDOLL

If one advances confidently in the direction of his dreams, and endeavors to live the life which he has imagined, he will meet with a success unexpected in common hours.

Henry David Thoreau

Most of us don't dream enough. If someone were to ask you, "What are your dreams this year? What are your hopes, your agenda? What are you trusting God for?" could you give a specific answer? I don't have in mind just occupational objectives or goals for your family, although there's nothing wrong with those. But what about the kind of dreaming that results in character building, the kind that cultivates God's righteousness and God's rulership in your life?

Here are a few more ideas about dreams. Dreams are specific, not general. Dreams are personal, not public. God doesn't give anyone else my dreams on a public computer screen for others to read. He gives them to me personally. They're intimate images and ideas. Dreams can easily appear to others as extreme and illogical. If you share your dreams with the crowd, they'll probably laugh at you because you can't make logical sense out of them. Dreams are often accompanied by a strong desire to fulfill them. And they are always outside the realm of the expected. Sometimes they're downright shocking. They cause people to suck in their breath, to stand staring at you with their mouth open.

This is the stuff of which leaders are made. If you don't dream, your leadership is seriously limited.

In the last days, God says, I will pour out My Spirit on all people. Your sons and daughters will prophesy, your young men will see visions, your old men will dream dreams.

Acts 2:17

To clean out kitchen drawers, use a can of compressed air
(like the type used for computer keyboards).

Bloom In The Heat

DONNA J. ADEE

When we cannot find contentment in ourselves it is useless to seek it elsewhere.

Francois de la Rochefoucauld

Gardening has always been my job on our farm. I love a large collection of rocks and driftwood with drought-resistant plants. In our area of central Kansas, we have lots of prickly pear cacti growing wild. But the beautiful, small, pincushion type is rare. Being rare made them special to me, so I kept looking for one to add to my rock garden.

While on one of our walking tours of the pastures, I spied a tiny pincushion cactus among the rocks. "Oh, there's one! Dig it up for me," I exclaimed to my husband.

"But I only have a pocket knife," hubby Ed complained. He managed to dig it out and I carried it carefully home in a piece of cloth. It looked so tiny among the large rocks and yucca plants, that I wondered if it would even survive.

The next summer I noticed one bright pink blossom, which later was followed with some baby pincushions around the base. The next summer during the hottest part of the day, I drove by the rock garden on my way to town. I was shocked to see the pincushion blooming profusely with hot pink flowers. In the morning when it is cool, the blossoms are tightly closed. I had thought it had quit blooming, but it was waiting for the hot sunshine. Heat seems to promote the best blossoms. The Creator had designed this plant to thrive in the heat.

If I could only be like that little cactus—content where I am planted and willing to thrive in difficult circumstances. Then I could show forth the beauty of God's creation while fitting into God's design for me. If heat brings out the true glory of God's cacti, trials should bring out the true glory of God's promises through His obedient children.

Give thanks in all circumstances, for this is God's will for you in Christ Jesus.
I Thessalonians 5:18

If you're getting rid of some books, sell them
to your used books store.

Shake Those Guilty Feelings
BARBARA JOHNSON

A guilty conscience needs no accuser.
English Proverb

If you can't shake guilt feelings, you can try separating true guilt from false. Lots of folks are carrying burdens of false guilt, thinking they have failed when they really have not. Again, moms suffer most from guilt feelings. They want to take on responsibility for everything their kids have done, and when they go wrong through their own choices, Mom still thinks, "It surely must have been MY fault."

So, how do we separate true guilt from false?" Sometimes it's simple; other times it's difficult, but you might want to try this solution: Why not give ALL your guilt to Jesus, the true and the false? Let Him separate it out and make the final judgments. Let Him decide what is true about the gray areas of your life, where the answers aren't in simple black and white.

You see, the good news is that Jesus was nailed to a cross so you could stop nailing yourself to a cross of true or false guilt. Accept His forgiveness and you can live a guilt-free life from here on out!

Therefore, there is now no condemnation for those who are in Christ Jesus.
Romans 8:1

If you use a lot of paper towels, use cloth napkins instead.

Abundance In Teen Trials Time
ELLEN BERGH

I can lead an abundant life even if my child is angry with me.
Dawn Curry

The rocky road of teen time with my daughter took me to the edge of my endurance. Raised in a troubled home myself, I yearned to help build Jenny's self esteem. She shrugged that off and thrived on hotly debating every issue of home life. Any family outing tortured her, while she pestered us for permission to go to vague destinations with dubious friends. "You are so rigid and unfair!" she growled.

Her barbs wore me down. "I've never been a mom before, let's get a second opinion." I suggested. She resisted but I insisted.

When we met with a Christian counselor, I winced when I saw her. How could this young mother of a toddler, counseling part time, understand my problems with a teen? But Dawn was my divine appointment. Only ten years out of her own teen time, and in the throes of mothering a two-year-old, she could relate to both of our struggles. She explained that we parents want our children to like us, but parenting is not a popularity contest.

Then Dawn helped us set boundaries of civilized behavior. Jenny journalized her requests for outings with who, what, where, and when information in a courteous manner. We wrote our responses. That way we had a written commitment of the parameters of outings and no misunderstandings.

When my daughter distanced herself from us as she went into high school and took a part-time job, Dawn challenged me to prepare for my empty nest future. I headed back to school to earn an AA in liberal arts, but prayer and counseling helped desensitize me to my minor's mockery. So what if I was hopelessly corny and outdated? I could lead an abundant life! Jenny and I graduated the same day.

Ten years later, our mom and daughter relationship is restored and we can look back with wry laughter at the conflicts we weathered. The skills we learned serve us today and I have the restored respect and encouragement that I had despaired of ever enjoying. God gets us through the tough times.

Maybe your putdowns aren't coming from a child, but from a parent or a partner. Be encouraged that you can lead an abundant life by seeking out the passions God planted in you, gathering encouragers and going forward.

I will lead the blind by ways they have not known, along unfamiliar paths I will guide them; I will turn the darkness into light before them and make the rough places smooth. These are the things I will do. I will not forsake them.

Isaiah 42:16

At the close of the day, jot down a list of the
top seven things you want to accomplish the next day.

Time Wasters

MARY WHELCHEL

*Great men never complain about the lack of time.
Alexander the Great and John Wesley accomplished everything
they did in twenty-four hours.*

Fred Smith

Think about some of your common time wasters. My guess is that interruptions would be near the top of the list. If phones didn't ring, people didn't ask questions, or unexpected meetings weren't called, we could get more done. But let's be realistic: these interruptions are never going to be eliminated entirely. They're part of the job.

Since we can't stop the interruptions, what can we do to "work smarter"? Remember: time is a gift from God, a resource provided to each of us in the same, daily measures. While some interruptions are unavoidable and even necessary, we can do some proactive things to minimize our interruptions.

Group your activities, for example. Return and place phone calls at certain times, all together. Go to the copier and the fax machine once or twice a day instead of ten times a day. Interrupt yourself for coffee or refreshments at specified times to help you stay on task longer.

A good time manager has a daily plan for activities and priorities, written down and followed. It can be in an informal format, like a calendar or a pad of paper, or a structured plan like a Day-Timer. If you consistently use a daily activity plan, you will use your time much more effectively.

Remember, despite all the difficulties you're going to face today, make the best use of your time; because once you spend time, you can never replace it.

Make the best use of your time, despite all the difficulties of these days.

Ephesians 5:16

For one week, keep a record of how you spend every fifteen minutes of your time. Then evaluate what needs to change.

To Sweep Or To Vacuum?

MARTY MAGEE

The haste of the fool is the slowest thing in the world.
Thomas Shadwell

We were having company from New Mexico in three days. Anyone coming to sunny California expects to enjoy a nice cool, blue, backyard swimming pool. Since I'm the resident people pleaser, I decided to do my part to get the pool ready. Until then, my husband David and I had an agreement. He would keep the pool maintained; I would swim in it. This worked.

But since I wanted it done on time, I decided I should do my part. That afternoon I went to the backyard. Hanging on the wall outside was a long blue tea strainer. I took it off its rack and skimmed the leaves off the top of the water.

But then I realized this was just the beginning. Hanging on the same rack was a long, hollow metal pole with two holes at one end. I knew this had something to do with pool maintenance. I took it off its holder. I had to find the right contraption to go on the end of it. I looked in David's storage cabinet and found a brush, of sorts. It had two knobs that clipped into the holes of the long pole. Now I was making progress. I maneuvered the thing until I got it in the pool. I went all the way around, sweeping like a proud new housewife. I even scrubbed the sides of the pool like I'd seen David do. Then I found another device; this one had wheels. I tried to make it fit somehow into the brush thing. I thought maybe the wheels would make the brush work more smoothly. But I couldn't figure it out. I found another brush, thinner, but stronger, and it worked. Again a few times around the pool.

I am so good at this, I probably won't even need David's help, I concluded.

But then I noticed lots of dirt swirling in the water. *I'd better turn the pool pump on so the dirt will go down . . . wherever it goes.* I couldn't wait for David to come home and see how well I was doing.

"What are you doing?" were the first words out of his mouth. Not "You sure are working hard!" Not "You've got most of the work done for me. Thanks!"

"Honey," he continued, "I was planning to vacuum the pool as soon as I got home from work."

Vacuum? What's wrong with sweeping?

He explained, "Because you swept it and stirred up the dirt, I'll have to wait until tomorrow to vacuum, which does a better job. You've simply swished it around, which could clog the filter."

Do I ever stir things up and get things clogged so that some wiser Christian has to wait until the dust settles before he can correct my futile attempts at doing God's work?

Let's be sure that we're doing what God wants us to do and then we'll know when to sweep and when to vacuum.

> *For I can testify about them that they are zealous for God,*
> *but their zeal is not based on knowledge.*
> Romans 10:2

> If you find yourself in a tizzy, stop and ask for guidance;
> it's there—in God's Word, through prayer,
> and from fellow Christians.

A Few Well-Chosen Words

H. Norman Wright

Gratitude is the memory of the heart.

Jean Baptiste Massieu

Often at funerals and memorial services one or more family members or friends deliver a eulogy. They share the positive qualities, characteristics, and accomplishments of the deceased. They extol the person's virtues and go into detail as to why the person will be missed. Sometimes you wonder if they (the deceased) knew while they were alive that this is how others felt about them. You wonder how much of what was shared at the memorial service was ever told to them directly. In most cases, it probably wasn't.

So many parents and children end up saying, "If only I had told them how much I loved them, what I appreciated, how much they meant to me . . ."

"If only . . ."— words of regret and sadness over missed opportunities. The presence of positive words can motivate, encourage, and lift up. The absence, well, perhaps they would never know what they missed. Or they could have been living with the longing for a few well-chosen words. We can't change the times we've missed, but we can fill our family members' lives now and in the future. Who needs words of love and encouragement from you? And who do you need to hear from? What others hear from you may help them do likewise.

> *Let the peace of Christ rule in your hearts, since as members of one body*
> *you were called to peace. And be thankful.*
>
> Colossians 3:15

Use a crystal dish or candy dish for a soap dish
and make the bathroom sparkle!

Choosing Who We Are

Naomi Rhode

*All mothers have their favorite child. It is always the same one: the
one who needs you at the moment.*

Erma Bombeck

"Because you are our very cherished daughter, I made a special gift for you,"
my father told me during his presentation ceremony the night before I left
home to go to camp for the first time. "I want you to accept this gift as a very
special sign of our love. *When you look at it, remember who you are.*"

Even though I was only twelve, I knew that in our family "remembering
who you are" meant we were children of wonderful people with great ances-
tors of deep spiritual faith.

After his speech of affirmation, my dad presented me with a piece of wood
he had carved and painted into the shape of an animal that resembled a
penguin. He named the carving Goofus.

The next day I went to camp with Goofus in my suitcase as a reminder
that I was a special person. Raised in an atmosphere of high trust and low
fear, I was assured of my parents' confidence in me to make good choices.

While at camp I met a fourteen-year-old boy with whom I became so
enraptured that I gave him Goofus. As an adult I don't understand that choice,
but as a child it made perfect sense.

"Dad, I gave Goofus away to the boy I am going to marry," I proudly explained when I got home.

Dad's response was classic: "He must be a very special person."

Rather than degrading, disciplining, or reprimanding his twelve-year-old daughter
for thinking so little of his gift, he accepted my choice. Unfortunately Dad died a
year later, so he didn't live long enough to experience the reality of his statement.
The boy's name was Jim Rhode, and seven years later I married him. We kept
Goofus as a reminder of my dad's confidence in my ability to make the right choices.

Though I'm not saying that any twelve-year-old is capable of making a decision about marriage, my dad's attitude toward me was important. While raising my own children, I frequently thought of Goofus and the confidence my dad always had in me, as I trusted and affirmed my children's decisions.

And this is my prayer: that your love may abound more and more in knowledge and depth of insight, so that you may be able to discern what is best and may be pure and blameless until the day of Christ.
Philippians 1:9,10

Take advantage of your local library's used book sale
to increase your book collection.

Friends Forever

HELEN LUECKE

Friendship is one of the sweetest joys of life.
Charles Spurgeon

My car was in the shop, so I hurried to catch the early bus to make it to work on time. I boarded and sat behind two young women. The nearly empty bus made their voices seem loud and I couldn't help but overhear their conversation.

"I don't think I'll ever talk to Susan again. I'm so mad at her."

"What's the matter? Isn't she your best friend?"

"She's supposed to be, but she uses me. I'm someone to fall back on in case of an emergency. She thinks I'll always be here."

The bus came to my stop. I stepped out into the brilliant sunrise. *I'm glad I don't have a friend like that*, I thought. Then the truth hit me hard and I felt a twinge of guilt. I was a friend like that—at least with the Lord. How many times had I turned my back on my Friend and grabbed at worldly pleasures? Only when my cares pushed me to my knees and no one else would listen would I again call out to Him.

Tears burned my eyes. Jesus waited to forgive me. My Friend would never leave me or forsake me. He is constant.

If you've been that kind of friend, He also wants to forgive you and help you be a more faithful friend.

Jesus Christ is the same yesterday and today and forever.
Hebrews 13:8

> Call a friend or send them a card to let them know
> that you are thinking of them.

Consider The Ant ✓

MARCIA VAN'T LAND

I am only one, but I am one. I can't do everything, but I can do something. And what can I do, that I ought to do. And what I ought to do, by the grace of God, I will do.

Edward Everett Hale

It was March 1983, and I had just returned home from a long and difficult hospitalization. Our three young children were glad Mom was home again. When the mail arrived that day, I opened an unusual envelope and out came a tube of swarming, wild, red harvester ants.

"Oh no!" I said as I dropped the tube. Then I remembered my promise to our children that we could set up an ant farm. Thankfully, the tube didn't break.

I didn't really feel I had the energy for setting up an ant farm, but I had to abide by my own words to our kids, "We must always keep our promises." Besides, the angry ants wouldn't wait.

The kids held the "Uncle Milton's See-Through Ant Farm" as I added the sand and water into the plastic form. Then we added the ants, which proved to be exciting, as some of the ants almost escaped.

Somewhat dazed, the ants took about one minute to orient themselves and immediately set to work. What fun we had watching these ants scurrying back and forth, up and down. They never stopped. Each ant had a job to do and they did it carrying one grain of sand at a time in their mouths.

As I watched the ants' progress in the next week, I noticed how focused they were. They never wasted time or meandered around, not knowing what to do. The whole situation reminded me of my grandmother saying, "Never walk empty-handed." My energy level was often quite low so I took that saying seriously and never went empty-handed.

The ants also reminded me that God wants us to be focused on what He wants us to do with our lives. Each ant knew its job and accomplished its assigned work. We don't have to do big things for God. He honors each small accomplishment for Him—each grain of sand moved.

And just as some of the plastic farm buildings inside the ant farm were soon buried under the sand, so our Lord Jesus covers our sins with His blood and they disappear—they are no more.

What is meaningful for you about the workings of ants? How could that lesson strengthen you to have a more abundant life?

Go to the ant, you sluggard; consider its ways and be wise.

Proverbs 6:6

If you spend a lot of time on the telephone, consider buying a cordless unit with a headpiece.

Facing And Overcoming Fear

Nelda Jones

The only thing we have to fear is fear itself.
Franklin D. Roosevelt

One day, as I washed the dishes at the kitchen sink, I overheard our pre-school daughter, Tracy, out on the patio talking to the chickens.

She said, " I know you, old red rooster, I've known you for thousands and thousands of years." The rooster, perched upon the picnic table, cocked his head as if listening intently to her, as she continued, "If you'll be my good buddy, I'll be your good buddy."

Suddenly our dog Missy spotted the cows by the fence and ran out barking at them to scare them away. Startled, Tracy ran toward the steps, almost tripping over the dog in her haste to get back to safer territory. Tracy cried out, her voice trembling, "Missy, you sure are nervous."

I smiled as I watched Tracy trying bravely to make friends with the chickens and overcome her fear of them. Even though Tracy was still frightened, this was a big step for her. When our son Mark had first gotten the chickens, Tracy liked to go with him to the pen and "help" feed them. But one day Tracy had taken a pan of potato peelings and scraps to the pen by herself to give them. Suddenly, I heard her screaming. Fear gripped my heart as I ran to check on her. The chickens had swarmed all over her, trying to get to the pan of scraps in her hand, knocking her down in the process. She thought they were trying to hurt her and came flying across the garden, screaming in terror. Although unhurt, she was hysterical with fear. It took me a while to calm her down and reassure her that the chickens were not intentionally "attacking" her. For a long time after that Tracy refused to go near the chicken pen, and if the chickens were out in the yard, she was afraid to even play in the backyard.

However, she overcame her fear, and got to the point where she would play in the backyard. If the chickens came too close, she would retreat to the patio or go into the house.

Now, as I listened to her making friends with the chickens again, my heart rejoiced, for I knew she was over the biggest hurdle. She had faced her "enemy," just as we all must do, before we can completely overcome our fears.

So must our Heavenly Father rejoice also, when He sees us, His frightened children, standing bravely against what we perceive to be our "enemies." We might need to risk speaking about Jesus to a friend or ask for prayer about a temptation that is overwhelming us. But as we do acknowledge our fear and take steps to overcome it, God will give us victory.

I sought the LORD and He answered me; He delivered me from all my fears.
Psalm 34:4

> Ask your local dry cleaners whether they will take back your extra hangers.

Wonderwoman Wannabe
Ellie Kay

Goodness consists not in the outward things we do but in the inward things we are.
Edwin Hubbel Chapin

As a girl, I watched Lynda Carter in the television series, *Wonderwoman*. She could lasso any villain that got in her way with her magic rope. She jumped over life's obstacles without letting her *little* costume fall off—a feat worthy of Superhero Status. As a former "Miss World," Lynda had the perfect body, perfect boyfriend (although he was a wee bit one-dimensional),

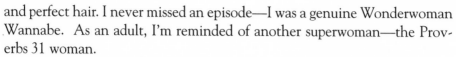

and perfect hair. I never missed an episode—I was a genuine Wonderwoman Wannabe. As an adult, I'm reminded of another superwoman—the Proverbs 31 woman.

I remember one day in particular when I was feeling like a Proverbial reject. On that morning, five-year-old Daniel climbed a forty-foot pine tree and wouldn't come down for the baby-sitter. The sitter called me during the class I was taking at a university and I rushed home to find Daniel—riding his bike.

At lunch, three-year-old Philip ran off to join the postal service. He was pulled out of the mail truck just before he committed a federal crime—destroying the mail. Later that afternoon, two-year-old Bethany climbed on top of Bob's dresser, pulled his Air Force Academy sword off the wall, and used it as a walking stick—pointed side up. Thankfully, I retrieved it before she was hurt.

The Kay guardian angels were working overtime and so was Mom. The angels succeeded, but I felt like a failure. In the midst of these circumstances, how could I possibly keep the Proverbs 31 woman list?

That evening, I wearily pulled on my tee shirt with the slogan: "I am woman. I am invincible. I am tired." What I needed was a pick-me-up. I put on the coffee and began raiding the cupboards for chocolate.

At that moment, the Great Chocolate Search was interrupted by singing. It was Bethany rehearsing a self-composed operetta in F major as she walked into the kitchen. My two-year-old sang dramatically. *"I like to eat potato chips. But Papaaaa . . . he got dem first and ate dem all up."* Verse two added depth to her plight. *"I saw de angel flying in de airplaaaane . . . and he was . . . verwy happy, eating Papa's potato chips."* (With a pilot for a father, how else could angels fly?) Verses three through thirty went much the same way.

I watched my blond girlie and thought, *She is so incredibly precious.*

That's when it happened. There was no bolt of lightning, no burning bush—there wasn't even a UPS truck. Nonetheless, God sent me a message—through a singing telegram.

A still, small voice spoke to my heart. *Ellie you are just as precious to Me. The way you see your little girl is the way I see you.* My self-pity was replaced by incredible comfort. I realized that God didn't require perfection, He only asks that I persevere. In my hectic, busy days of mothering, God sees me and smiles. He looks upon me with affection—He thinks I'm precious. He thinks I'm cute.

So, I rest in Him.

Come to me, all you who are weary and burdened, and I will give you rest.
Matthew 11:28

> If God were to give you an endearing nickname, what would it be? Think about how special you are to the Father and rest in Him today.

Memory Verse Tag

HELEN E. KESINGER

We must use time as a tool, not as a couch.
John F. Kennedy

I'm terrible at memorizing Scripture. I dutifully write Bible verses on index cards and stick them on the bathroom mirror, in my car, on my bedroom wall, in my purse, or use them as bookmarks. Within two weeks the cards have disappeared, only to mysteriously reappear a year later when I clean out that special kitchen drawer. You know which one I mean.

Then one day I read how Moses, in preparing the people to enter the Promised Land, encouraged them to keep the Word of God constantly alive in their daily lives. One way he recommended in Deuteronomy 6:8 was to tie the commandments as symbols on their hands.

How? I prayed. God revealed a simple solution.

Buy a plastic ID tag. I bought mine for 59 cents at a hardware store. It came with a little key chain. Or you can get them with key rings in the automotive section of discount chain stores. Print, by hand or computer, the scripture you want to memorize. Cut and slip it into the ID tag. The scripture tag can be used as a separate key chain/ring or attached to your favorite key ring, slipped onto a necklace chain (like a dog tag—but let's call this a God tag) or colored twine, or a zipper. I attached mine to a plastic spiral key holder that goes over my wrist. I am so optimistic with this little memorization tool that I printed off a whole page of different Bible verses using the label tool on my computer.

I'm sure you can come up with all sorts of ways to utilize the memory verse tag. It's especially a great way to memorize Scripture while walking or jogging!

Let love and faithfulness never leave you; bind them around your neck, write them on the tablet of your heart.
Proverbs 3:3

Consider asking that your dry-cleaned clothes be returned to you in your own garment bag, rather than using more plastic. If plastic must be used, make sure you recycle it.

Grandmother's Quilt
GEORGIA CURTIS LING

The most important thing that a human being can do is pray, because we've been made for God and our hearts are restless until we rest with Him. And it's in prayer that we come into contact with God.
Mother Teresa

I have a confession to make. I have a favorite blankie. Yes, I'm a closet cuddler. When I married, I had to give up my teddy bear, but I kept my blankie incognito, as an extra blanket at the foot of the bed, just in case it got too cold.

It's a special, one-of-a-kind blanket. It's a quilt, hand-crafted by my Granny Curtis and my great-grandmother, Mommy Duck. (Yes, you guessed it, she waddled like a duck—hence, the nickname.) It was a family tradition to make each grandchild a quilt when they were born.

To me, it's not just a quilt, it is a patchwork treasure box filled with wonderful memories.

Both of these godly women are gone now, yet are so close as I cuddle my soft, worn-out blankie. I can visualize them around the quilting hoop, hard at work as they chat about their family and the latest grandchild. Dreaming of what the future would hold for her. Hoping to share many years in her life, and saying little prayers as they stitched away, stitch, by stitch, by stitch.

It reminds me of Hannah, who each year made a special cloak for her son Samuel, whom she promised to God, and gave him to the priest Eli, to help serve in the temple. You can imagine Hannah designing this coat in her mind, then spending long hours clipping the sheep, brushing the wool clean, painstakingly crushing root and berries to boil and dye the wool brilliant colors, and then weaving the yarn so tightly, bringing it all together, forming a beautiful masterpiece. Stitching it ever so carefully and with each stitch, praying for her son, stitch, by stitch, by stitch . . . *Stitching Prayers*, if you will, asking God's blessing on her son in her absence.

Do we have simple stitching prayers for our children and those we love, offering them up continually in prayer? Anything we do needs to be stitched in prayer. It's the thread that holds our lives together. It strengthens, comforts, encourages, heals, and gives us peace of mind, as we give everything to God.

Remember, a stitch in time saves nine.

> *Be joyful in hope, patient in affliction, faithful in prayer.*
> Romans 12:12

When you get a run in a nylon stocking, tie the stocking into a gentle knot when putting it away. That way, you'll know it's use is limited.

Serenade

Patsy Clairmont

Home that our feet may leave, but not our hearts.
Unknown

Some of the most soothing sounds during our family's Kentucky vacations were created by the serenade of my grandmother's home. Summer mornings in the South often turned into sultry afternoons, causing the pace of our days to slow dramatically. Family members would sit on Mamaw's shaded porch with tall drafts of iced tea, while others of us would doze lightly inside.

I loved to nap on Mamaw's generous featherbed spread across her aging mattress. There I would dreamily listen in on summer as ice rattled against frosty tumblers, rocking chairs moaned from the strain of guests, and buzzing bees tended to the clover outside the open windows. A small table fan whirred sweet relief while stirring the lace curtains in swishing patterns against the peeling wallpaper. Interspersed in this summer symphony was the melody of the creaking screen door as folks would amble in and out for additional re-freshments.

Lulled by the safe sounds of family I would dangle in that delicate space between awake and asleep, every cell of my being at ease. Then ever so gen-tly I would drift off, cradled in a languid lullaby.

All sounds in our spheres, however, are not soothing lullabies. In fact, some can be quite jarring, such as shattering glass or screeching tires. Oth-ers are bothersome: the incessant dripping of a faucet, the shrill whistle in the pipes each time the water is turned on, or the neighborhood dog that won't quit howling. I've noticed all homes seem to have varied noises that range from delightful to discordant. And sometimes what is music for one is disruptive to another.

Trains rumble frequently through our little town. For my husband and me the late-night train whistles are like tranquilizers that deepen and sweeten

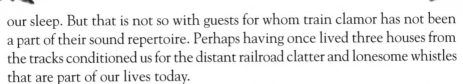

our sleep. But that is not so with guests for whom train clamor has not been a part of their sound repertoire. Perhaps having once lived three houses from the tracks conditioned us for the distant railroad clatter and lonesome whistles that are part of our lives today.

Recently a guest stopped by for a first-time visit. As she walked through my dining room the hardwood floor creaked under her feet. She stopped and applauded the noise. Then she leaned forward and back, replaying the golden oldie that flooded her with thoughts of yesterday. "Oh," she exclaimed, "what a wondrous sound. It brings back a thousand childhood memories."

I wish I could have captured her face on film as it lit up when that noise touched her ears and then her heart. I personally love the lively floor sounds that serve as people-tracking devices, helping me to hone in on everyone's whereabouts.

Have you thought about orchestrating the sounds in your home? Stop and listen. What do you hear? Does it please you? Does it set you on edge? Could you add or subtract some notes to enhance your atmosphere?

The sound of rejoicing in Jerusalem could be heard far away.
Nehemiah 12:43

For free coupons over the internet, check Quick Coupons
on www.qponz.com.

Waiting For Applesauce

ANITA VAN DER ELST

Let us then, be up and doing,
with a heart for any fate;
still achieving, still pursuing,
learn to labor and to wait.

Henry Wadsworth Longfellow

In the fall, one of my chores as a child growing up on a farm, was gathering up the fallen apples under our two Gravenstein apple trees. While picking up the bruised, oozing spheres, I delighted in the springtime memory of the fluffy, puffy, white blossoms adorning the gnarled branches above. And it was exciting to observe throughout the summer the little hard green balls ripening and maturing into fragrant, red-streaked yellow, juicily tart fruit. Boxed and stacked in the garage, what a heady aroma we enjoyed through winter months.

We also looked forward to the applesauce-making sessions in my mother's kitchen, usually with Grandpa turning the handle of the handy apple corer-peeler and Grandma quickly and deftly slicing apples while Mom stirred the pot of softly cooking apples. With just the right amount of sugar, no store-bought applesauce could compare.

From dead, brown, winter leaflessness to steaming hot, fresh applesauce, the process covered several months, a span of time which to a ten-year-old could seem like an eternity. Yet I never questioned the patience that was needed in the waiting.

God has a similar message for us. Just as apples are not produced or manufactured immediately ripe or mature, He wants us to accept the time it takes for us to grow. Rather than being impatient with our inadequacies or critical of what we perceive as a lack of growth in others, Jesus tells us to rely on Him for the changes He is causing slowly. He promises a rich harvest. We can look forward to His version of hot applesauce.

I am the vine; you are the branches. If a man remains in Me and I in him, he will bear much fruit; apart from Me you can do nothing.

John 15:5

Peel, core, and slice several Granny Smith or similar type apples into a saucepan with a small amount of water covering the bottom. Cook on low heat, stirring frequently. Let the aroma remind you to rely on Him. Add sugar to taste. Enjoy!

Feeding The Spirit

JACQUELINE CAIN

Kindness is the golden chain
By which society is bound together.

Goethe

Some people make such an impression on us that we never forget them, no matter how many years go by. I met Mary Edith and Thelma the summer of 1959, when I became a secretary at the company where they worked. Eighteen and fresh out of high school, this job was my entry into the adult world. When my boss, Mr. Dempsey, introduced me to my fellow employees, everyone was cordial even though it was obvious that they were in a state of turmoil. My being a new employee must have even brought tears to the eyes of some, especially those who'd received laid-off notices. This was my first encounter with "ageism," although then I didn't know it by its proper name. Neither, I suspect, did my elders. They only knew they would be losing a job they'd had for many years. The company was cutting expenses by letting go of higher paid employees and bringing in younger ones at much lower salaries.

This was especially worrisome for Mary Edith, since she had diabetes and needed the health benefits the job provided. To look at her, though, one would have never suspected the unrest she was going through. There was a radiance about her, a kind of inner glow that lit up any room she was in. An inveterate collector of wise sayings, she shared them with others by writing them on the office bulletin board. One I still remember is: *It is better to be more than you seem, than to seem more than you are.*

Like Mary Edith, Thelma was in her mid-forties but looked years older because her skin was prematurely wrinkled by too much Arizona sun. She wore a perpetual smile and had memorized what seemed like an endless supply of good, clean jokes. I can still hear her throaty giggles and see her hazel eyes crinkling up as she told one. Humor helped her forget her troubles and lightened up the atmosphere for us all. Still, she was plenty worried about losing her job.

"What company is gonna hire an ol' gal like me?" I overheard her saying to Mary Edith. "This old gray mare just ain't what she used to be, that's for sure!"

Concerns over being laid-off never got in the way of their treatment or attitude toward me, however. They were nurturing in their actions and instilled a "can do" attitude in me that's never left.

"We all make mistakes," Thelma soothed, whenever I worked the switchboard and inadvertently cut a caller off. "You mustn't let it get you down so!"

"Dictation is hard," Mary Edith would say, whenever I moaned over getting bawled out for making errors in transcribed letters. "You've got the makings of an excellent secretary."

The two women mothered me in other unforgettable ways, taking me out to lunch, throwing a party on my birthday, and both serving refreshments at my June wedding. This was no easy task, since the air conditioner stopped working and it was so hot in the reception room that the frosting on my wedding cake melted. Mary Edith even crocheted an exquisite basket for the little flower girl to carry. Since my own mother had passed away two summers before my marriage, their caring presence at my wedding meant everything.

By September of 1960, their jobs had ended, and a year later, so did mine, due to being, as Mr. Dempsey phrased it, "in a family way." Why I didn't stay in touch with my two friends escapes me. But being a new wife and then a mother were the most probable reasons.

Time has taught me that Mary Edith's and Thelma's gestures of friendship, when their own lives were in such a turbulent state, were acts of great generosity. They made my entry into the adult world a positive experience. My fond memories of them are a testimony to the everlasting power of kindness in a young person's life.

Is there someone whom the Lord wants you to reach out to with His generous love? Don't hesitate to do so, for you'll never know fully the tremendous impact you'll have upon that person.

Be kind and compassionate to one another, forgiving each other,
just as in Christ God forgave you.
Ephesians 4:32

Write a thank-you note immediately so that you won't forget
and so that you can express the warmth
you feel at the moment.

The Tooth Angel Keeps The Tradition Going
BETTY CHAPMAN PLUDE

The things that count most in life
are the things that can't be counted.
Unknown

My friend, Veronica, thought quickly during her five-year-old son, Nehemiah's (Miah), first experience with the Tooth Fairy. After days of Miah having a tired tongue from wiggling his loose tooth back and forth, it became a family project. Everyone wiggled the tooth. Finally, Dad was the hero. Miah's first baby tooth was out.

Miah was so excited he washed his little tooth till it sparkled, tucked it carefully under his pillow, hopped into bed, and said his prayers. He wanted to fall asleep quickly, anxious for morning to see what his tooth would be worth. Sleep was hard coming because he was curious, wanting to see the Tooth Fairy.

Around midnight, Veronica tiptoed into Miah's bedroom to slip a dollar under his pillow. Miah jumped up surprised and said, "Mommy, you are the Tooth Fairy!"

Veronica was shattered. She had blown the first chance at this fantasy. She sat on the side of the bed running her fingers through Miah's dark, soft hair. Thinking quickly, she began, "Son, you are a very smart boy and you found the secret out early."

Miah looked puzzled as his mom continued.

"When the rest of your teeth come out, we will celebrate with surprises from the Tooth Angels. Mommy and Dad will be the Tooth Angels. Under your pillow we'll tuck money, a video, a book, or a toy. We can even make it a treasure hunt. We will leave a note under your pillow and you will start on the treasure hunt. The note will say. 'Miah, look under your bed. There you will find another note to tell you where to go until finally you find a surprise. Won't that be fun?'"

Miah's eyes were sparkling as he reached into his mouth to start wiggling the loosest tooth he could find. Snuggled in for the rest of the night, he drifted into a sweet sleep.

Anxious to hear an update, I asked Veronica, "What's new with the Tooth Angels?"

With a little chuckle, Veronica explained, "Miah has lost a few more teeth. When we decided to do the treasure hunt, Noel and I questioned how we would do it since Miah can't read. But we came up with a plan. When Miah awakened and lifted the edge of his pillow, he found a toothbrush."

They asked him, "Miah, where does your toothbrush go?" Off he went to the bathroom. There he found a spoon. "Miah, where does the spoon go?" In the kitchen he found a cassette tape. He had the hang of it then and quickly carried the tape to the entertainment center with a sense of excitement. There it was—a video he had been asking for.

Miah, eyes sparkling, said, "Thanks, Tooth Angel, that was fun!"

If you'd like to substitute a Tooth Angel for the Tooth Fairy for the lost teeth of your children, introduce it to them from the beginning and you may all enjoy it.

I will instruct you and teach you in the way you should go;
I will counsel you and watch over you.

Psalm 32:8

For a catalogue of practical organizing products for jewelry, undergarments, and socks/hosiery, contact Neatnix Organizers at (800) 683-6328.

Pondering "Pet" Sins

KAREN POLAND

What makes resisting temptation difficult for many people is that they do not want to discourage it completely.

Franklin P. Jones

I am sitting in a quiet and peaceful house right now, but it has not been this way for the past few days. Our family is dog sitting, if you can call this eleven-week-old bundle of energy a dog. The puppy herself is not so much trouble. It's the anxiety that this houseguest has caused for my five- and six-year-old daughters that has upset the peace.

If the girls liked the dog, that would be great. If they hated the dog, that would be all right, too. The dilemma is that they are as drawn to her as they are frightened of her. The pull toward this puppy is as equal as the desire to run from her. Every ten-minute period they are displaying an extreme opposite emotion (and they are quite heavy on the dramatics). One minute they are shutting her into the laundry room, only to be influenced moments later by her audible cries to be let out. They simply cannot decide what to do with her.

As impatient as I am with this experience, I am faced with how it applies to my own struggles with sin. Am I not equally drawn and repulsed by the sin in my life? Am I not equally as fickle at times too? Do I not run from sin at one moment, only to run to it the next? Do I not put it away only to pick it up again?

Perhaps you, too, can relate to this struggle. Consider the "laundry room" of your heart. What sinful attitudes have you kept locked up, only to be drawn to let out again? Perhaps a particular sin remains just behind a closed door, but is tugging at your heartstrings. Is your own lack of peace today a result of indecision about what you will do with the sin in your life?

Make a decision to get rid of those secret sins and disobedience. You'll be thrilled to experience a new sense of peace without those temptations calling you from the laundry room.

No temptation has seized you except what is common to man. And God is faithful; He will not let you be tempted beyond what you can bear. But when you are tempted, He will also provide a way out so that you can stand up under it.
I Corinthians 10:13

Compile a list of Scriptures that will help you when you face temptation.

On This Rock

Marilyn J. Hathaway

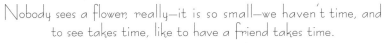

Nobody sees a flower, really—it is so small—we haven't time, and to see takes time, like to have a friend takes time.

Georgia O'Keeffe

Peter was my laid-back child, the one who missed the morning school bus as we searched for a lost shoe, coat, cap, school bag, comb, whatever. He was also my baby. When he fixed me with his innocent deep brown eyes I could forgive the little towhead's every transgression.

Regrettably, I was as uptight as Peter was unabashed. An obsessive-compulsive perfectionist, I believed in a place for everything and everything in its place. In small quarters with a husband and three youngsters this was impossible. It's the stuff children's nightmares are made of.

I'm also a creature of the night, falling asleep late and, too soon awakened, a grumbling zombie. School mornings were bad hair mornings all around, especially with Peter's double cowlick. I was a loving mother but not one to brag about.

During the children's growing years we lived on a mountain road on the east side of Salt Lake City, where many yards were dotted with large immovable boulders. A gigantic rock marked the school bus stop. In winter the many neighborhood children huddled near that rock for warmth, though, with icy indifference, the boulder gave little but hope. By spring the rock was abandoned, as the children played tag in the roadway.

On Tuesdays, I also left home early for a Bible Study at an uptown church. The children usually skipped the bus and I dropped them off at school on my way, saving much hassle. Therefore, I was startled one chilly spring morning when Peter appeared in the kitchen, red parka zipped to the chin, stripped sock cap pulled over his ears, and announced he was leaving for the bus stop.

"This is Tuesday," I chided.

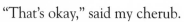

"That's okay," said my cherub.

Instead of complimenting his togetherness, I grew impatient. "It's Tuesday," I insisted.

"I know," he said. Then discerning that I was in need of help, he added, "I want to climb the rock and listen to the birds sing."

I stared a long moment. Silenced, I gave him a bear hug and sent him on his way.

I was late for Bible Study that morning. Standing at my kitchen window, I watched the red form sitting on the distant boulder, his knees tucked under his chin. The rising sun glistened on his golden head as the cap dangled from still fingers. He was deep in his own peaceful world until the chugging bus arrived.

Minutes later, I stopped my car to retrieve the crumpled cap lying in the sun at the base of the rock and wondered when I had last listened to the birds welcome the morning.

Pressing the warm cap to my cheek, I drove on to the church, but deep inside I knew that God had already delivered my life's lesson. If I was ever to experience the abundant life God has promised, it was time to get my priorities in order.

What rock have you sat on lately to listen to the birds sing?

From the lips of children and infants you have ordained praise . . .
Psalm 8:2a

> When you are a guest somewhere
> and are wondering if it is time to leave—it is!

Entering His Courts With Praise

SUZANNE J. GRENIER

I keep my attention on God in a simple, loving way.

Brother Lawrence

The church I attended before the Lord led me elsewhere was entrenched in a ritualistic, stagnant form of praise and worship. So when the music sounded at this new interdenominational church and people raised their hands, I was baffled. I had seen this once before and yet felt even more uneasy trying it. However, the awkwardness dissipated when I learned that it's one way of blessing the Lord. In recent years I also learned of other ways of pleasing Him by exercising the active verbs of praise found in the Psalms—clap, sing, laugh, leap, dance, and shout.

If you desire to promenade from His gates into His courts, here are some suggestions. If your church isn't very demonstrative, and you believe the Lord is drawing you into higher praises, practice at home. Since corporate praise and worship ushers in greater joy, eventually you may seek a church that more freely expresses their love to the Lord.

- Determine that this is your time to be with your first love, Jesus.
- Hide your petition list.
- Repent of any unconfessed sins.
- Thank Him for your blessings, especially if you don't feel like it.
- Play any type of musical, worship tape/CD. I prefer one that begins with an upbeat tempo so that I can begin to disengage myself from scattering thoughts.

When I can't stay focused, I pray: *Father, in Jesus' name, by the power of the Holy Spirit, I command my mind, body, soul, spirit, and strength to yield to You.*

My sole aim is to bless the Lord. When my mind wonders, I don't berate myself, I simply pull my thoughts back to Jesus.

As the music continues, I may or may not sing along with the songs, but I listen intently to the words. In addition, I stay attuned to the Spirit for my next movements which may be to clap, shout, lift my hands, dance, etc., periodically alternating or simultaneously combining these heartfelt displays of affection. Often my hands and arms rhythmically grace the atmosphere like a ballerina's. It may or may not be the same for you.

> *For the kingdom of God is . . . righteousness, peace and joy in the Holy Spirit.*
> Romans 14:17

Express your praise to God in a new way today.

The Memories Of The Golden Years
LEEANN S. YAMAKAWA

As we go through life, each of us is taking a notebook of memories, whether we put our notes on paper or only on the pages of the mind.
Unknown

I have fond memories of childhood visits to my grandmother's house. I would spend hours looking through many photograph albums that lined the shelves of her living room. In them, I found many old pictures of distant relatives I hardly knew, and pictures of my father and other close family members. Many of those pictures had stories behind them that fascinated me. I never grew tired of looking through those treasured books and hearing the stories behind the pictures.

II Timothy 1:5 tells us about the positive influence Timothy's grandmother was in his life. Paul writes, "I have been reminded of your sincere faith, which first lived in your grandmother Lois and in your mother Eunice. . . ." You may never know how much your example of godly character will influence generations to come.

As you enter the golden years of your life, your grandchildren can learn valuable lessons from you if you share with them what you have learned over your lifetime. Children almost never get tired of listening to stories, especially those that are about people they know and love. You can share the blessings that God has showered on you over the years. You can also share the mistakes you've made and the consequences you have experienced as a result of your actions. The memories you share may have a significant influence on them in the future when they are faced with similar decisions or dilemmas. You might even consider recording some particularly memorable life events on a cassette tape that your grandchildren can listen to for years to come. Grandparents are important people!

Children's children are a crown to the aged,
and parents are the pride of their children.
Proverbs 17:6

Plan today to write a letter to a grandchild
and share a learning experience from your past.

Word Perfect

ALICE KING GREENWOOD

What the heart delights in, the memory retains.

Charles H. Spurgeon

Personal computers baffle me, but that does not stop me from enjoying mine. With it, I can send e-mail all over the world, write music, draw colored pictures, keep a recipe file, play games, store financial records, find definitions in a dictionary, and check the stock market reports. There is one thing, however, that I cannot do. I cannot pull up photographs. Why? Because without a scanner, I cannot store them on a disk. Some day I will buy a scanner, and then I will be able to enhance genealogical records and annual Christmas letters with family pictures. They will always be at my fingertips any time I want to use them.

In a similar way, my spiritual life can be enhanced by knowing God's Word. As long as I have a Bible in hand, I can locate in a concordance the verses I need. There is one thing, however, that I cannot do. When I am away from my Bible, I cannot pull up any verse that is not stored in my memory. The solution to this problem is simple: I must program my human computer to activate my memory disk; then God's Word will always be available for the Holy Spirit to bring to my remembrance.

Perhaps you are a person who thinks you cannot memorize easily. I believe that most people can do so if they have the desire and discipline to spend a few minutes each day on this activity. Let me suggest ways by which you will be able to memorize many scriptures.

- Have a genuine desire to do so and ask God to help you.
- Set apart a certain time each day to work on memorization.
- List the Scriptures you want to learn first, along with their "addresses" (references).

- Start with the most familiar verses. You probably already know several.
- Write out long verses to help you learn them more quickly.
- Say aloud the verses with their references at least once each day.
- Fill a looseleaf notebook with graph paper or plain paper marked off into squares. Write one reference on each line.
- Make a diagonal mark in the graph squares each time the verse is repeated.
- Add new verses as soon as the first ones are mastered.

As time goes by, so many Scriptures will be on your list that it may take several days to say all of them at one time. You will be thrilled with what you are learning and you will not want to stop. Memorizing Scriptures will become a lifelong habit.

God's Word is the first thing I think of each morning; it occupies my last thoughts at night. Throughout the day, the Holy Spirit continually pulls up Scriptures from my memory disk. Every situation I encounter reminds me of something God says; each problem has an answer, each experience a Biblical precedent. For all my needs and all my joys, the Word of God is perfect.

Oh, how I love Your law! I meditate on it all day long.
Psalm 119:97

Invest in computer software with which you can create greeting cards for your family and friends. Your personalized messages, along with appropriate Scriptures, will be treasured by the recipients.

Where Two Or Three Come Together

Myrna L. Baldwin

God would have us put on a cheerful courage, and even in our
worst times, rejoice in His love and faithfulness.

Streams in the Desert

It was 4:30 A.M. and I simply could not toss and turn in bed one more
minute. My friend Donna in New York had offered more than once, "If you
ever need to talk, night or day, don't hesitate to call." She was sincere, but I
never wanted to bother her.

Why was I so desperately discouraged anyway? The restlessness couldn't
be controlled. I needed help. As good as my friend's suggestion sounded,
there was a shy and proud hesitation inside me.

Excuses began entering my head. *Surely I can handle my feelings by myself.
She is a busy pastor with plenty of people calling for prayer. It's absolutely too
early.* But after several hesitant attempts, I completed dialing the number
and my sleepy-sounding friend politely answered.

"Donna, hi," I blurted out. "I'm sorry if I woke you but can we pray together? I'm falling apart and don't have a clue why. Usually I sense God is
watching over me but I have a deep loneliness oppressing me. I can't back up
and can't go forward. What should I do?"

She took a few silent moments to seek the Holy Spirit and then began her
thoughtful prayer with, "Lord you said when two or three come together in
your name, you'd be there . . ."

The words suddenly relaxed me. It was like a soft warm pillow which I'd
been groping for in the dark, had been found. What seemed so overwhelming and uncontrollable only a few moments ago gradually began to subside. I
felt an uplifting peace. My tears came easily and honestly.

"Thanks, my friend, for being there for me," I finally said. "God bless you
for listening to my frustrated sobs."

"You're very welcome. I have to tell you, during our prayer, I kept seeing Jesus holding His arms out beckoning you. Let Him embrace you until this emotional storm passes."

Immediately in my spirit, I felt what she had seen through the Father's eyes. I rejoiced again in the wonderful gift of prayer. God had used her insight to set me free but I had to be willing to let her look behind my "mature Christian" door where the frightened child occasionally comes out from hiding.

Have you allowed pride or pain to prevent you from seeking God's help and peace through the loving prayers of another Christian? Permit yourself to risk. The power of two or more joining their spirits with the Lord's Spirit brings great results.

> . . . "Not by might, nor by power, but by my Spirit,"
> says the LORD Almighty.
> Zechariah 4:6

Ask yourself, "How much of my time am I spending on tasks that no one cares about?" Then stop doing those chores.

Thrive, Don't Just Survive

DORIS STERNER YOUNG

Those of you who are happy can choose to have faith.
Those in darkness must have faith.
Unknown

The nurse walked into my hospital room at 6:30 A.M. and startled me by asking, "Mrs. Young, do you know where your husband is?"

Having just called him at home and not gotten an answer, I said, "He's either in the shower or on his way to work."

"Wrong," she replied, "he's in the Emergency Room downstairs. He came in during the night complaining of severe back pain. Looks like he is going to be admitted. Maybe we can get you a double occupancy rate," she joked.

But it was not a joking matter. The CT scan showed a malignant tumor in his spine. During the previous year he had his first cancer surgery and was told the operation would extend his life by a year or two. Maybe three. Now we knew. The timetable was the short version. He was given only weeks to live.

When he passed away only three weeks later, I tried focusing on the blessings left in my life, but all I could see was the emptiness. The empty chair at the table, the empty side of the bed, the empty slippers. Even the air seemed empty without the sound of his voice. Where was God's abundance in this? Abundant loneliness is what it looked like to me. This was the second husband taken from me by death. I wondered, "Why me?"

Then it began happening. The dozens of phone calls from family and friends. The special cards and personal notes, flowers, and contributions to charity in my husband's name, invitations to lunch or dinner, and multiple visits from family members who traveled thousands of miles to visit. Truly an outpouring of love and concern.

As surely as night follows day, I knew the day would come when the calls and visits would let up and the mailman would be back to bringing bills instead of encouraging notes, current reminders of the illness that took my love. Then what?

For me, that's when I had to make a choice. I could feel abandoned by God, which would lead to the kind of sadness that makes getting out of bed in the morning a chore. Or I could choose to live again, putting one foot in front of the other, doing what needed to be done. I could choose to take care of the never ending stream of bills and phone calls relating to my husband's last hospitalization, even though it seemed too overwhelming.

I realized I could make those painful choices because one day, I would wake up feeling the love with which God has always surrounded me and know that it had been there all along. Even when I couldn't feel it, it was being delivered to me by God's messengers, the people in my life.

If you're grieving any kind of loss and wonder if you'll ever feel God's love again, take heart. Although your pain is real, God hasn't abandoned you or forgotten you. Moment by moment, ask for His help and you will reach the other side of grief.

> *. . . His compassions never fail. They are new every morning;*
> *great is your faithfulness.*
> Lamentations 3:22–23

For those grieving the loss of a love, read, *To Live Again,*
by Catherine Marshall

How To Beat The Time Gobblers
TINA KRAUSE

Lost time is never found again.
John H. Aughey

Have you ever resented the intrusion of an unexpected visitor? A long-winded telephone conversation? An untimely request for a special favor? Or the nagging obligation of attending home parties or other borderline events that extract valuable time? I call them the "time gobblers."

Consider this. All week you've anticipated taking the kids to the park for a picnic. You're packed and ready to go, when the telephone rings. It's Joanne again. You told her you were about to leave, but she continues to talk about her problems. You listen politely as the kids whine and tug at your sleeve. You know what you should do, but you don't. Consequently, the time designated for your children is short-changed.

Or does this sound familiar? You bake the best apple pies in your church. One Friday morning the president of Women's Ministries calls. "Can you help me?" she pleads, "I need more pastries for the bake sale tomorrow and you make the best . . ."

Ordinarily no problem, but you made plans for the day. Graciously, you try to explain. "Well, my husband and I were planning to leave this afternoon to go to . . ."

"Please," she insists. Though you bristle under the strangling noose of an untimely favor, you reluctantly agree.

As Christians, how do we distinguish between serving others and allowing "time gobblers" to rob us of valuable time? Here's a few tips:

1. Take time out. Even Jesus "went up on a mountainside by himself to pray," Matthew records. Do you need more time in prayer and Bible study? Everyone needs "down time" to refresh and restore weary bodies and spirits.

2. Learn to say no politely and firmly. Women have trouble with this because we allow ourselves to feel guilty. Realize that self-serving people tend to control us by monopolizing our time. In the leaving-for-the-picnic scenario try saying, "I'm sorry, Joanne, I must go now. I'd be glad to call you later when I have more time." Then hang up.

3. Be honest. For instance, if asked to host a Tupperware party when you'd rather not, don't make excuses. Simply say, "I'm sorry, I'm not interested, but thanks for thinking of me anyway."

4. Determine the reason for your lack of control. Is your drive to please others based on fear of rejection or disapproval? Does your desire for acceptance override your ability to say no? If so, in the words of Paul, ask yourself: "Am I now trying to win the approval of men, or of God? Or am I trying to please men? . . ." (Galatians 1:10 NIV).

5. Prioritize. What do you value most? Your relationship to God? Time with your children, grandchildren, or husband? Time to pursue career goals or a hobby? Time to relax? Discover who and what your priorities are, and then stick to them.

6. Avoid excesses. Are you a couch potato? Are you a compulsive house cleaner? Do you tinker with the computer too much? Pray for a balanced interest in the activities you enjoy.

7. Seek God's wisdom. Sometimes God wants us to alter our plans or priorities for someone in need. When we follow the Holy Spirit's leading, rather than the inducement of pesky intrusions, our lives will be blessed and our time multiplied.

> . . . the wise heart will know the proper time and procedure. For there is a proper time and procedure for every matter . . .
>
> Ecclesiastes 8:5–6

Always sort your mail over a trash can and immediately throw away anything unworthy of your attention.

Let Your Light Shine

WILMA KENNEDY

Each day God gives you a twenty-four-hour slice of time in which your investments have eternal repercussions.

Joni Eareckson Tada

My younger daughter gave me a journal for Christmas. It's called, "Reflections From a Mother's Heart" and it has questions on just about every aspect of life. I try to answer one or two questions every night after I do my gratitude journal and read a chapter in the Bible. One page asks me to share some insights from Scripture that have guided my spiritual journey.

One of the first memory verses I learned was Matthew 5:16, *Let your light so shine before men that they may see your good works and glorify your Father who is in heaven.*

As I was thinking about this verse, a vision of the moon popped into my head. The moon is the loveliest light in the sky, inspiring poets to write beautiful words and scientists to do ambitious deeds. But the moon has no light of its own; rather, it reflects sunlight. It seems to me that we are to be like the moon, reflecting Sonlight. So often our lives are filled with the daily routine: clean the house, shop for food, prepare meals, go to work, pick up the kids, etc. There isn't time to write that inspiring series of books and we don't have the talent to whip the church choir into a one-hundred-voice work of art. We have no great deeds to our credit and haven't won any gold medals.

But does God ask that of us? I think not. What He asks is that daily, we reflect Sonlight. As Joni Eareckson Tada points out, something we say or do, some small word or deed, may have an effect for a thousand years. And it's the little things that make up our days, the minutiae of daily living that build the path we lay. It's a cheerful "Good morning!" every day that our children will remember, a warm handshake for a visitor at church, patient forgiveness when another driver cuts us off. We can lighten many a dark corner if we let the Son reflect off our lives.

How will you reflect Sonlight today, even in a small way?

In the same way, let your light shine before men, that they may see
your good deeds and praise your Father in heaven.
Matthew 5:16

Keep a "tickler file" labeled with 1 through 31. Use each file,
having it correspond to the day of the month on which
something needs to be taken care of.
Then look each day in that particular file number.

Our Inheritance

DEBORAH SILLAS NELL

Hope is the best part of our riches. What sufficeth
it that we have the wealth of the Indies in our pockets,
if we have not the hope of heaven in our souls?

Bovee

"Our land covers all the fields up to that tree line," said my brother-in-law
Tom as he pointed across several corn-filled, ten-acre fields. Sitting next to
me in the front seat of the pick-up was my sister-in-law, Marty. The gravel
from the road under the truck tires created a cloud of dust as Tom drove
through the Nell land pointing out the perimeter of the property.

In the back of the pick-up truck, sat my husband, daughter, nephews, and
several in-laws. For the first time, we all were seeing the total footage of the land
that belonged to the Nell family. The total acreage was one hundred sixty acres.

My husband and I had been living on the land in Tom and Marty's house
for almost two months. We had walked some parts of the land, but today was
different. The magnitude and the beauty of the fertile soil, forest areas, possible wet land areas, and potential homesites were tangible realities that we
could see and touch.

That night, we sat Indian style on the front room floor and brainstormed
about the possibilities for the land.

"If we created a lake through the wetland area, we could build cabins
along the sides of the lake. It would be beautiful," said Marty.

"And we could use the lake for a campsite for underprivileged kids from
the city," said my sister-in-law Helen.

"We could farm and live off the land. If we all worked together, we really
could make a living here," said Tom.

Ideas like sparks ignited in all of our brains. We were excited.

In the next twenty-four hours, I had time to contemplate our discussion and the tour of the land. What was most difficult for me to believe was that all that beautiful, corn-filled, forest-lined property belonged to all of us. My husband, Craig, was a descendent of the first owner of the land. Like all his seven siblings, he was an heir. I was married to him, so through him, I had an inheritance also.

As I pondered the awesome privilege of this, I also pondered the inheritance we as Christians have in Christ. Peter tells us that our inheritance is incorruptible and undefiled. It will not fade. It is reserved for us in heaven.

I could see this earthly inheritance on the Nell property and it was awesome. But how much more awesome is the inheritance we have in Christ. And what a day that will be when we meet Him face to face. On that day Jesus will be our tour guide and show us what is laid up for us in heaven. That is our incorruptible and undefiled inheritance. All else will fade away. For as beautiful as this earth is, it does not compare to the beauty of God's love for us.

Though you have not seen Him, you love Him; and even though you do not see Him now, you believe in Him and are filled with an inexpressible and glorious joy, for you are receiving the goal of your faith, the salvation of your souls.
I Peter 1:8, 9

Surprise your husband and have a candlelight dinner waiting for him when he arrives home from work. It makes for a special evening at half the price of a date out on the town.

Bowling Blunder

CELESTE DUCKWORTH

If someone were to pay you ten cents for every kind word you ever spoke about others and collect five cents for every unkind word, would you be rich or poor?

Unknown

Bowling is a boring sport. When you have finished with your turn, there's not much else to do but look around or slurp your diet soda. On this ill-fated Wednesday night, everyone was busy up and down the lanes but me. To entertain myself, I began to observe the bowling style of one of my opponents. Faye, with her four-foot-nine frame, would begin her approach much like Fred Flintstone in his bowling days, with the pirouettes and tiptoes. She would elevate her twelve-pound, pink bowling ball at a one-hundred eighty-degree-angle straight above her petite head. As she danced to the fast approaching foul line, her pastel orb would swirl from its lofty height and leap six feet in the gaping air halfway down the wooden lane, as it left her tiny fingers. The ball crashed on the lane with a bang, then with a jolt, lobbed on down it's crooked path toward the white chipped pins at the runway's end. Slowly, her ball hit its mark, the pins slovenly heaving over and reluctantly tipping onto each other. Only two pins remained for Faye to pick up on her second throw.

"This is just too funny!" I thought as I chuckled to myself. "Maybe she made a mistake on her approach."

I continued to watch as Faye threw not twice but many times in the same fashion as she did for her first performance.

What a time I had in my own little world observing Faye and giggling as she labored over her score for the rest of the game!

At the end of our first game, my friend came down from her lanes at the other end of the house.

"What's up?" she asked.

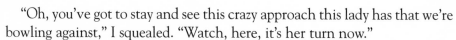
"Oh, you've got to stay and see this crazy approach this lady has that we're bowling against," I squealed. "Watch, here, it's her turn now."

Faye did her thing, as if on command. I fell apart, laughing hysterically out loud, happy to share my find with my friend. But my friend wasn't responding to Faye the same way I was.

"What's the matter?" I asked as I teasingly slapped her on the shoulder, "Wasn't that the funniest thing you've ever seen?"

My friend never flinched when she glared at me with her nose slightly tilted heavenward, "No, it was not!"

"Why on earth not?" I asked confused.

"Because that's my mother!" And it was.

I learned that day to watch my words and attitudes because God wants us to speak kindly to everyone and of everyone. The next time you're tempted to do less than that, remember my humbling lesson.

Let your gentleness be evident to all. The Lord is near.
Philippians 4:5

If appropriate, write the information directly on the letter requesting it, and send it back. Be sure to photocopy it for your own records.

Why We Need Each Other

KIMN SWENSON GOLLNICK

Life is short and we never have too much time for gladdening the hearts of those who are traveling the dark journey with us. Oh be swift to love, make haste to be kind.

Henri Frederic Amiel

Headed for home, it was my turn to drive that last day of our family vacation. We dallied a bit too long during our stop at the Gingko Petrified State Park along I-90. Night descended as we piled into our minivan and started the long climb into Washington state's Cascade mountains, a three-hour drive still ahead of us. I smiled when I noticed my husband's head bobbing next to me as he drifted to sleep. The kids had already zoned out.

Alone with my thoughts, I reflected on our recent switch to a new church. The process was painful and reminded me of other loved ones' experiences with other churches. I loved the Lord deeply, but I struggled to grasp the value of organized church bodies at all.

The rough landscape caught my attention. Jagged peaks rose in black silhouette against a navy blue sky dotted with stars, but the moon was absent. Dark clouds billowed across the left side of the cliffs, surrounding the peaks. I wondered if they signaled a coming storm, and prayed we'd reach the other side before it hit.

Inky darkness swallowed the unfamiliar interstate in front of me. Unnerved, I slowed from the posted 70 mph limit to a ridiculous 55 mph. Beyond my headlights, I couldn't see if the road went up or down, left or right. Fear grabbed my heart as I imagined various accident scenarios.

A group of cars approached from behind. I let them pass, wondering how they could drive at what seemed an excessive speed. Not until their taillights disappeared did I realize my mistake. Their combined headlights had helped illuminate the lanes. Ahead of me, their taillights had

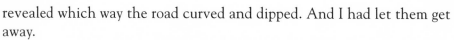
revealed which way the road curved and dipped. And I had let them get away.

Aware of my sleeping family and their trust we'd get home safely, I prayed for more cars so I wouldn't have to drive alone. Soon another group caught up, and I pulled behind a friendly looking truck. I tagged him my "driving buddy," keeping pace with him and the pack, up over the pass and down the mountain together. The group had a rhythm—cautious where needed on sloping roadway, yet picking up speed on safe stretches so we could all reach our destinations in timely fashion.

As I drove, the Holy Spirit whispered how this experience mirrored why I need other Christians around me.

My private life wasn't the only thing that mattered to God. As a Lone Ranger Christian, I could see how I might be committed to following the right path, but the way is hard and the going slow without the support of other believers. In committing to a God-fearing church where members practice a sincere and authentic faith, I could see how I might find my way through life's storms more easily. And just as I experienced on the mountain pass, I could see how I might draw courage from the light of my Christian brothers and sisters around me on our joint journey toward righteousness. We are also less apt to make a wrong turn.

Are you alone in your Christian walk? Even the Lone Ranger had Tonto. Seek out a body of believers soon.

Let us not give up meeting together, as some are in the habit of doing, but let us encourage one another—and all the more as you see the Day approaching.
Hebrews 10:25

For those hectic mornings when your child has "sleep hair," keep a small squirt bottle filled with water and one teaspoon of hair conditioner. Spritz on unruly hair and comb smooth.

A Heart Of Praise

DONNA CLARK GOODRICH

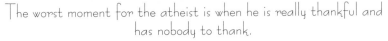

The worst moment for the atheist is when he is really thankful and has nobody to thank.

Dante Gabriel Rossetti

"Develop an attitude of praise," our pastor told us in his Sunday message. "It will change your life."

I tried it. If it rained, I tried to be thankful it didn't flood. If it was too hot, I gave thanks for our air conditioner. For the ornery boy in my Sunday school class, I thanked God that his parents cared enough to bring him. It seemed to work—for awhile!

Then in the next few years, I found it harder to be thankful. My mother died of cancer. My husband had a serious car accident, which put him out of work for three months. Then, a few years later, he had a heart attack, which, along with a number of other health problems, led to his retirement at the age of forty-eight. Having three teenagers for seven years increased the stress.

"How can I be thankful?" I often asked myself. Then one day while listening to the words of a song a friend was singing at church, the answer came to me: Being thankful is for *things* God gives to us; but a heart of praise is giving thanks for *who He is.*

Have we lost our sense of awe when we are in God's presence? I remember when our family first moved to Arizona. All baseball fans, we were thrilled to learn that several major league teams held their spring training in our area.

My son grabbed his baseball autograph book and we took off for a batting practice where young players were more than happy to sign their names. Suddenly a tall, imposing figure walked toward us. I stopped, frozen in my tracks. *Joe DiMaggio!* I couldn't speak, but our son, who knew no fear, ran up to him. "Hey, Joe!" he yelled. "Can I have your autograph?"

I thought later, if I felt that much awe for a man who merely played baseball, how much more awe should I feel when I come before God?

I can still have an "attitude of gratitude," but now I realize that God deserves my highest praise—not because of what He gives me, but because of who He is.

Devote yourselves to prayer, being watchful and thankful.
Colossians 4:2

If you want to cancel a magazine subscription, you can. The publisher should send you a refund for the future issues.

Evening Dreams
ESTHER M. BAILEY

It is not the years in your life but the life in your years that counts!
Adlai Stevenson

When asked to teach a class of young people, Fay thought the Sunday school superintendent was joking. Earlier in life she had taught youth for twenty-eight years, but she hadn't taught since her husband died twenty years before. She expected her comment about the incompatibility of gray hair and youth to close the matter.

A few days later the chairman of the board of Christian education surprised Fay with a second request that she teach. "I've already taught some of the children of my first students. I don't want to start in teaching the grandchildren," she said.

"Well, pray about it," the chairman said.

From her halfhearted prayer, Fay didn't expect to hear from God because

she believed she already knew the answer. It wasn't until the pastor challenged her to accept God's call to teach that Fay decided to pray in earnest.

For a couple of weeks Fay received no direction, so she decided to set aside a whole day to plead her case with God. By evening she still had no answer. Somewhat discouraged, she opened the Psalms at random. In amazement, she read, *Even when I am old and gray, do not forsake me, O God, till I declare your power to the next generation.* (Psalm 71:18, NIV).

With doubts about age and gray hair erased, Fay began teaching the grandchildren of her former students.

As Fay learned, the aging process is not an excuse to discontinue involvement in ministry. God doesn't offer retirement benefits. In fact, the opportunity to fulfill a dream of doing something for the Lord is even greater after ending a secular career. It's never too late to dream big for God.

Of course, health or other factors may dictate a reduction in the things we choose to do but our term of service is for life. Activities that require minimum energy could include: mentoring a new Christian or a child, visiting or sending cards to shut-ins, volunteering to work in the church office, telephoning lonely people, making gifts for children, sewing for missions, praying for specific needs within the church, or asking someone on the church staff for other ideas.

Staying involved in Christian service helps us maintain the feeling that we are worth something to God, to others, and to ourselves. To really experience God's abundance, we need to invest ourselves in something that continues to pay dividends beyond the grave.

> . . . *he who began a good work in you will carry it on to completion until the day of Christ Jesus.*
>
> Philippians 1:6

Pamper yourself with a new hairstyle or a professional make-over. Enjoy feeling younger.

Chattering Voices

Sharon Raivo Remmen

Silence is golden.

Unknown

"I'm sorry I can't hear you. The voices in my head are making too much noise."

Most of us have likely heard this quip and many of us are distracted by our own inner "voices." I know I am.

My mind's voices are not particularly harmful; they just chatter a lot. "Maybe I should have worn the blue shirt instead of the red. When am I going to find time to have the car serviced? I hope there isn't a layoff at work. Should I plant tomatoes in my garden this spring?" And on it goes.

Even as I take a walk in the park or even as I lie down for an afternoon rest, the voices rattle on as noisily as ever. How can I stop it so that I can relax? Then it came to me. Memorize and mentally recite Bible verses. So I have. And guess what? Concentrating on special verses quiets my mind, gives me peace, and stills my soul. And in the process, I am learning many beautiful and comforting passages from the Bible.

What verses could you use to quiet the chatter in your mind?

. . . He will quiet you with His love . . .
Zephaniah 3:17b

I keep a duplicate copy of my address book in our safety deposit box. In case of fire or other damage to our home, I still have those hard-to-replace addresses and telephone numbers of friends and relatives.

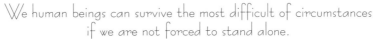

Obedience Vs. Sacrifice

KAYLEEN J. REUSSER

*We human beings can survive the most difficult of circumstances
if we are not forced to stand alone.*

Dr. James Dobson

When my husband John came down with the flu a few hours before milking time, I was frantic. Our hired helper had the night off and I had not been in the barn since our baby was born a few months before. John insisted he could do the work with my help so I phoned Katie, our teenage baby-sitter, to ask her if she could care for Mandy during that time. With little experience and a sick instructor, I envisioned us being busy 'til near midnight.

Katie's mother, Connie, answered the phone. I explained the situation and she surprised me by asking if their family of five could come over to help us. I hesitated since they did not live on a farm or have animals. It was also Wednesday and their family always attended church services. She insisted, however, and I told her what time chores would begin.

Their family arrived promptly and John, who hung weakly onto the milk tank for support, assigned all of us jobs. Connie and her eight-year-old daughter fed the calves buckets of milk in the nursery area. Roger and his teenage son helped John in the parlor, lifting milkers and washing the cows. From where I stood, feeding cows in the barn, I could hear Mandy's squeals of delight as Katie swung her in the yard. I relaxed, knowing everything was going well.

Light chatter and serious work filled the next three hours. Finally, John turned off the milk house lights and everyone met in the barnyard. Every job had been completed without mishap. Our friends offered to return for the next morning's milking, but John said he would feel better, and he did, enough to complete the job himself.

When our friends chose to get their hands dirty, instead of folding those same hands in prayer at church, they chose to show love. It wouldn't have been wrong to attend church; but their choosing to help us instead was love in action.

The next time you have the opportunity, show God's love with more than just words, but with action.

. . . to obey is better than sacrifice . . .
I Samuel 15:22c

On Sunday, visit a shut-in who can't come to church.

The Swing
SHERYL L. HILL

Blue skies with white clouds on summer days. A myriad of stars on a clear moonlit night. Tulips and roses and violets and dandelions and daisies. Bluebirds and laughter and sunshine and Easter. See how He loves us!

Alice Chapin

As a young girl I had the privilege to spend summers on the Minnesota farm of my grandparents. I would spend hours playing outside in the fields of their two-hundred acre farm.

One day, my grandfather made a swing for me out of a flat 2 x 4 board and some rope. He hung it in a huge oak tree beside the back door. I spent hours on that swing. Closing my eyes I imagined that swing taking me up into the clouds. Stretching with all my might, I dreamt of traveling in the faraway hills, never once fearing the swing would break.

That is what our Heavenly Father wants us to do. God wants us to close our eyes and depend on Him to soar though life's daily challenges. As our challenges take us to new places, we can take a minute to look up to the clouds, close our eyes, and ask our Father for guidance and strength. In doing this, we are free to be children again, while we soar on the swing and let go to trust God in His provision for us.

I lift up my eyes to the hills—where does my help come from? My help comes from the LORD, the Maker of heaven and earth.

Psalm 121:1–2

Take a walk and go to a park and get on a swing
and close your eyes as you soar through the clouds.

Restoration

MARY ELLEN WRIGHT

All I see teaches me to trust the Creator for all I do not see.

Unknown

Our Silver Maple trees, which have been attacked almost every year by green worms, were attacked three times in one season. Presently, they are in the process of putting on new Spring-green leaves, for the third time in about six months.

At the height of the invasion, piles of wriggling green worms gathered at the base of the trees. Tree trunks were transformed into a moving mass of green and in the evening white moths appeared on the lawn like scattered popcorn.

We put poison out, we crushed the moths and we fertilized the trees. We did everything we knew to do. In spite of all of our efforts, the trees were stripped again and again. We even consulted an expert who said the worms attacked the trees because of an imbalance in the soil or in the moisture. This was frustrating because we had taken extra care of the trees.

Then I realized the spiritual message. Imbalance for me has occurred when God has not been my focus. When I've not spent time with Him in prayer, in His Word, or isolated myself from the Body, I've been more vulnerable for attack. At those times, I have been stripped of my peace, joy, and faith. Faced with the reality of putting other things before my relationship with Him, I've fallen on my face in repentance, crying out for help. In answer to my cries, He renewed my hunger to be with Him. Spring-green sprouted in my life again.

At other times, the stripping has come even when I've been following His will. It has come strictly as an attack to cause me to question His faithfulness and love. Then I've found myself digging deeper into His Word, using it for warfare against the enemy and standing firmly on His promises. My place in Him has become richer, and regardless of the circumstances, I've grown in the assurance of His love and His ability to restore me.

Therefore we do not lose heart. Though outwardly we are wasting away, yet inwardly we are being renewed day by day.
II Corinthians 4:16

Enhance your Scripture study time with fragrance. Spray a favorite perfume on an index card and insert it in your Bible. Move it from time to time. It will permeate the Word with sweet aroma.

Enough Is Enough

MARGARET PRIMROSE

Since my eyes were fixed on Jesus, I've lost sight of all beside.

Mary D. James

At the airport my nephew opened the car trunk, hesitated, then turned to me. "I hate to tell you, but . . . it's not there," Dave said.

"It" was the suitcase that was usually too full to close until I sat on it. We knew almost immediately why it was missing. Eighteen miles from his farm, we had stopped at the county hospital where his wife works. We forgot the luggage when we changed cars and headed for Omaha.

Dave quickly offered to make the 300-mile round trip for it but that did not sound to me like a good idea. It was summer, a farmer's busiest season. Nor did I want to waste money by sending it on a later flight. After considering several different scenarios, I finally asked, *Can I get along without it?*

Without too much thought, I decided "yes." *I will enjoy the trip without all of the trappings.* And I did, thanks to a good hostess, one new dress, and little else. At the end of my trip, a used throwaway bag held the few things I had to carry home.

I didn't simply travel, I traveled simply—and it was more fun.

The next time your luggage somehow manages to travel without you, or you without it, relax. It's not as bad as you think. Just travel simply and you may find it's actually the abundant way to go.

But whatever was to my profit I now consider loss for the sake of Christ.

Philippians 3:7

Think of something that is more of a burden than a necessity to you and give it up.

Vacations For Moms?

LETTIE J. KIRKPATRICK

As we once again hit the vacation trails this summer, committed to having family fun (no matter how much pain...and suffering it entails), our hours...can be triumphant! Remember to be prepared, which translated into Mom's language means to plan.

Linda Dillow and Claudia Arp

Reality descended upon us immediately after we arrived at our lovely lodge. Five boys, hovering dangerously close to starvation, clamored for me to fix them lunch. I also needed to put away boxes of groceries and disperse the various pieces of luggage to the appropriate bedrooms. In the midst of all that, the scent of a dirty diaper drifted my way. And the van still wasn't completely unloaded! The question once more sprang from the recesses of my cluttered mind, "Are there *really* vacations for Moms?"

Consider these tips to bring the possibility of vacation closer to reality—for moms.

Developing Reasonable Expectations

The nature of many moms is to feel responsible for everyone's happiness. We also develop picture-perfect fantasies of the "ideal vacation." Reality is:

1. The stress of preparations, change of routines, and close proximity to one another may escalate, at least temporarily, already existing tension between siblings or spouses.
2. Moms are *not* accountable for the choice of other family members to be malcontented, self-centered, or complaining. We are, however, responsible for our response to those attitudes.

3. Vacations can be wonderful times of closeness, renewed communication, and shared memories. But they are most likely to happen in relaxed moments, not in a rigid atmosphere that demands a successful vacation.

4. As nurturers and family managers, mothers continue to bear a larger share of the work load, even on vacation. My victory in this area came when I asked the Lord to give me a servant's heart toward my family and trusted Him to meet my own needs.

Packing

1. Avoid procrastination. Prepare early enough to prevent the pressure of having to throw everything together at once.

2. Make lists. Write down the items needed for clothing, recreation, travel, medical supplies, and food. Use these lists to pack.

3. Involve your children. Give each their own travel bag. The ones who read can have a list telling them what to include. For example:
   • designated amount of underwear
   • swim suit
   • sleep clothes
   • socks
   • short sets
   • jacket
   • toothbrush
   Follow up briefly to make certain they have complied.

4. Keep it light! The K.I.S.S. (keep it simple, sweetie) motto definitely applies to packing for vacation.

Traveling

1. Night travel. Some families insist that driving at night while children sleep is the only way to achieve peace. However, others divide the time on longer trips over several days.

2. Individual tote bags. Include reading material, small toys, snacks, and portable art supplies. Little ones may also be motivated by small surprises from mommy's bag.

3. Play together. Family car games and conversation stretchers like add-a-sentence stories help time to pass on the road.

4. Consider vacations close to home. Our family's age diversity (ages 3 to 19) doesn't travel long distances well. So we confine most of our vacations to short distances. We have found plenty to do and see within three to four hours of home. It's also cheaper!

5. Prepare for sibling rivalry. In close proximity of each other, siblings will antagonize one another. Provide distractions, but insist on accountability for disruptive behavior.

What changes can you make in your thinking, attitudes, and plans so that your vacation can be the best it can be? Work toward that now.

> *. . . he said to them, "Come with me by yourselves to a quiet place and get some rest."*
> Mark 6:31b

Meal expenses on vacations can be reduced by eating the main meal in the middle of the day. Lunch menus are less expensive than dinner and often contain the same choices.

Apology Accepted

C. ELLEN WATTS

Most of us follow our conscience as we follow a wheelbarrow. We push it in front of us in the direction we want to go.

Billy Graham

God's abundance often pours into our lives in ways we might never have imagined. Sometimes, we must first make room for that to happen.

During our youngest daughter's adolescent years, we lived in a house where fill dirt for the backyard had been brought in from the sparsely forested foothills nearby. Along with that soft brown loam came an army of black widow spiders bent on establishing a fort beneath the siding beside our back door.

That summer, our daughter declared war on the invaders. Armed with a spray can, she positioned herself on the back steps each morning and refused to budge until at least one spider had dropped to its death behind the petunias. Needless to say, life became simpler for her after the last "enemy soldier" lay curled in the dust.

A "spider" of a different variety once wove its web in my life. My unkind words had all but severed a special friendship. I'd tried acting as if nothing had happened, but my friend refused to buy such behavior. A flurry of ceaseless activity failed to cover my intense feelings of remorse. Still, I could not bring myself to apologize. I had never before apologized to anyone. I did not know how.

Perhaps my lack came from having grown up in a large family where minor infractions sometimes fell by the wayside due to the busyness of my good, though non-Christian, parents. Besides, none of my siblings ever apologized, so why should I? As a result, I learned early on to imagine that every infraction on my part must surely have been the other guy's fault. If faking innocence failed to work, I could always distract people through humor.

While "Love means never having to say you're sorry" once leapt off the pages of a book to become a well-known quote, quite the opposite is true. Love sometimes has everything to do with speaking aloud those words that help to make amends.

My "spider" bit the dust the moment I claimed ownership to my mean-spirited words and apologized to my friend. Her forgiving response gave me courage to make past wrongs right and to put into practice my new belief that love means having a genuine desire to make amends quickly. Ridding myself of webs woven on behalf of self-protection not only simplified my life but left room for God's abundant approval.

Are there any spider webs of spiritual deception lurking in your mind or heart? It can come in a variety of forms: anger, defensiveness, pride, or self-ishness. Why not wipe those webs away now?

. . . a broken and contrite heart, O God, you will not despise.
Psalm 51:17b

After finishing a book you intend to read only once, decide
who might also enjoy it, then give it
to that person immediately.

The Upward Climb

Marie Chapian

*Since there's nothing new under the sun,
creativity means simply putting old things together in a fresh way.*

Unknown

It may seem like an upward climb, but we can make our everyday lives creative. We move a step up every time we choose to creatively handle situations and tasks at hand. We can make even the act of sweeping the floor a creative expression.

Personally, I find doing the laundry a creative task which I take pleasure in. I like the smell of the detergent. I like the sound of the washing machine, the softness of the clothes when I pull them out of the dryer. My family's clothes are precious to me because my family is precious to me. I have a sense of satisfaction in the task as I pray for those who will wear the clothes, use the towels, sleep on the sheets.

Think of the everyday tasks you perform that until now you've considered low on the ladder of importance. Now imagine each task as a creative expression of yourself. Washing the car, buying groceries, making the bed, polishing your shoes—these are not meaningless tasks, they are the upward climb that can sweeten your creative mind if you allow them to. The activities that fill your days have the power to lift you to new heights of creative expression.

*"Behold, I will create new heavens and a new earth. The former things will
not be remembered, nor will they come to mind."*

Isaiah 65:17

If you travel frequently, consider having a second collection
of all your toiletries already packed to take with you.

Fall

Oh, the crisp air. The falling leaves. The billowy clouds. Fall, or Autumn, is an enchanting time of enjoying God's creation. For many, it is the time when the children go back to school, and it culminates in Thanksgiving. In this section, we will also include selections about Christmas as we near the end of the book—and the year.

As the year winds down, may you be blessed with new hope, knowing that with God, every day is a new opportunity for abundantly knowing how much He loves us and never gives up on us.

Listening With Your Heart

BECKY FREEMAN

One of the great similarities between Christianity and marriage is that, for Christians, they both get better as we get older.

Jean A. Rees

It is a rare and precious evening. My husband, Scott, and I are curled up on an overstuffed love seat, our legs outstretched and intertwined together on the giant ottoman in front of us. He's drinking a mug of hot, black coffee; I'm sipping herbal tea from a china cup. In the background, romantic music from the 1940s is playing: "Sentimental Journey," "You Made Me Love You." The room is softly illuminated by the light of a lamp and a glowing fire in the hearth.

After traveling all day and speaking to a gathering of bankers' wives, my feelings tonight are a mixture of gratitude, relief, exhaustion, and satisfaction. Ruby Kathryn, the benevolent woman who organized the day's events has seen to it that our time here in Mississippi includes plenty of southern-style pampering. Knowing Scott was accompanying me, she arranged for our stay in this charming bed-and-breakfast. She even sent a dozen red roses and a gargantuan basket of goodies to our room. Tonight I feel like saluting the South, its charm, and all its Ruby Kathryns.

Not only is this evening special because of the romantic setting away from home, kids, and the phone, it is unusual because I'm not in the mood for talking. I've talked nonstop all afternoon and for now, anyway, have grown weary of the sound of my own voice. I'm in a curious frame of mind—I'm in the mood for *listening*. For a few moments there's silence between us, except for Nat King Cole's crooning, the crackle of burning logs, and an occasional sigh of contentment.

Then something remarkable happens. I ask my husband a couple of questions. Then I focus on his face, listening attentively to his answers. Allowing Scott all the time he needs, I do not interrupt or interject my own thoughts, as is so often my habit. Oh, occasionally I throw in a piggyback question or encouraging comment, but mostly I gently bat the conversational ball back into his court. Amazing. Like a bud opening to flower, I sit in this cozy atmosphere and observe my husband come to life.

My reserved husband is smiling as he chats away the hour. One might even say he is *animated* as he pours out several dreams, plans, and ideas he's been mulling over for months. He is relating on a deeper level than he has in a long, long time. I realize how happy he seems at this moment—how starved he's probably been for the listening ear of a wife who, of late, has been far too preoccupied with herself.

I also realize another truth: Men probably don't stop talking because they aren't "talkers" by nature; they stop talking because we stop really *listening*. They stop talking because when they do talk we criticize them or tease them about their subject choice, judge them, or interrupt them with our views.

A man who lacks judgment derides his neighbor, but a man of understanding holds his tongue.
Proverbs 11:12

Have a box in the garage to gather discarded clothing.

The Abundant Life
MARGARITA GARZA DE BECK

Don't sweat the small stuff . . . and it's all small stuff
Richard Carlson

Not again! Not another day of getting stuck behind a slow driver. Chugging along at 45 miles an hour was not my idea of how to get to work in decent time. There were so many curves and hills on River Road that it was almost impossible to pass. I had been working my new job for over a week and almost every morning I managed to get behind a slowpoke. By the time I got to work, I was usually exhausted and quite frustrated.

I looked again around the the car ahead of me for an opportunity to pass. At that moment my eye caught the brilliant autumn colors of the trees which lined both sides of the road. Strange that I hadn't noticed the changing leaves before.

As I rounded each curve and crested each hill, the beauty and variety of colors of the trees fascinated me. Some of the trees still had most of their deep green leaves. The leaves of other trees were red, or orange, or yellow, or magnificent combinations of these colors.

The next morning, I was eager to get back on River Road to see what new color patterns I would discover. And the next morning. And the next. It was a few days before I realized that instead of arriving to work in a grumpy mood, I was actually humming a song. That morning I'd even waved to the slowpoke in front of me when he glanced in his rearview mirror!

The road to work was still curvy and hilly. I still encountered slow-moving vehicles, but I no longer dreaded the trip. My situation hadn't changed. But I had! I discovered that when I focused my attention on the positive aspects of my trip, I scarcely noticed the negative ones.

I got to thinking then. Some situations, situations of much greater importance than my River Road experience, may be slow to change, or they may never change. So if I was going to live the abundant life that Jesus promised us, I might be called on sometime to take a big risk. It's the risk of changing my attitude, even in the face of something exasperating that might not ever go away. I realized then that only I can change my attitude. The major key to a better future for myself is *me*.

The thief comes only to steal and kill and destroy; I have come that they may have life, and have it to the full.

John 10:10

F·A·L·L

> Use color-coded files for organizing your material.
> Possibilities: bills, red; letters, blue; needs immediate
> attention, yellow; children's school information, pink; etc.

Get Ready For Exciting Prayer

QUIN SHERRER

*Anything creative, anything powerful, anything biblical, insofar as
we are participants in it, originates in prayer.*

Eugene H. Peterson

I am more convinced than ever of the need to set aside a specific time each day to be with the Lord. I started with just 15 minutes, expanded it to 30, and before long wanted to lengthen it even further.

As active wives, mothers, and grandmothers, we sometimes complain we don't have time to pray. We send up "minute prayers" like spiritual arrows while we work at our office desks, iron clothes, make beds, drive carpools, or sit in waiting rooms. These prayers are commendable, but God wants quality time with us each day, too.

Whatever time you set aside for Him—morning, noon, or evening—it helps to have a few tools on hand: notebook, pen, Bible. Then you're able to record your prayers and God's answers. No "quiet time" is complete until you have not only talked to Him, but also listened to hear our Father's voice. Since we are all different, no two of us will use the same techniques in our personal devotional times.

> *Whatever you ask for in prayer, believe that you have received it,
> and it will be yours.*
>
> Mark 11:24

The next time you record an answer to prayer in your journal, put a big red star by it.

Instrument Of Ten Strings

MILDRED L. BARGER

The man who kneels to God can stand up to anything.

Louis H. Evans, Jr.

An old gray-haired man prayed, "O, Lord, we will praise Thee with an instrument of ten strings." He offered his eyes to look only to God, his ears for listening to God's voice, his hands for service, his feet for walking in God's ways, his tongue for bearing testimony of God's loving kindness and his heart for loving God alone.

Two eyes, two ears, two feet, one tongue, and one heart—a living instrument of ten strings!

With our *eyes*, we read in God's Word of His majesty and everlasting love. We see the promise of eternal life. Also, with our eyes we behold a glorious sunset. Surely nothing could be more beautiful, and yet the most gorgeous sunset is only a tiny sample of the glorious colors of heaven.

With our *ears*, we hear the gospel preached and voices lifted in praise. We hear the mockingbird's trill, a child's delighted laughter, a cascading waterfall, and the roar of thunder. We are reminded of God's great power and of His goodness.

We have *hands* to do His work and to lift heavenward in praise. Martha Snell Nicholson wrote a poem expressing that God took the things she treasured most from her hands. He then invited her to hold them open so He could fill them from His store of riches. Our hands are the only hands Christ has to do His work. When we lift them to Him, empty, and let Him fill them, the work we do for Him brings praise to His name.

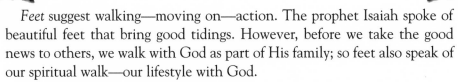

Feet suggest walking—moving on—action. The prophet Isaiah spoke of beautiful feet that bring good tidings. However, before we take the good news to others, we walk with God as part of His family; so feet also speak of our spiritual walk—our lifestyle with God.

In the Old Testament, the story of Enoch, who walked with God, illustrates a holy life. Enoch became God's man, sharing the peace and joy of God before he entered the eternal rest when God took him home. Enoch walked among men and at the same time walked with God. So with our feet, we praise the Lord as we walk in His way, doing His work.

God gave us only one *tongue* but it is mighty, for good or evil. No words are spoken without it, nor can a song rise from our lips. Whether we speak eloquently or stumble over each word, whether we sing off-key or with perfect pitch, God accepts our efforts for Him.

Finally, God has supplied a *heart* with which to praise Him. He sees our heart's deepest needs and longings. He knows our motives and judges our efforts for Him by our heart attitude. He values a heart that is broken, humble, and contrite. He delights in a heart lifted to Him in worship.

With our heart in tune, our whole instrument of ten strings may be used to serve Him. Which "instrument" do you use the most often? Which one would you like God to use to bring glory to Him?

> *I will sing a new song to you, O God; on the ten-stringed lyre*
> *I will make music to you.*
>
> Psalm 144:9

To save time, set the table as you unload the dishwasher.

My Daily Walks With God

Sandra Jensen

It is very helpful to make a habit of offering, morning by morning,
the troubles of the day to our dear Lord,
accepting His will in all things.

H. L. Lear

Anyone who has been a mother knows how harried family life can some-times be. As a mother of three children, I always struggled to find quiet time with God. As I was reading Matthew one day, a passage admonishing believ-ers to go into their room, shut the door, and pray to their Father made a great impression upon me. *I need to do this*, I told myself.

When the children seemed preoccupied with activities of their own, I tiptoed into my room, but even before the words *Dear Lord* formed on my lips someone was banging at the door. Other days I'd actually get so far as my first prayer request when a terrible racket from the other end of the house suggested wild Indians on the warpath. Praying in secret to my Father just wasn't working!

I was not easily defeated, however. This time I decided to get up early while the house was still quiet. I carefully slipped into the kitchen, made myself a cup of coffee, and curled up on the couch, eager to begin my day with the Lord. Invariably, one of my cherubs would sense movement and hurry out of bed to be with Mom. My quiet time with God was not happening!

It was around this time that I noticed my waistline growing faster than my children. I negotiated with my husband to watch the children for a half hour each morning before he left for work so I could go for a brisk three-mile walk. At first, it was a challenge to get dressed, run a comb through my hair, and extract myself from the throes of a toddler who was convinced Mom was never returning. The next thirty minutes were spent unwinding and letting a little peace drip into my veins before venturing home. But eventually my morning walks became routine, and when I closed the door behind me and set out down the road, I turned to God.

The only interruptions I dealt with now were the glorious sights and sounds of God's creation as I strolled down the bridle trail near our home. It was so easy to praise Him as I looked around at the trees still moist from the early morning dew, or watched the birds flitter from limb to limb. Once I had completed all of my prayer petitions, I still had plenty of time to listen to God. *Show me Your will, Lord. How can I serve You today?*

When I arrived home, I was completely at ease. I had started my day with God, and I was confident that He and I could handle whatever came my way. My morning walks, originally intended to provide some necessary physical exercise, now afforded me spiritual exercise as well. As Christians we are all "walking with God," but my brisk turns around the neighborhood literally became my daily walks with God, and His presence in my life offered me an abundance I had never known before.

Could your waistline benefit from a walk and could your spiritual armor benefit from a talk with God? Try putting both together on an early morning jog or stroll.

Show me Your ways, O LORD, teach me Your paths; guide me in Your truth and teach me, for You are God my Savior, and my hope is in You all day long.
Psalm 25:4, 5

Purchase a large chalkboard and hang it in your kitchen. Every week write a different Bible verse upon it. In that way, you will "bathe" your family in God's word. As your children get older, let them choose the verse and write it on the chalkboard.

A Simple Note

KACY BARNETT-GRAMCKOW

Our thoughts are not like God's thoughts. . . .
He has a different agenda.

Max Lucado

One day, on impulse—I thought—I wrote a brief but heartfelt note to a dear friend. I expressed my admiration for her terrific "people skills," her wisdom, and her ability to work through difficult situations with grace and good humor. I also praised her for being a role model I could trust.

I ended the note simply, saying, "I thank God for your influence in my life." Satisfied, I signed the note and sent it off, then—true to form—I forgot about it.

Weeks later, my friend reminded me of the note. "It arrived on a difficult day," she admitted. "I felt like the whole world was coming down on me. Honestly, I was ready to just throw my hands up in the air and say 'forget it! I give up!' But when I read your note, it made me stop and think about my life, and where I was going from here. . . ."

Almost in tears, my friend told me she had made several life-altering choices, the most profound one affecting her deepening walk with God. Listening to her talk, I was astonished, recognizing God's loving will at work in my friend's life. God had used my impulsive note of encouragement to urge my friend to step out in a new direction spiritually. And, as always, God's timing was perfect: the note had arrived when she needed it the most. His ways are marvelous, but his tools are so ordinary . . . simple as a note.

And he made known to us the mystery of his will
according to his good pleasure . . .

Ephesians 1:9

Write a note of encouragement to a special friend
or relative today.

The Kitten That Ran Away

Janie Jerman Bennett

*The great thing is to have our minds always in a childlike state when
we are considering or fixing our plans—and thus we shall know
that God is guiding our path, even if it were a mistaken one,
to very blessed issues.*

Andrew Murray

My neighbor and I were sitting around the dining room table chatting when she commented, "You know, I think sometimes people are like the kitten that came to our back door the other day."

"What do you mean?" I asked.

"Well, I heard this kitten in our backyard crying. I looked out the window and saw him at our back door. I figured he was hungry so I got a saucer of milk and opened the door to put it on the back step. As soon as I opened the door, it ran across the yard and into the bushes. I could see when he ran he was limping and I wanted to help him. But when I came near him he ran farther away. Finally I gave up. But I could have helped that kitten if he had let me. I'd even have taken him to a veterinarian."

"That was too bad," I said.

"That kitten either didn't understand I was trying to help him or he was afraid of me." She thought a moment. "I think some people are like that when it comes to asking God for help. They pray, asking God to get them out of a bad situation, but then don't respond to what God has for them."

That made me recall a family that visited our church. The father was out of work and he asked us to pray for them. We did pray and a job did open up for him. But he wouldn't take the job, saying it didn't pay enough. The family hasn't been back to church since then and we don't know what happened to them. I believe God wanted to help that family by giving the father an

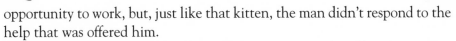
opportunity to work, but, just like that kitten, the man didn't respond to the help that was offered him.

Now when I pray I think of that kitten. I want to be able to recognize God's help when He answers my prayer.

> *For I was hungry and you gave me something to eat, I was thirsty and you gave me something to drink . . .*
> Matthew 25:35

The next time you pray and ask for God's direction, commit to obeying what He says.

One Gangrenous Foot
ARLENE CENTERWALL

Temptations discover what we are.
Thomas á Kempis

Screams pierced the air as the elevator door opened that day in October 1972. The hospital ward buzzed with activity. I was burned out with all the problems and now this. I sighed as we put Roger, a forty-year-old heavy diabetic smoker to bed. I waited for orders for the pain in his gangrenous foot.

I frowned when I read the orders. Plain Tylenol every four hours was hardly enough to dull the pain.

"This wouldn't be enough to put an emaciated mouse to sleep," I muttered to no one in particular.

Three days later, Roger continued to cry out with pain. He cursed the nurses for not doing anything. My staff, disgusted with the poor medication control, came to me and demanded that I do something about it. I agreed and called the surgeon.

When he appeared on the ward, I told him of our unhappiness with his treatment of his patient.

"For heaven's sakes, do something for that poor guy's pain. He's driving us nuts with his screaming," I groused.

"I want him to have that much pain so that he'll demand to have his leg removed. So far he refuses to have it amputated and you know as well as I do that it'll kill him if I don't amputate"

I explained all this to my staff and they understood. It gave us the ability to tolerate the abuse.

At last, Roger agreed to have his leg amputated. It saved his life.

Suddenly the light dawned on me. I thought of how often I simply want to dull the pain in my own spiritual life rather than allow God to amputate the root of the problem. I want to go a different way than the way God wants me to go. Only when I allow Him to amputate the root of my old nature in a deeper way am I able to have a deeper spiritual life!

What source of temptation or struggle are you resisting having amputated by your Great Physician? Don't just ask for the pain to go away, get rid of the cause.

"Why are you sleeping?" he asked them. "Get up and pray
so that you will not fall into temptation."
Luke 22:46

> Replace cosmetics between six months and two years,
> depending upon the product. Blush and eye shadow
> can last longer but mascara can become contaminated
> within three to six months.

Capsules Of Marriage Joy

DAVID AND CLAUDIA ARP

Marriage is not an achievement which is finished. It is a dynamic process between two people, a relation which is constantly being changed, which grows or dies.

Walter Trobisch

Our secret for a happy marriage? Practice preventive medicine by nurturing a spirit of rejoicing, looking for the positive and treating your spouse like a friend. In the process you'll be giving your mate marital vitamins!

Concentrating on the positive seems so simple, but anyone who has tried to do so knows, it's not that simple. But it is very effective. So add that extra touch of health to your marriage by giving each other marital vitamins. What's a marital vitamin? It's anything we do to encourage our mate. Just showing kindness and being considerate of each other can add to your marital health!

Our friend, Joe, literally gave his wife marital vitamins. He bought thirty empty capsules, typed out thirty compliments for his wife, and put one in each capsule. On the bottle he wrote, "Take one a day for encouragement."

Dave tried to do this. "I actually went to a pharmacy and asked for empty capsules. The pharmacist stared at me like I was a drug dealer, so I quickly left without my marriage vitamin capsules! I had to come up with another idea so I folded little pieces of paper and put them in a jar."

Claudia's response: "They worked!"

Everyone needs encouragement. It's got to start somewhere, so why not with you?

A wife of noble character who can find? She is worth far more than rubies.

Proverbs 31:10

Take a couple of minutes right now to make a list of ways
you can build up and encourage your mate.
Put them in a jar and tell him to pick one out each day.

Bloom

KAREN GRONVALL LARSON

The eagle that soars in the upper air does not worry itself
how it is to cross rivers.

Gladys Aylward

The crisp Rocky Mountain air wafted the tang of the evergreen trees. Chilled, we kept hiking through the meadow between the mountain ridges, stepping over snow piles left by the previous winter. We headed for the twin falls, enjoying the pristine beauty in the remote valley beyond the hiking trail.

Coming closer to the falls, a splash of yellow caught my eye. At the edge of the stream, a large clump of yellow buttercups stood in full bloom. Very few people would see the brilliant display. Some animals would pass this patch of blossoms. But God saw. The flowers bloomed to their fullest, doing what they were designed to do right where they were.

Just like those buttercups, we may not be noticed in this life. Our lives may be routine. Our jobs behind the scenes. No large audiences applaud our speeches. Only the kids and the dog hear our views on things that matter to us.

It's okay. We glorify God by doing our daily duties with joy and praise to the Heavenly Father just like those buttercups hidden away in the mountains. But the blossom of our lives reflects God's love as we carry out those mundane activities with a spirit of abundant cheerfulness.

Every day I will praise you and extol your name for ever and ever.
Psalm 145:2

Are you blooming? Praise God for one particular blessing
and write it on a card taped to your bathroom mirror.

Changing Your Mindset
PAM FARREL

There is more to life than increasing its speed.
Mohandas Gandhi

Earlier in our marriage, Bill worked as an architectural draftsman. He was also a student and a youth pastor. We had two tiny boys at home, and life was definitely a whirlwind. One day I was upset at Bill because he seemed so sullen and withdrawn. That evening our conversation hurt my feelings. I went to our room to cry. Then I started to pray. Suddenly God impressed upon me that this night was a turning point and I couldn't let the argument die.

I went out to the living room and saw Bill sitting in a chair studying.

"Bill, this is bad. We're fighting just like average married people, and we don't want an average marriage. What's going on?"

Seeing the distress on my face, he said, "I don't know, Pam, and it bothers me, too."

"You do all the right things, honey. You even brought me flowers last week and you are busier than you've ever been. But it feels like you're not *here*.

"You aren't the Bill I fell in love with. When you handed me my flowers, you just held them out with no expression on your face and said, 'Here, I brought you these.' No kiss, no hug, nothing! Lately it's like you are a Bill clone or a robot or something."

"That's it, Pam. I'm so stressed over meeting graduation deadlines, work deadlines, and ministry stuff that I have nothing left. I'm too tired to feel."

"I can understand that. But we can make it—and I can help, if I just know what's going on. I can lower my expectations of you. I'll help in whatever way I can."

The discussion went on. Bill realized for the first time that his coping mechanism during stressful times was to shut down his emotional center. I gave him permission to do that if he communicated that to me. I also made a commitment to lower my expectations to almost nothing, with the promise of a celebration at the end of the stress in a few months. I just needed light at the end of the tunnel.

Now, if either of us senses that we're in one of those "bury your head and run for the goal line" modes, we know we have made a commitment to communicate—to let the other partner know. This way, Bill's emotional atrophy won't wound me and my typical preoccupation and flurry won't wound him. We give space to one another with the commitment of celebrating the goal together at the end. After the celebration, then we regroup for the future.

Love is patient, love is kind . . .
I Corinthians 13:4

If you put out guest soaps that have lost their fun shapes
by the time the guests leave, use them for yourself,
and put out fresh for your next guests.

Above The Clouds

MURIEL LARSON

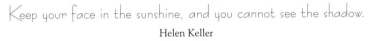

Keep your face in the sunshine, and you cannot see the shadow.

Helen Keller

We lived on the highest ridge in the scenic southwestern section of Wisconsin. One day I decided to drive down to town to get some groceries. The beautiful sunshiny day lifted my spirit as I drove toward the asphalt road that led to Boscobel. But as I headed down the steep hill I saw clouds spread out across all the land below.

Shifting into second gear and turning on my lights, I prayerfully continued on. It was pea-soup fog all the way down. In comparison to the ridge above, the town looked dreary indeed, what you could see of it!

I bought groceries and headed back up through the cloudbank—and when I got near the top, I broke through it into the golden rays of the sun.

"When I was under the clouds in the lowland," I thought, "things looked dreary indeed. But above the clouds the light restores my spirit."

That's just the way it is in life, isn't it? When we're going through trials, things tend to look gloomy and depressing. *How long will this go on?* we wonder. What's going to happen? And while we're asking that question, we're imagining the gloomiest scenario possible!

As Christians, however, we have some great resources. As I went toward that cloudbank, I shifted gears and put on the lights. So when we see trouble coming, or start into it, we can "shift gears" and "put on the light."

How? When things are going smoothly, we take life for granted. But when we encounter trouble, we're wise to wake up and switch to "prayer mode," and start praying about every detail involved in the troubling situation. We also can put on the light by running to our Light, our Lord, and being conscious of His presence with us through it all. Prayer and walking with Jesus will see us through the darkest night or spiritual cloudbank.

When I went down into that cloudbank, I knew the visibility would be poor and I had better keep my eye on the road. I knew also that I would be returning to the beautiful sunshiny day. So it is with trials. We face the fact that we will go through them and we're wise if we keep our eyes on our attitudes and outlooks.

If we allow ourselves to get angry, bitter, and resentful, we'll wallow in depression and gloom; our lives will be miserable. But if we resist ungodly attitudes and keep looking to Jesus, life won't fog up our vision. We can remember that above the clouds the sun is shining—and this trial will also pass. God is the father of lights, and with Him there is no shadow of turning!

So do not fear, for I am with you; do not be dismayed, for I am your God.
I will strengthen you and help you; I will uphold you
with my righteous right hand.
Isaiah 41:10

If you have children at home, have a calendar in a central place that everyone can write down their activities on.

The Joy Of Reading
KATHRYN THOMPSON PRESLEY

Richer than I, you'll never be. I had a mother who read to me.
Strickland Gillilan

In my Dust Bowl, Depression childhood, there was no money for entertainment, so we learned to appreciate the simple pleasure of good books. Nearly every Scots Irish home on the Southern frontier had three books—the King James Bible, *Pilgrim's Progress*, and *Ivanhoe*—and we read these over and over, memorizing chunks of them. We also worked our way through every volume in the meager library at my two-room country school. Sunday afternoons were usually devoted to reading. In the drudgery of our lives, those hours around the table reading, often by lamplight, were a welcome oasis.

When I was thirteen, my teacher gave me *Root Out of Dry Ground*, by Argye Briggs, an Oklahoma preacher's wife. In it, Jansie, the protagonist, was a devout Christian and came from a poor farm family like mine. She grew up in the Southwest as did I. Chris, the orphan she raised, did well in school, worked her way through college, and set out to help her impoverished people. Though it took twenty-two years to get my first degree, there was never a doubt I'd be a teacher after reading that book. Knowing the power of a good book, I've found one of the great joys of teaching (and mothering and grandmothering) is introducing children to beloved books which have molded my life.

In our television-oriented society, teachers can quickly identify the minority of students who have been read to in their homes. They always have a "leg up" in the academic and business world. In fact, the superintendent of Chicago's public schools once lamented: "If we could get parents to read to their preschool children fifteen minutes a day, we could revolutionize the schools."

We must teach our children integrity, love, compassion, justice, and courage. They learn these by our example—and by the long-term process of reading good literature. Reading to children improves both their listening and verbal skills and lengthens their attention span. They will have a varied vocabulary, good grammar, rich vicarious experiences, and the ability to empathize with people who are different from them. Good reading is as essential for the mind and spirit as exercise is for the body.

When was the last time you read to a child? Try it again; you'll enjoy it.

Blessed is he who reads . . .
Revelation 1:3a

> Find a good bibliography such as *Honey for a Child's Heart*
> by Gladys Hunt so that you can pick a good book
> to read to a child—and yourself.

The Carpool's Waiting
SUZY RYAN

Have I a strange god—not a disgusting monster, but a disposition that rules me? More than once God has brought me face to face with the strange god . . . I got through the crisis by the skin of my teeth.

Oswald Chambers

I admit it—I am not a morning person. It is painful for me to lumber out of bed and marshal my three young children to school by the 8:05 bell. I also confess that carpool mornings burn up my patience faster than the gasoline in our waiting Volvo. Since I dread dropping the kids off at school with the memory of me screaming, "Hurry up or we will be late" (or worse), I developed a system to change my natural reaction to the school morning routine.

- First thing in the morning, I pray for God to orchestrate our morning and convict me of any frustration before it sets the mood for the day. Some days, we have to "stop, drop, and pray." This halts the downward spiral, and starts our day over with joy.
- I read a passage from the Bible before we leave for school (or my second-grade son does this in the car).
- We take turns saying our blessings and reviewing some attributes of God. (Sometimes this is also done in the car.)
- We load the next day's supplies before falling into bed. Backpacks (with umbrella and sweatshirt), homework, sports equipment, piano books, and

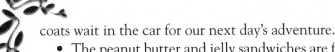

coats wait in the car for our next day's adventure.

- The peanut butter and jelly sandwiches are frozen for the week (whole wheat bread, with a thin spread of low-fat PB on each piece of bread, sealed with fruit spread jelly).

- Bottles of water are frozen each night. They thaw just in time for lunch. (During the winter months, I freeze half the bottle and fill the rest of with water in the morning.)

- Clothes are laid out the night before.

- The kids check off items on their "job chart," after accomplishing their morning chores. When all the kids get ten checks, we do something special as a family.

- The kids make breakfast in the morning. They put in their own waffles. (They have not realized that butter and syrup belong on waffles. Shhh! Don't tell them.) I have milk cups filled and apples washed and ready to eat.

- After arriving at school, I pray a special blessing for protection and wisdom for each child while lathering sunscreen on their faces.

School started several months ago, and unbelievably, I am actually enjoying the school routine. Careful planning, organization, and cooperation from my children enable us to claim victory most of the time. Let's face it, though, I will never be a morning person.

With God's help, you too can begin each day with gratitude and confidence. Excuse me now, gotta run—the carpool is waiting.

> *I do not understand what I do. For what I want to do I do not do,*
> *but what I hate I do.*
> Romans 7:15

Determine to start the day reading your children
a chapter of the Bible. Have them make a picture
of the story and then file it in a three-ring notebook.

A Pink Cap
And Wedding Dress Memory

DEE HYATT

When there is an original sound in the world,
it can make a hundred echoes.

John Shedd:

Some people think to make a difference they must accomplish something spectacular. In truth, the tiniest of actions can bring enormous results.

At the time of my wedding, my grandma's health was too poor for her to attend, at least not physically, but she was there in spirit. I promised that I would visit her in my wedding dress at the nursing home after the wedding.

As I walked toward my grandma with my wedding dress and veil on, her eyes were gleaming from underneath her bright neon baseball cap, given to her on Mother's Day. We hugged each other with tears of joy.

I twirled around letting her see my dress with the long train. Her eyes danced with pride and love as she fingered the pearled sequins. Grandma and I were floating on cloud nine as we made our way down the hallway. My new husband, Ted, joined our procession pushing her wheelchair.

Everyone asked, "Who are you?"

I proudly held Grandma's hand. "I'm Rena Sanger's granddaughter." Grandma beamed as they congratulated her.

I had transformed a nursing home into a reception without knowing it. I hadn't been prepared for the outpouring of attention. I had only wanted to show Grandma my dress.

The overwhelmed residents stood in the hall cheering and laughing. Their eyes had looks of nostalgia, women sighing and reliving their own wedding days.

The dingy hallway was filled with smiling faces and hands reaching out to feel the dress as they wanted to be part of the moment. Even the residents that usually sat with frowns were smiling and joining in.

Grandma felt like a queen that one day. She was young again, no aches and pains to concern herself with. She sat and enjoyed being a grandma, laughing more than I had seen her laugh for many years.

Grandma is in heaven now.

My wedding album holds a picture of my proud grandma sitting next to me with her pink cap, me with my wedding dress. We have the same smile, one of love for each other.

It can be hard to watch your loved ones grow old. But they too are on a journey and no matter what our age, we all have lessons to learn and to teach if we are willing.

God's love will enrich our lives every moment of every day if we ask him. When we do small things, they sometimes turn into one of the most beautiful memories we will ever have. Is there someone in your life that you can make a memory with today?

But if a widow has children or grandchildren, these should learn first of all to put their religion into practice by caring for their own family and so repaying their parents and grandparents, for this is pleasing to God.
I Timothy 5:4

When visiting grandparents, ask them about themselves and write it down. You will have a wonderful gift for your children from their great-grandparents.

Doctor God

Nora Lacie Abell

For there was never yet philosopher that could endure
the toothache patiently.

William Shakespeare

"Ow, Ow, Ow!" I burbled, drooling saliva out of the corners of my mouth. The dental assistant slurped it up with her shiny little silver vacuum cleaner and the dentist continued with my "endodontic treatment, (dental talk for root canal). Right at the start of my much-anticipated Spring vacation, my tooth began to throb, not just a little twinge, but a wake-up-in-the-night, hand-a-total-stranger-the-pliers type of toothache. Fortunately, my dentist worked me into his schedule, and I had to admit that, though uncomfortable, my "treatment" didn't really *hurt* as much as the painful toothache. Now I sat tipped back in the big dental chair, having the diseased nerve of my offending tooth carefully removed with small, precise reamers. None of the necrotic tissue could be left behind, or it would re-infect and cause more painful swelling. The expert dental team sterilized the empty nerve canal and filled it with a medicated paste that smelled of cloves. A final x-ray confirmed my completed treatment, and after the paper bib was removed, I was courteously shown out of the office. What would I have done without those pain-relieving experts?

Who is the expert pain-reliever in your life? When you ache, emotionally or spiritually, do you put off treatment hoping it will just go away? Spiritual pain, like a toothache, never just disappears. It may lie dormant for years, or like a severe toothache, grab your attention suddenly and painfully. It festers, swells, disturbs your sleep and causes excruciating pain in your heart until it is competently and thoroughly treated. The sick tissue must be removed! The Bible talks about "circumcision of the heart," but another way to look at it is a "root canal of the heart." What dentist would do that?

Would we attempt to drill or fill our own teeth? Of course not. It would be foolish, wouldn't it? Likewise, God has an abundant treatment plan for our spiritual pain. He is *the* expert in this sort of treatment! Not only does He fit us into His heavenly schedule, He sees us, listens to our complaints, understands our symptoms and treats us *immediately!* With His x-ray vision of the heart, He sees what infects us. He uses Godly methods to work every unGodly "nerve" out of its dark, diseased hiding place. While the treatment may occasionally be uncomfortable (we may even squirm and mutter, "Ow, Ow!"), we can trust Him. He never makes mistakes and is thorough and gentle. Diseased tissue removed, our hearts can be filled with the sweet-smelling medicine of grace. Forgiveness permeates the heart's secret hiding place, and the sting is gone! Best of all, He willingly accepts His Son's payment as our proof-of-insurance!

He heals the brokenhearted and binds up their wounds.
Psalm 147:3

Just as you floss, brush, and rinse your teeth daily,
remember to pray, praise, and forgive daily.
And don't forget periodic checkups!

Haunting Memories
LARAINE E. CENTINEO

Forget it. Put it away firmly. To leave the door of memory
even a bit ajar is to provide passage for grief. . . .
Marjorie Holmes

Looking at old photographs is fun. At times my family spends hours browsing through them. "Hey, Mom! It's Dad's fiftieth surprise party," my daughter smiles, lifting the photo for everyone to see. We all cherish happy memories.

But what about the memories of our past misdeeds—those we'd rather forget? Do they continue to haunt us? Do we still carry a mental scrapbook of guilt and shame? If we do, our negative recollections of yesterday serve as stumbling blocks to knowing God's peace in our lives today.

How sad that we allow former failures to weigh us down. It is never God's intention that we carry such a burden. On a cross, on a hill, over two thousand years ago, Christ paid the price for our sin and we were freed from self-condemnation and blame. Satan, our accuser, no longer has a hold on us. We need only claim the tranquility that is rightfully ours.

The next time you mentally begin to flip through your photo album of past sins, imagine the words "forgiven and forgotten" written across them in indelible ink. Then throw that scrapbook away!

And the peace of God, which transcends all understanding, will guard your hearts and your minds in Christ Jesus.
Philippians 4:7

Write a note thanking Jesus for writing the words
"forgiven and forgotten" across your
mental photo album of past sins.

God's Special Discipline
LISA L. KECK

"This is going to hurt me more than it hurts you."
Mom just before the spanking

We've all heard that one before, but did you know that it's a saying that could actually be attributed to God? After the people of Judah had been sent into captivity for repeated disobedience, God was sorry for having to punish them. He didn't want to punish, but His children needed to learn that there are consequences when rules are broken.

At a conference several years ago, I ran into the first teacher I worked with in special education. I was her aide in a diagnostic pre-school class. That means the children's abilities were assessed and she gave input on their elementary school placement. I admired her dedication and determination in fighting for the child's best interest. Sometimes it was special education and sometimes it was mainstreaming. Even though the students I had worked with had moved on, I asked Carolyn how they were doing.

Carolyn told me that Heather had gotten a "ticket" in her new grade school for running in the halls. She broke a rule; therefore, she received a consequence. But Carolyn told me about it with a smile on her face. You see, when Heather was in her class at age four she could barely walk! Now she'd gotten a ticket for running! But, unless Heather learned the lesson of the "ticket," she wouldn't learn to obey the rules.

Another tactic a teacher could have used would be to have Heather write one hundred times: "I will not run in the halls." That would have taken time to complete, time to reflect, while sitting still.

You and I are like Heather. Sometimes when we become empowered by God to do His will, we go beyond what He intended. We begin to "run" in our own power. Then God has to bring consequences into our lives so that we'll reflect on what got us into trouble and learn to depend only on Him.

Yet God always promises restoration when we sin or make mistakes. He wants to restore and strengthen us when we wander. He doesn't punish us; He trains us for future effective ministry in His power.

If you stay in this land, I will build you up and not tear you down; I will plant you and not uproot you, for I am grieved over the disaster I have inflicted on you.
Jeremiah 42:10

Plant tulip bulbs in the Fall. The results won't be immediate, but, oh, what a wonderful reminder of how God works in ways we cannot see.

Be Still

KAREN KOSMAN

*If we make God's will our law, then God's promise shall be our
support and comfort, and we shall find every burden light,
every duty a joy.*

Tryon Edwards

One morning, the mailman brought a big manila folder that I recognized as a critique from my editor. Susan's cover letter carefully made suggestions, offered corrections, and gave me encouragement. She closed by saying, "Remember, writing a book is like eating an elephant! Don't get indigestion."

I thought, *Lord, I think I already have indigestion. For weeks I've struggled to find time to work on my book project. Other things have come along in my life that I felt you wanted me to say yes to.*

My husband John and I said we'd teach a youth group on Sunday evenings. Tuesday evenings we have a Bible study at our home. Two days a week I take care of my granddaughters. Each task started out with joy. But confusion and frustration from being overextended was stealing my joy.

One evening, John said, "Karen, you look tired."

"I just can't seem to get organized."

"Maybe we need 'a getaway day,'" John replied.

I thought, *Sounds wonderful.*

"Karen, did you hear me?"

"Yes. I agree. I just don't know how or when."

"Nothing will get done if you get sick."

"You're right. So how about tomorrow?"

"Great!"

The next morning was gorgeous. After breakfast, we drove to the beach. A breeze blew through the open car window bringing the salty, clean smell of sand and ocean. Parking was free and the summer crowds were gone. The wind blew softly, just enough to make it enjoyable. We strolled hand in hand and watched a sandpiper seek and find a sand crab. Three baby sandpipers ran across the sand, close to the water's edge, their little legs swirling like paddle wheels. They seemed to instinctively know what direction to go. A seagull flew above swooping, and a pelican dove into the ocean, fishing. I glanced around the beach and thought, *This is all God's creation.*

We sat down on a wall close to the jetty where the sound of the waves created a symphony. A peaceful, quiet moment, I heard God's spirit within whisper, *"Karen, let go. Stop and listen. Be still and know that I am God."* My tired muscles relaxed, and a peace filled my being. God's abundance surrounded us. I made a decision at that moment to stop being superwoman and take time for tranquil moments with God.

Are you feeling stressed? Does it seem like there's too much to do? If you are in God's will, He promises to provide everything you need to accomplish His plan. And maybe that should include a little getaway. Why not today, if only for an hour?

"Be still, and know that I am God; I will be exalted among the nations,
I will be exalted in the earth."
Psalm 46:10

Create your own spa. Use aromatherapy in your bath water (a drop of rosemary oil). Soft music and candlelight creates an atmosphere where your mind, body, and spirit relax.

Waste Not

Lou Ann Prosack

Conservation: The wise use of the earth and its resources
for the lasting good of men.

Gifford Pinchot

It is celebrated in November each year. It will come and go without much fanfare and little notice. Yes, *Use Less Stuff Day (ULSD)* will quietly pass with no big tickertape parade debris to be cleaned up and no disposable holiday decorations to be thrown away. Actually, that is what ULS is all about: using less.

A number of years ago at a church service I attended, the minister spoke about the waste generated by using paper products such as paper towels instead of tea towels and paper plates instead of regular plates. While I haven't been able to give up using paper towels, to this day, I cannot buy paper plates for home use. Every time I take them off the grocery shelf, the image of the minister goes through my mind and back on the shelf they go. While this is only a very small contribution, it's good to know there is finally a day to celebrate the effort.

Use Less Stuff is a program started four years ago by Partners for Environmental Progress and includes among its sponsors the EPA, Keep America Beautiful, and various cities and counties throughout the country.

To assist you in waste reduction efforts, the Partners for Environmental Progress offers *42 Ways to Trim Your Holiday Wasteline* at the following website: http://cygnus-group.com.

*In the beginning God created the heavens and the earth. . . . The land produced
vegetation: plants bearing seed according to their kinds and trees bearing fruit
with seed in it according to their kinds. And God saw that it was good.*

Genesis 1:1,12

Millions of trees are destroyed each year to produce products made from wood, trees which help clean the air and provide shade from the heat. Set a goal—plant a tree this year.

Yards Of Blue Cotton

DORIS HAYS NORTHSTROM

When December days get hectic and there seems no room for
more
There is always a place in the inn of your heart's door.

Doris Hays Northstrom

As grandmother and narrator, I was in charge. Or so I thought. It was the morning of Christmas Eve and all five grandchildren were with me in the kitchen as their parents did some last minute shopping. Brian, our youngest, their teenage uncle, helped me keep everyone occupied. Brad and Tyson sorted gumdrops for gingerbread cookies; Amy and Bridget plunked out carols on the piano; Shannon, feisty four-year-old, elbowed her way to the frosting bowl.

Earlier in the week, we had enjoyed the Sunday School Pageant, gone caroling on a hay truck, and made ornaments and candles for giving. This was our "home" day, warm and filled with Christmas sounds and smells.

Looking at Shannon, who was needing more direction, I said, "Let's plan a pageant. Would you like to be Mary?"

Her eyes glistened as she ran into my arms. "Yes, Grandma, yes! Can I get the costume box?"

While Shannon pored through yardage, the rest of us finished decorating cookies, decided on parts, and collected candles and greens. Their parents and great grandma, Dorothy, would be the audience.

Brad pulled on a wig and a play-weary jeweled crown while Tyson dressed in burlap as Joseph. Amy and Bridget tied garlands in each other's hair and pranced around the living room, flapping their wings with angelic secrets in their smiles. Brian dressed as the Innkeeper and took charge of music.

Shannon stopped giggling and calmed down as I draped her in yards of blue cotton. Her eyes softened as she brushed the cheeks of the baby doll with her lips. A holy kind of hush engulfed us as we watched her cradle the face of the baby Jesus, then hum softly in his ear.

I opened my Bible. "Okay, kids, let's begin. Mary and Joseph traveled from Nazareth to Bethlehem to be taxed." I patted Shannon's shoulder, "Walk with Tyson, honey, you're tired from a long journey." She complied, impatient to get on with the story of the baby.

Brian turned up the cassette as they walked toward the simple nativity we had created. Strains of "O Little Town of Bethlehem" reached out to childhood memories of my own. The purity of the children's voices reflected the heart and true meaning of Christmas. I saw on their faces that they could feel the wonder, too.

Brian, our Innkeeper, stood tall and persuasive. "There's no room for you here."

Mist glazed Shannon's eyes as I continued the scripture, "Because there was no room for them in the Inn."

Shannon stormed out of the room, returning with her favorite threadbare blanket. "There is too room, Grandma," she bellowed as she stood with her hands on her hips. Then she picked up the babe, already propped in the manger, wrapped him carefully, snuggling his head under her chin, and carried him back to her bed.

We all stood there looking at each other. Wind rustled the patio chimes, candlelight danced across the greens and empty manger. My heart bowed. Christmas had come.

Yet to all who received Him, to those who believed in His name, He gave the right to become children of God.

John 1:12

F·A·L·L

After reading an issue of a magazine, give it immediately
to your local library if they don't have a subscription
to that particular magazine.

The Christmas Crook

NAOMI WIEDERKEHR

*The simple shepherds heard the voice of an angel and found their
Lamb; the wise men saw the light of a star
and found their Wisdom.*

Fulton J. Sheen

The shepherds took their crooks and were the first to visit the newborn Christ Child. The crooks were present for that first worship service.

The Christmas crook comes to your house every Christmas. It is one of the most traditional candies at Christmas time—the familiar red and white candy cane. The crook, the shape of the candy cane, can rightly be called one of the first symbols of Christmas.

The colors of the candy cane have meaning. The broad red stripe stands for Jesus' blood that He shed for our sins, while the smaller stripes remind us of the sacrifices we make as Christians in serving Jesus. The white color speaks of the pure white heart Jesus gives us.

The sharp, but sweet, peppermint flavor makes us think of the cleansing and of the healing Jesus brings to our hearts and lives.

The history of the candy cane is traced back more than 900 years to its first appearance at Germany's Cologne Cathedral. In 1670, during a church service, a choirmaster is said to have given out white candy sticks with one end bent to resemble the shepherd's crook.

Around 1850, a German-Swedish immigrant in Wooster, Ohio, is credited with introducing the candy cane to America by giving samples to his nieces and nephews.

Why not use your own imagination to decorate some candy canes? The only supplies you will need are the plain white candy cane, an artist's small paint brush, food coloring, and chocolate. Below are a few suggestions in addition to making the usual red and white.

1. Paint different color stripes at various widths. Be sure one color is dry before adding another.
2. Paint polka dots.
3. Paint the cane all one color.
4. Paint a multicolor cane which may be used as an object lesson. Black stands for sin, red for Jesus' blood, white for pure heart, green for Christian growth, blue for royalty, and yellow or gold for heaven.
5. Dip in melted chocolate.

You can make a variety of these to hang on your Christmas tree or give to your friends.

So they hurried off and found Mary and Joseph, and the baby,
who was lying in the manger.
Luke 2:16

Make rice krispie squares with chips of candy cane stirred in.

F · A · L · L

Cards That Comfort

LETTIE J. KIRKPATRICK

A written message is a tangible expression of love. Your written words represent you—your time and your love for others.

Gloria Chisholm

A well-chosen, well-worded card can become a powerful voice of hope, comfort, and encouragement to a needy person. Cards are always a gesture of caring. Choosing, signing, addressing, stamping, and mailing them takes time, which itself is a precious gift. I was grateful for every card during the illnesses and following the death of my daughter. But there were some that so spoke to my heart they have been saved and reread.

These guidelines will increase the possibility that your cards will truly become a ministry.

1. *Include a personal message.* Even carefully selected, beautiful verses don't have the impact of brief lines from your own heart.

If you are extending sympathy, share a personal memory that you have of that person. Or mention something about their life that touched yours. One friend wrote that every time she saw a Six Flags commercial, she remembered our Shela. They had been together there.

Encourage the caregiver, affirming their faithfulness to their loved one. Don't just say, "I'm praying." Name some exact ways you are praying. It might be for healing, strength, comfort, or for the doctors to have wisdom. Share a specific scripture, if God leads you. In dark days, I clung to some of the verses my friends wrote to comfort me.

2. *Seek God's timing in mailing cards.* Almost three weeks to the day after my daughter died, cards stopped coming. This is normal. But how precious were those seemingly "late" ones that arrived on days I was overcome with loss such as her birthday, the anniversary of her death, and difficult-to-face

175

holidays. Sometimes an isolated card at a strange time can touch a life in an exceptional way.

3. *Enclose pictures if you have them.* I was delighted when others shared copies of pictures that included our daughter. We eventually made a memorial album of her life.

4. *Don't neglect sending a card or note for fear of doing or saying "the wrong thing."* Most of us understand how awkward people feel in the face of pain. I appreciated every expression of caring. And sometimes "practice makes perfect"!

> A word aptly spoken is like apples of gold in settings of silver.
> Proverbs 25:11

Watch for bargains and keep a variety of appropriate cards on hand. Store these in a pretty basket with pens, address labels, stamps, and your address book.

Twelve Ways To Make Christmas Memories

LETTIE J. KIRKPATRICK

Christmas should be a joyous celebration of our Lord's birth. We want our children to grow up with treasured memories of family times at Christmas—times when Christ is honored in our family.

Ann Hibbard

Here are twelve ways to make Christmas memorable and even more meaningful.

1. Purchase an advent calendar and open a window of the project each day.
2. Keep a basket of Christmas music close by and create a festive or worshipful mood during baking, wrapping, and decorating.
3. Burn candles and fragrant potpourri throughout the season.
4. Pray for those who send cards to your family.
5. Draw names in the family and become Secret Angels—reveal yourselves on Christmas Eve.
6. Gather weekly around an advent wreath. Light candles, read Scripture, and sing carols while discussing different aspects of the Christmas story.
7. Set out a basket of Christmas books containing colorful pictures with the retelling of the birth of Christ or other related stories.
8. Put only gifts for others under the tree until closer to Christmas. It keeps the focus on giving.
9. Encourage secret or spontaneous acts of kindness throughout the season. Take cookies to a service provider (pharmacist, doctor, owner of a favorite restaurant, or grocer) with a note of appreciation. Let school children choose a needy classmate to receive an anonymous gift.
10. Plan several projects focused on reaching out and meeting needs:
    • Giving to a mission offering
    • Church ministries to struggling families
    • The Shoebox Ministry sponsored by Franklin Graham and The Samaritan's Purse. It is a great family project for Christmas.
11. Plan a family night out and take in some light extravaganzas or a nativity re-enactment. Or plan a family night "in" and watch Christmas movies or just "crash."
12. Make a toy nativity set available so little ones can recreate their own version of Jesus' birth.

Which activity would you like to use to make Christmas time more focused on the true reason for the season?

But Mary treasured up all these things, and pondered them in her heart.
Luke 2:19

Have a birthday party for Jesus, complete with cake,
napkins, and song.

Knock, Knock . . .

PATTY STUMP

Christ is not valued at all unless He is valued above all.
St. Augustine

We've all had the experience of hearing an unexpected knock at our door
and wondering who's there. Often we peak through a window before decid-
ing whether or not to open our home to the visitor. Scripture refers to Christ
knocking on the door of our heart waiting for us to invite Him in. Often we
postpone letting Him into our moments, preferring to prioritize other activities or thoughts. At other times we welcome Him, desiring to exchange otherwise ordinary moments for a holy encounter. Once we set aside our agenda,
prioritizing the important rather than the urgent, the concerns of life dim as
we pause in the presence of Christ.

Quiet moments with Christ shape our day from the inside out, affecting
our perspective, attitude, priorities, relationships, and our direction. A few
simple moments invested wisely each day will bring divine dividends! Consider the following as you open your heart to Him:

Pray before your time together, asking for clarity of thought and discern-
ment. Ask Him to give you discipline in prioritizing your time with Him and
wisdom to hear His leading.

Select a book of the Bible, study resource, or devotional guide to read. Some variety in your quiet time will keep it refreshing. Listening to or singing praise music can help you develop an attitude of worship. He will give exciting insights as you take the time to look, listen, and learn!

Keep a notepad handy to jot down thoughts that cross your mind. Some thoughts may pertain to things Christ reveals to you in your time together. Others may pertain to things you need to take care of and don't want to forget. After jotting them down, continue your fellowship time with Christ.

Try to choose a time and place for your devotions that is quiet, away from distractions. You may decide to rise early while others are sleeping or set aside private moments during a break at work or home. Or the evening may be more suitable for you. Whatever time and place works best, stick to it!

A notebook or journal can be useful to record prayer concerns as well as answers to prayer. It is exciting to look back and see how the Lord creatively responded to your prayers. In your time of study and prayer, be expectant!!

Last, be sure to not only talk to God, but listen to Him as well. He desires a personal relationship with you that involves two-way communication. He will speak to your heart. We must be committed to letting Him in, being still, and listening.

Here I am! I stand at the door and knock. If anyone hears My voice and opens the door, I will come in and eat with him, and he with Me.
Revelations 3:20

Take an outing to your local bookstore and purchase a journal. Begin recording your prayer requests to the Lord, His answers, and the insights He gives regarding His work in your life.

The Blessings Of Memorization
ERMA LANDIS

Sin will keep you from this Book. This book will keep you from sin.
Dwight L. Moody

People often assume the primary reason to memorize Scripture is to have it embedded in your mind and therefore have it with you all the time. For most of us that's not the way it works, unless you have an extraordinary mind. If yours is like mine and resembles a sieve, take heart. Very seldom have I been able to retain a portion of, or a book of Scripture, more than six months, but I have found the *process* of memorization holds some of the most valuable blessings that have ever enriched my life.

Blessing Number One: The repetition of the same words every day (I aim for eight to ten times daily) eventually penetrates your mind until it impacts your spirit to the core. Sometimes I find my heart pounding as the message reaches my inner spirit. I began to realize how exciting learning God's Word can be.

Blessing Number Two: Saturating one's mind with God's thoughts (His Word) enables us to more readily have the mind of Christ. Psalm 1:2 says a godly man meditates on His Word day and night. Saturation makes us able to view life through God's perspective and that is having the mind of Christ.

Blessing Number Three: Memorizing God's Word gives us a greater sensitivity of right and wrong. Frequently we are unaware of the long-range effects our decisions have on us and the world around us. Having this sensitivity is very important in daily living.

Blessing Number Four: Our hunger for God's Word is increased. If you've ever had a deep yearning for a taste of your favorite treat you know the delight of satisfying that yen. You are satisfied but you find yourself looking forward to the next time you will have that treat. So it is with God's Word. It is satisfying, yet you still find yourself longing to know more.

Finally, and most importantly, memorizing helps to keep your mind focused on God. Our world moves so fast and it is easy to lose one's focus of Him. Without even being conscious of it, we can become so self-sufficient that we forget to depend on God alone. By repeating His thoughts morning and evening, we concentrate on Him more often.

Even if you don't have one of those extraordinary minds that retains your memorized passages for a long time, the blessings of memorization can still be yours. And don't you forget it!

Your word is a lamp to my feet and a light to my path.
Psalm 119:105

Commit to learning one verse of Scripture this week.

Blue Christmas Trees
RONICA STROMBERG

It is life near the bone where it is sweetest.
Henry David Thoreau

Christmas at Grandma's always held a bit of mystery for me as a child. The mystery surrounded her sugar cookies. While the Santa Claus figures had the expected red and white frosting and the stars and bells were frosted yellow, the Christmas trees were always blue. *Why doesn't Grandma frost the Christmas trees green?* I pondered, year after year.

Grandma *did* have peculiar ways. She had a hard time parting with old rubber bands, string, used aluminum foil . . . almost anything. She had lived through the depression, a bona fide member of the "waste not, want not" generation.

Gifts from her came wrapped in a patchwork of used paper with bows salvaged from Christmases before. The gifts themselves were often revamped garage sale toys. Not that I minded. When I received a gift from Grandma, I knew that chances were I would not be merely the first kid on the block to own the toy, I would be the *only* kid on the block to own the toy. My paper doll collection was a constant source of envy of neighbor girls.

As I grew older, the mystery surrounding Grandma's cookies dissolved. The Santa Claus figures changed from red and white frosting to blue. I was old enough then to realize that Grandma had not been making green Christmas trees because her green food dye had run out years before. Now her red dye had also run out. Grandma had apparently been trying to use up the dye in her cupboards before buying more.

A little older, I came to yet another realization: Grandma had not just been frugal, she had been poor. Funny how this realization had escaped me as a child. I must have thought the homes of the poor were all filled with misery and heartache. But my grandma's home—the home with the blue Christmas trees—had been filled with love and joy.

Love and joy are not dependent upon the amount of money anyone has. My grandma proved that. Have you experienced the same?

> Better a dry crust with peace and quiet than a house full of feasting,
> with strife.
>
> Proverbs 17:1

For a soft, tasty frosting on sugar cookies, use the same frosting you would on a wedding cake. Here is a simple recipe: Mix two cups powdered sugar with two tablespoons shortening. Add enough milk (a little more than two tablespoons) until the frosting is smooth and easy to spread.

What Makes Us Valuable?

Joy Anna Rosendale

Souls are God's jewels, every one of which is worth many worlds.

Thomas Traherne

Sometimes my shoulders tense and knot, and pain crawls up my neck and throbs in my forehead. "Oh, no! Another tension headache! Why am I stressing out again?"

Usually I'm trying to do something that I hope will look impressive enough to prove my worth. I struggle with the fear that I'm not important and my abilities don't count for much. But I'm sick of the tangled confusion and stress of constantly trying to prove myself. Is there a better way of finding that I'm valuable?

Recently, I gained insights by reading about edelweiss, the tiny, white, star-shaped flowers cherished in Switzerland as the national emblem. I'm surprised the Swiss don't choose their mountains to represent their country. The massive stone bastions, which tower two miles up into the clouds, and the jagged peaks and plunging precipices have made Switzerland famous throughout the world. But living among the rocks, high above the meadows and forests, above the timberline and near the frozen glaciers, the edelweiss are hidden too far away for anyone to see them—insignificant white specks lost in the vastness of the rugged mountains.

Fiercely cold winds whip the mountain peaks and the ground beneath the edelweiss lies frozen year around. Thick clouds blot out the sunshine for months on end. The edelweiss grow most of the time in gloomy fog, bravely unfurling their six slender petals, like little white stars shining in the snow. They are able to stay alive only because God personally takes care of them.

I picture Him kneeling down on the sides of the mountains to spread invisible blankets over His little flowers. He makes their petals thick and wooly to keep them warm. He melts the snow, and their tiny rootlets sip water from His warm hands. And in the bitter winter months when they hardly ever see the sun, God smiles on the edelweiss. In the light of His love they blossom and flourish, pure white and tender, glowing with joy upon the mountains. These flowers are treasured in Switzerland because they symbolize God's care for little things.

How simple and peaceful my life becomes when I content myself with being little. My value isn't based on what I try to *do*: it's based on what God *does* for me. I'm valuable because God holds me in His tenderness and expends His greatest efforts on me. When I simply drink in His loving care, I start to blossom naturally—just the way He wants me to. I can stop trying to be impressive. I can enjoy being His little mountain flower: small, but dearly loved and lovely.

God cherishes us. When we feel small and insignificant we should remember that God lavishes His special love on little things. As He is caring for the edelweiss, He stoops down to take care of us. His tender touch confirms our worth and demonstrates forever that we are valuable.

I praise you because I am fearfully and wonderfully made;
your works are wonderful, I know that full well.
Psalm 139:14

Find a white silk edelweiss flower and place it somewhere
to remind you of your value.

Sweet Smelling Rainbows

CAMILLE SCHULER

What is the price of an afternoon when a small girl is soothed in your arms, when the sun bolts through a doorway and both you and the child are very young?

Dorothy Evslin

"What a beautiful picture," declared the flight attendant as she peered over the shoulder of my five-year-old. "I'll bet it's going on your refrigerator at home."

Isabelle affirmed the woman's perception with a bashful smile. The flight attendant moved on and my daughter went back to work on her latest "masterpiece."

I watched as she colored with her "smelly" markers. Holding each pen up to her nose as if it were the latest perfume, she inhaled deeply before she continued drawing. When she was finished with the color, she'd sneak one last sniff before replacing the cap. Since her case was in the lap of her dozing daddy, she silently slipped each color into the package, careful not to wake either him or her little brother in the next seat.

"Here, Mommy, smell this one," she whispered. My daughter's delicate little fingers waved a felt tip just under my nose. It smelled delicious. I nodded my approval and she returned to her project. I lingered there in the land of pigtails and bubble gum blue.

I'd seen Isabelle color before, almost every day for the last few years. But looking down at her light brown hair as it hung over the multi-scented rainbow, I enjoyed my daughter in a new way. I had always taken great pleasure in her accomplishments, big or small. Whenever she would come bounding over to me, excited to share her latest work, I'd draw a happy face at the top of each picture—a sign of my blessing on her achievements. Then I would display her creations in a place of honor on our refrigerator door.

But today was different. For the first time I was not looking at what she drew. Rather I was enjoying the process of being a part of her world without all the distractions that can clutter a day. Sitting on an airplane, I had no phones to answer, no meals to prepare, no clothes to wash. I indulged myself in the luxury of gazing at my daughter.

It came to me then, that my Heavenly Father takes the same liberties with me. He considers my prayers and efforts as sweet as the scent of bubble gum waved under His nose. He enjoys who I am simply because I am His daughter. And He delights not only in what I accomplish but also in watching me as I draw the drama of my life. Maybe that is what is hanging on the door of Heaven's refrigerator alongside a box of sweet smelling markers.

For the LORD takes delight in his people . . .
Psalm 149:4a

When was the last time you stopped everything just to smell a rose, to gaze at a rainbow, or simply to watch your child at play?

Dot To Dot
ANDI SMITH

A picture is worth a thousand words.
Unknown

The simple activity of drawing lines between numbered dots to create a finished picture delighted me as a child. I lacked the confidence of drawing freehand, but through following the guidance of the numbers I felt like a real artist. The anticipation of a surprise picture spurred me on to the last dot. As an adult, I now see that moving from the invisible to the visible gave me a sense of fulfillment I didn't understand at such a young age.

I often see life with faith in God much like a dot-to-dot picture. Each day offers a new opportunity to connect the dots of spiritual truths from the invisible kingdom of God to the visible dots of my life on this earth. As I receive the word of God from reading the Bible or feel an inner nudge from the Holy Spirit, I then connect to the next dot by responding to His instructions.

It's an exciting process. "What image is emerging?" I ask myself. "How will the complete drawing appear in the end?" I anticipate my future the same way I anticipated a finished drawing as a child. I become co-creator with my Creator, holding on to the promise that He will complete the work He has begun.

As a result, I face each new day with expectant wonder. What new picture will be revealed in my life? What characteristics of Christ will become evident to others? The Lord helps me make a beautiful work of art out of my life, as I respond in faith to His revealed truths. Faith to works; heaven to earth; dot to dot. I simply connect the dots of my life one at a time as the Lord reveals them.

How is your life's dot-to-dot picture coming?

In the morning, O LORD, you hear my voice; in the morning I lay my requests before you and wait in expectation.
Psalm 5:3

Create the habit of looking forward to each new day with expectation. Rise early enough to take a few minutes to communicate with the Lord in prayer. Meditate on His Word, knowing He will be faithful to give you the direction you need.

God's Studio

Lynn Thigpen

God's fingers can touch nothing but to mold it into loveliness.
George MacDonald

Michelangelo is famous for his work as a sculptor and painter, especially for his statue of David and the ceiling of the Sistine Chapel. He is also famous for the number of his unfinished pieces. Only once did Michelangelo sign a work. Even that inscription was left with one letter missing, giving the feeling of an unfinished project, a work in progress.

As creative as Michelangelo was, he is surpassed by one other sculptor. This creator's works are innumerable. His creations are intricately and delicately designed. We are a part of them. He calls us His workmanship. When I think of the Creator working like Michelangelo, I realize life is His museum or a glimpse at His studio.

With the great Creator claiming us among His works, why do so many of us feel like one of Michelangelo's unfinished pieces? Why do we feel like chunks of rock waiting for the right person to recognize the potential inside us? I don't often think of myself or others as masterpieces until I realize what an insult my misconception is to God's greatness. Paul disclosed the wonderful promise that God is still chiselling on us, never giving up, always keeping us in His studio. This truth offers hope for abundance in my life and in the lives of those around me.

> *Be diligent in these matters; give yourself wholly to them,*
> *so that everyone may see your progress.*
> I Timothy 4:15

At least one time today, look at the inadequacy or mistake of another person with a new view: as an unfinished project of God's.

Missing Something?

Pat Verbal

Don't forget! Life is about 10% how you make it . . .
And 90% of how you take it.

Barbara Johnson

A friend recently shared a new recipe with me during a visit to her home. Here's the recipe she gave me.

Raisin Walnut Muffins

1 cup molasses
2½ cup bran cereal
1 cup boiling water
½ cup applesauce
1 cup raisins
1 egg

2 cup buttermilk
2¾ cup flour
2½ tsp. baking soda
½ tsp. salt
½ cup chopped walnuts

Heat oven to 400° F. In medium bowl, mix 1 cup bran cereal, raisins, and water. Set aside. In large bowl, combine remaining ingredients. Mix in bran-raisin mixture. Pour into greased muffin pan. Fill two-thirds full and bake for 20 minutes. Remove muffins onto rack to cool. Yield: 48 muffins.

Weeks later, I lined the kitchen counter with the needed bowls, spoons, measuring cups, and pans. I poured boiling water over the raisins. Then I carefully measured and mixed the applesauce with the molasses. Then I sifted the flour, baking soda, and salt. Next came chopping the nuts. After pre-heating the oven, I put the forty-eight paper liners in the muffin tins and poured the thick batter filling the cups two-thirds full. Proudly, I popped my masterpieces into the oven and set the timer to twenty minutes. Then I turned to survey the mess left on the kitchen counter.

The buttermilk! There sat the carton of buttermilk—unopened. I scanned the recipe: "add two cups buttermilk to the dry ingredients." I gazed hopefully at the oven door trying to convince myself that the finished product would be fine without buttermilk. The batter wasn't dry. It tasted okay when I licked the spoon. I don't even like buttermilk. Who needs it?

My rationalizations, however, failed to calm my rising panic. Grabbing the oven mitts, I rescued the pans from the 400-degree oven. I quickly dumped the murky water out of the mixing bowl I'd put in the sink to soak. Frantically I began digging the muddy mixture from the paper liners, which were warm on the bottom. Hoping the baking soda hadn't already reacted to the heat, I promptly splashed the chilled buttermilk into the cooling batter. (Martha Stewart would no doubt faint in my kitchen!) I hid the flattened cups and promptly filled the tins with clean new liners.

Soon the smell of fresh baked muffins filled the room. I reached for my daily devotional book as I waited for the uncertain results. The day's passage came from the Apostle Paul in Philippians 3:12: *Not that I have already obtained all this, or have already been made perfect, but I press on.* I was reminded that Paul admitted his imperfections. As hard as I try to be a perfect wife, mother, teacher, and friend, I never seem to get it right.

The timer on the stove rang out, reminding me of my latest blunder. I cautiously examined the flat, steamy muffins. They smelled okay. In the taste test, they weren't as good as my friend's, but they were edible.

Next time maybe I'll get it right . . . or maybe not. Either way, it's okay. The important thing is that I "press on." Perfect cooks (or perfect Christians) aren't required.

We live by faith, not by sight.
II Corinthians 5:7

If you work at a computer,
be sure to back up your system once a day.

You Can't Get There From Here

LESLIE WHITWORTH

Living a spiritual life makes our little, fearful hearts as wide
as the universe, because the spirit of Jesus dwelling
within us embraces the whole creation.

Henri J.M. Nouwen

Just as dew sparkles at dawn and then vanishes like a mirage, so there is a fragile, crystal silence in our house just before daybreak when everyone is asleep but me. I set up the coffeepot at night so I will not risk waking anyone. While I wait for it to brew, I often go out on the porch to watch the sun rise. The night noises have faded and all nature seems to be mesmerized, wondering where the golden orb will peek up today.

One damp morning, there was a hummingbird trapped in the screen porch. Recent rains left the door swollen and it stuck open just a crack. She flew against the screen, desperate to be free. I tried to shoo her over toward the door, but she refused. She was drawn to the rosy sliver of warmth and light growing on the horizon, but the door is on the north side. I went up behind her and gently placed my finger under her feet. I could hear my heart pounding in my ears. What a treasure to touch a hummingbird. I felt the prickle of sharp claws clinging to my skin. Her sticky feet reminded me of a beetle. I turned to go out the door and she flew off, back toward the sun.

Startled, I said, "I know what you want, but you can't get there from here. Let me help you." Again, I reached out and she perched. This time I placed my thumb and forefinger on either side of her iridescent back, trying not to damage her buzzing wings. Pushing the door with my hip, I released her into the glistening morning.

Back inside, I could still feel the tickle of a tiny talon on my finger. I held my steaming coffee and watched the sun's ascent.

How many times had I beaten my head against a barrier in pursuit of a goal that seemed obviously good? I was recently divorced and my ex-husband had possession of our children. How could a mother be separated from her children? I felt frantic, irrational in my need to be with them and know the minute details of their lives. Did my son sleep through the night? Did my daughter eat all of her breakfast? Did they both have enough covers as they slept? Yet, in that morning's experience, I felt the gentle hand of God leading me. I would have to find new ways of loving my children. I could not break down the barriers that divorce created in our lives. But if I could be still and allow myself to be led, God would bless us. Sometimes God has to release us from the prison of our own perceptions before we can be free.

I can do everything through Him who gives me strength.
Philippians 4:13

Practice silence. Turn off music, TV, computer, conversation, and thinking. At first it may seem impossible to go even a couple of minutes without thinking, but doing so creates an opening in the soul where God's peace floods in like a shaft of light through a parted curtain.

Simple Variations On A Theme

Susan Kimmel Wright

These I have loved: white plates and cups, clean-gleaming.
Rupert Brooke

We got married in the early, do-your-own-thing seventies. We didn't register at the bridal department of the local stores. Instead of china and crystal and silverware, we received sand candles, fondue pots, and place settings painted with big flowers—in shades of avocado, rust, and harvest gold.

As the years went by (and those "groovy" flowered plates broke one by one), we thought about replacing them with something more elegant and less dated. But every time I went to the store to check out a china sale, I found it hard to justify spending so much on dishes. We only entertain casually, and are still raising a group of adolescents who have already contributed their fair share to the dinnerware breakage.

Still, I yearned for a lovely table—even if it was just a quiet family break-fast. As I wrestled with my dilemma, I ran across a suggestion that appealed to my love of simplicity and beauty, as well as frugality. A woman had as-sembled her china service piece by piece by selecting unmatched all-white items. Some she purchased at yard sales and flea markets. Others were gifts from family and friends.

The basic white color theme unified her table, and the subtle variations in design lent a quirky charm. Even a company dinner looks appealing with the addition of a good tablecloth and a bunch of flowers or a dry arrangement. Some small, but trendy restaurants have discovered this idea, and gone even farther, by mixing good-quality china in different color and pattern schemes.

Once I discovered the concept of variations on a theme, I found other ways to incorporate it into other aspects of my home. One of the most wel-coming kitchens I've seen used a mismatched assortment of old, carved oak chairs in place of a factory-fresh set. I've also applied it to people. Just as the people in my life are unique and beautiful individuals, their places at my table are quietly distinctive.

By appreciating differences and variations, whether in place settings, deco-rating, or people, you and I can gain greater abundance through acceptance and unconditional love.

Better a little with the fear of the LORD than great wealth with turmoil.
Proverbs 15:16

Don't be afraid to use your imagination and creativity in furnishing your home, and remember to give thanks.

Keep It Simple

MILDRED WENGER

Remember that Jesus is the reason for the season.

Anonymous

It was a few days before Christmas, and I had a big list of things to be done before the 25th arrived. But the phone call from my daughter changed all that. Rachel's babysitter needed the day off. This left Rachel with no one to keep her baby while she was at work. Would I keep him?

Of course I said yes. One never allows family to be "out on a limb." But this baby was the "no nap" kind. He was awake and demanding attention most of the day. My list would have to wait till the next day.

When that promised day arrived, I received another phone call. My daughter-in-law wanted me to keep Matthew while she went shopping. Matt had a cold and fever, and couldn't go to school. Of course I said yes again, but I began scheming which items on my list I could do while playing with him. One of these items was to try out a fancy dessert recipe. I figured that if it turned out okay, I could make it for the big family get-together.

Matt brought along a computer game and wanted me to play with him. I'm not so good at computer games, but we started. I also got the dessert started. I raced back and forth between the table and the stove, trying to play and cook at the same time.

After I poured the fruit into the blender jar, I couldn't find the little glass center for the lid. So I held my hand over the top, and turned the motor on. Instantly I realized my mistake. The little glass center was in the blender jar, and in those few seconds the blades had shaved slivers of glass into the fruit. My fancy dessert was ruined!

In that moment, I realized my priorities had been all wrong. Fancy desserts are not what Christmas is about. Giving a little boy good memories of time with Grandma was far more important. After that, I gave him my undivided attention.

It's easy to fall into the world's pattern of celebrating Christmas. Expensive gifts, spectacular decorations, beautiful cookies, and fabulous meals are the world's way of saying "happy holidays." But Jesus' love is the reason for the season. We should try in all of our Christmas activities to demonstrate that we are followers of the lowly Carpenter of Galilee. I believe this means refusing to be caught up in the excesses that characterize much of the world's celebration.

I also believe that a good place to start is to cut down on the amount of fancy foods we serve. A little trimming of the amount and number of dishes would be better for everyone. And it would allow us more precious time to devote to the people in our lives who need our attention.

Today in the town of David a Savior has been born to you;
He is Christ the Lord.

Luke 2:11

When planning a fancy holiday meal, ask yourself:
"Who will remember this ten years from now?"

The Edible Christmas Wreath Recipe!
MILDRED L. BARGER

I do hope your Christmas has a little touch of Eternity in among the rush and pitter patter and all. It always seems such a mixing of this world and the next—but that after all is the ideal!

Evelyn Underhill

Why do we decorate with wreaths at Christmas? Does it stretch the imagination too much to think of Christ as we fashion our Christmas wreaths?

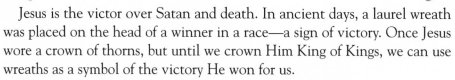

Jesus is the victor over Satan and death. In ancient days, a laurel wreath was placed on the head of a winner in a race—a sign of victory. Once Jesus wore a crown of thorns, but until we crown Him King of Kings, we can use wreaths as a symbol of the victory He won for us.

Wreaths may be fairly plain or ornately decorated. They may be huge or small. They may be studded with candy so guests may help themselves. Some wreaths hang outside with bits of food for birds to enjoy.

I enjoy making an edible Christmas wreath because it adds color and form to our table of goodies. Whatever form a Christmas wreath may take, and for whatever reason we use them, may our spirits rejoice in God our Savior. I don't know who originated the following recipe but it came to me from a woman in her 80's.

EDIBLE CHRISTMAS WREATH

1/3 cup margarine or butter	1 tsp. green food coloring
10 oz. regular marshmallows	6 cups corn flakes
½ tsp. vanilla	red cinnamon candies (red hots)

Melt the margarine in microwave or three-quart saucepan. Add marshmallows and stir constantly until melted and syrupy. Add vanilla and coloring. Add corn flakes and stir until well-coated. Form into wreath (on plate), shaping by hand, or by pressing into a ring mold. Sprinkle with red cinnamon candies. Place candle in center. Makes a dinner-plate size wreath. A sprinkle of coconut adds snow on this edible wreath.

And Mary said: "My soul glorifies the Lord and my spirit rejoices in God my Savior."
Luke 1:46

Keep a map book in your car. You never know when you'll need it.

The Smell Of Christmas

Eva Marie Everson

Spread love everywhere you go: first of all in your own house. Give love to your children, to your wife or husband, to a next door neighbor...

Mother Teresa

The basket with the large holiday bow greeted me as I returned from another weary Christmas shopping spree. The "to buy" list in my purse had grown shorter, but not nearly short enough. Growing more short was my holiday spirit and the true reason for the season was diminishing in a blur of tree lights and tinsel.

And then, there was this basket; an unexpected gift from my newest neighbor, Jo. Nestled in the red and green tissue paper was an interesting assortment of grocery items: one tea bag, a bound teaspoon of whole cloves, an apple, a lemon, an orange, and two cinnamon sticks. Attached to the handle by curling ribbon was a recipe card that read: Christmas Smell.

Quarter fruit and place ingredients in boiling water.

What a sweet idea! I thought. I turned and saw that the front door of each house on our oak-lined block was graced with Jo's thoughtful gift. Even better than the surprise was the delightfully soothing holiday aroma that met my family later that afternoon. As I breathed it in, the excitement of the holidays returned.

Jo's Christmas Smell Basket has continued to be a favorite over the years. I don't recall the other gifts I received that year, but in one simple gesture, Jo provided me with a Christmas memory that would last a lifetime. Now the fun is in returning the gesture to others.

A gift given in secret soothes anger . . .
Proverbs 21:14a

For a key on your keychain that you know won't be used often (and thus forgotten what it's for), put a different dash of fingernail polish on each one and then label an index card with the different colors and what door they open.

Frantic Or Focused?

BARBARA J. ANSON

Drop thy still dews of quietness
Till all our strivings cease;
Take from our souls the strain and stress,
And let our ordered lives confess
The beauty of thy peace.

John Greenleaf Whittier

I love the weeks leading up to Christmas. Abundance seems to fill the air and reign in hearts. Goodwill abounds, as do decorations, gifts, parties, church and school programs, beautifully decorated cookies, and rich melt-in-your-mouth candies. Before getting caught up in the frantic whirlwind of your own preparations, consider God's preparation for sending the most extravagant gift of all . . . His gift of Jesus.

God's preparations were not hurriedly crammed into a few frantic weeks. He took centuries to prepare the world for the birth of His son, and the last four of those centuries had been filled with silence. At last conditions were perfect. They included Roman rule that had brought peace to the known world and an extensive network of roads to expedite travel. It was exactly the right time for God to enter human history in the form of baby Jesus.

The setting through which Jesus entered the world was not the magnificent palace of a major capitol. No trumpets blew elaborate fanfares to an-

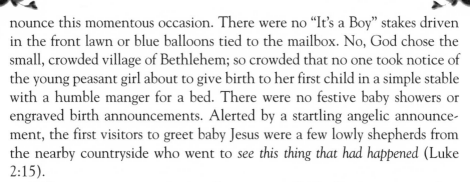

nounce this momentous occasion. There were no "It's a Boy" stakes driven in the front lawn or blue balloons tied to the mailbox. No, God chose the small, crowded village of Bethlehem; so crowded that no one took notice of the young peasant girl about to give birth to her first child in a simple stable with a humble manger for a bed. There were no festive baby showers or engraved birth announcements. Alerted by a startling angelic announcement, the first visitors to greet baby Jesus were a few lowly shepherds from the nearby countryside who went to *see this thing that had happened* (Luke 2:15).

God's ways are not man's ways. I cannot match God's extravagant gift to mankind, nor do I have centuries to prepare my surroundings for the celebration of Jesus' birth. I can make careful preparations in my home so the focus is on Jesus rather than my lavish displays of beautiful decorations and carefully wrapped packages. The setting for a Christ-centered celebration is right when I refuse to be ruled by hectic schedules and excessive expenditures of time, energy, and money, planning instead for the beauty of a peaceful atmosphere where simplicity replaces complexity.

Don't allow frantic preparations to steal your joy and peace this Christmas. Covenant with God to simplify your preparations and make His gift of Jesus the focus of your celebrations.

> *Let us therefore make every effort to do what leads to peace*
> *and to mutual edification.*
> Romans 14:19

As part of your decorations this Christmas, lay out a Bible opened to Luke 2 and read the Christmas story aloud each day.

The Christmas Box

SANDRA JENSEN

The most important part about Christmas is the first six letters.
Unknown

Amidst the national focus on Santa, gift giving, holiday parties, and tasty treats it's easy to forget our Savior. Every Christmas I look for ways to demonstrate to my children the true meaning of the season.

Frequently our family "adopts" a needy family who doesn't have the ability to purchase gifts or goodies for one another. I take my children along to help deliver the Christmas provisions so they can see for themselves how some families manage with much less than we have. I also want them to understand what it means to give without expecting anything in return.

Last December, harried from decorating and shopping, I stopped to visit a friend from church who owns and operates her own hair salon. Like any other store at that time of year, it was decorated with an assortment of Christmas finery on windows and walls. But the most eye-catching decoration was an enormous and beautifully decorated Christmas box, complete with a magnificent red bow, prominently displayed in her shop. No expense had been spared to decorate it. Its size and splendor were what every child dreams of finding under his Christmas tree.

But there was something that set this box apart from a typical holiday package. As I moved closer, I could see slips of white paper glued to the box. On them was written various Bible passages. Standing beside the box I noticed such verses as: *To those who believed in His name, He gave the right to become children of God.* Another verse read: *For it is by grace you have been saved, through faith . . . it is a gift of God.* Still another read: *But with everlasting kindness I will have compassion on you says the Lord,* and still another: *Never will I leave you; never will I forsake you.* I walked around the box several times, fascinated with the numerous passages with which my friend had chosen to adorn the box. These verses were God's promises—those He offers every believer through the simple act of faith in Jesus.

I went home that day, and with the help of my children, we made our own Christmas box. It, too, is decorated with handsome paper and bows. Whenever a guest arrives they are immediately drawn to its size and beauty. They love to *ooh* and *aah* over it, but I'm hoping their lasting impression will be God's promises—those that reveal the true meaning of Christmas, hand-delivered by a newborn babe 2,000 years ago.

I bring you good news of great joy that will be for all people . . . a Savior has been born to you; He is Christ the Lord.
Luke 2:10b, 11b

Purchase several packages of dried baby's breath from a craft or florist shop. Carefully pull apart each twig and insert it between the branches of your Christmas tree after all other decorations are in place. It lends an old-world charm to your tree.

No Room
KENDRA PRINCE

The trouble with some of us is that we have been inoculated with small doses of Christianity which keep us from catching the real thing.
Leslie Dixon Weatherhead

One of the most maligned characters in the first Christmas story is the innkeeper, who did not have room for Mary and Joseph. They were forced to stay in a humble stable, which became the birthplace of Jesus, the Son of

God. His bassinet was a feeding trough for the animals. His layette was strips of cloth. That night, the animals offered His lullaby. If the innkeeper had realized Mary was carrying the King of Kings, do you think he would have made room?

At the time of Christ's birth, Caesar Augustus had issued a decree that a census be taken of the entire Roman world. This required that everyone return to their hometown to register. No doubt, Bethlehem was teeming with families returning for the census. The innkeeper probably had never had so many paying guests. A wonderful opportunity, but focusing on the present caused him to miss out on the future.

Are we so different from that innkeeper today? Most of us lead hectic, demanding lives. Our jobs claim (at least) eight hours of our day and our families often get what is left. So where do we fit in the Savior? Just as He did not fight for the deluxe suite in Bethlehem, He will not fight for first place in our lives. He waits for us to make accommodations for Him in our day. And like the innkeeper, we are the ones who miss out when we do not make a place for Christ.

There is one difference between us and the innkeeper. While he may not have realized the important guest he was relegating to the stable, we do know who Jesus is and the kind of lodging He deserves. All the more reason for us to make room for the Savior in our lives today.

While they were there, the time came for the baby to be born, and she gave birth to her firstborn, a son. She wrapped him in cloths and placed him in a manger, because there was no room for them in the inn.

Luke 2:6, 7

> When storing your luggage, attach the key to your luggage to the inside lining of the suitcase with a safety pin for safe keeping.

Paper Chain Art

Sarah Healton

God walked down the stairs of heaven with a Baby in his arms.
Paul Scherer

Paper chains are fun, easy to make, inexpensive, and have may uses. They can be made into a flag using red, white, and blue strips. They can also be used to decorate a Christmas tree, or count the days to Christmas. Children of any age can make them and you can use it as an activity to prepare their minds for the real reason for Christmas.

Tools and materials needed per child:

- glue
- paper clips
- an assortment of strips of colored paper such as construction paper, typing paper, wrapping paper, or paper that goes with a theme. Cut the paper into strips about 6 inches by 1 inch.

1. Choose one strip of each color.
2. Make a circle of the first strip and glue it together. Press the two ends together until the glue holds.
3. Take the next color and put it through the first circle. Make a circle out of it and paste it together just like the first one.
4. Do the same with each strip.

Counting The Days To Christmas Activity

Make your own special way of counting the days until Christmas. First make a chain of twenty-five loops. Next, draw a Christmas picture and write a Christmas jingle or copy this one:

I'm counting the days 'til Christmas
with this paper chain.
Each day I take one loop away
Then I count the ones that stay.
When they're all gone,
Hooray! Hooray!
It's Christmas Day.

For other holidays, make a chain of orange and black for Halloween or pink and blue for Easter. To decorate a miniature Christmas tree or an Easter egg tree, the strips can be made shorter and narrower.

Therefore, prepare your minds . . .
I Peter 1:13

When young children are making chains,
you may want to hold each loop with a paper clip
until the glue dries.

The Gift We Give

DARREN PRINCE

You can never truly enjoy Christmas until you can look up into the Father's face and tell him you have received his Christmas Gift.
John R. Rice

All this wrapping makes for pretty trash!
Ribbons cover boxes for a time . . .
Until the day they're torn and tossed aside.

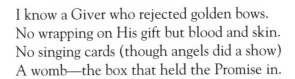

F·A·L·L

I know a Giver who rejected golden bows.
No wrapping on His gift but blood and skin.
No singing cards (though angels did a show)
A womb—the box that held the Promise in.

The Greatest Gift came not in grand display,
Not finely dressed or heavenly adorned,
But rags and infant skin alone were worn.

We wrap ourselves as Christmas gifts.
Made nice (high priced),
All "oohhs" and "ahhhs"
Until the sparkle fades.

This tinsel-troubled soul could spend
a lifetime wrapping emptiness
unless
the Greatest Gift
could rest within

That alone is what we give the world.
All bows and ribbons softly grace the floor.
And in the end we're nothing more
Than what we are unwrapped and unadorned.

But the angel said to them, "Do not be afraid. I bring you good news of great
joy that will be for all the people."
Luke 2:10

Don't buy any more new wrapping paper
until the old paper is used up—even the leftovers.

Secret Meaning Behind
A Popular Carol

KATHY IDE

*I wish we could put some of the Christmas spirit in jars
and open a jar of it every month.*

Harlan Miller

The edict is official. Your faith is illegal. You are prohibited by law from any practice of your religion—public or private. If you are caught with anything in written form that indicates you still practice your beliefs, you could be imprisoned, hanged, beheaded, or drawn and quartered.

Most of us have wondered how we would react to this type of persecution. Would we recant or hide our beliefs if faced with the alternative of torture and death? We'd like to think our faith would be strong enough to withstand the threat. But if we die as martyrs, who will teach these beliefs to our children? On the other hand, if we continue to teach, we place ourselves and our children at tremendous risk.

During the persecution in Great Britain between 1558 and 1829, Catholics faced this very struggle. The most difficult time of year for these persecuted believers was Christmas. Catholics were afraid to even hum their favorite carols.

One clever believer devised a unique solution to the predicament. He wrote a song—a Christmas carol. The lyrics told the story of gift giving during the holiday season. The composer carefully chose "gifts" that would appear innocuous, yet be filled with meaning to those who knew the translation. What was this innovative song? "The Twelve Days of Christmas."

The "true love" mentioned in the carol referred to God, the giver of all good and perfect gifts.

God the Father "gave to me," first and foremost, "a partridge in a pear tree," representing Jesus Christ, God's only begotten Son.

Although sources vary somewhat, the other symbols in the song represent the following gifts from God:

2 Turtle doves: The Old and New Testaments
3 French hens: Faith, hope, and love, the three gifts of the Spirit (1 Corinthians 13)
4 Calling birds: The four Gospels (Matthew, Mark, Luke, and John) or the four evangelists
5 Golden rings: The first five books of the Old Testament, called the "Pentateuch" or the "Books of Moses" (Genesis, Exodus, Leviticus, Numbers, and Deuteronomy)
6 Geese a-laying: The six days of creation (Genesis 2)
7 Swans a-swimming: The seven gifts of the Holy Spirit (1 Corinthians 12:8–11, Romans 12, 1 Peter 4:10–11) or the seven sacraments
8 Maids a-milking: The eight beatitudes (Matthew 5:1–12)
9 Ladies dancing: The nine fruits of the Holy Spirit (Galatians 5:22–23)
10 Lords a-leaping: The Ten Commandments (Exodus 20:1–17)
11 Pipers piping: The eleven faithful apostles
12 Drummers drumming: The twelve points of doctrine in the Apostles' Creed

The song was first taught to young catechism students. This enabled the children to learn and recite their lessons in a fun, unique way without fear of persecution. But since "The Twelve Days of Christmas" sounded like rhyming nonsense to the legal authorities, it could be sung by young and old alike without fear of imprisonment. And the catechism it taught was general enough that it could even be claimed to be Protestant, if the authorities detected any religious overtones!

At that time, people celebrated twelve days of Christmas—the days between Christmas and Epiphany (January 6), when the wise men were believed to have found Jesus. The Feast of Epiphany began in the second century. By the sixth century, the traditional twelve days of Christmas had become a way of celebrating the turning of the year. Exchanging small, inexpensive gifts on each of the twelve days became a favorite holiday tradition among families of the time.

The author of "The Twelve Days of Christmas" maintained his anonymity so well that his identity remains a mystery to this day. But every year, these lyrics are sung throughout the world by both Christians and unbelievers.

This Christmas, when we sing this familiar carol, may we be reminded of the sacred message hidden behind its encoded lyrics. May we thank God for the freedom to sing all the beloved carols of the season. And may we be inspired by this anonymous composer to come up with our unique, imaginative ways to proclaim the birth of our Savior, Jesus Christ—truly the greatest gift ever given.

Preach the Word; be prepared in season and out of season; correct, rebuke, and encourage—with great patience and careful instruction.
II Timothy 4:2

Give your children a Christmas ornament each year with the year written on it and then those will be their ornaments when they move out.

Shepherds Came That Christmas Down

LINDA CUTRELL

*Christmas is a gift from God that a man cannot keep
until he gives it to someone else.*

Dorothy Cameron Smith

Four years ago when my husband died at age 49, many people tried to comfort me by saying, "Linda, you have so many close and wonderful friends." This remark, however, did little to ease my pain as I grieved.

Now, it was my fourth Christmas without my husband and my first without my children. Although my college age son, Josh, came home for the holidays, he had much to do with his friends. He, of course, didn't realize how lonely or depressed I was. I hid my depression from everyone, ashamed because I didn't want them to think my faith was weak.

On December 26, I hit rock bottom, crying the whole day, not caring if I lived or died. "How wonderful," I thought, "if I could be with my husband in Heaven."

I made myself put away the Christmas decorations. As I dismantled the nativity scene, wrapping each piece in tissue paper, I dropped a lamb. One of the sheep that had contentedly laid beside Baby Jesus in the manger bounced on the carpet. As I reached down for the porcelain animal, I thought, "I'm as lost as you are, poor little sheep."

The shepherd scene in Luke 2 flashed in my mind, how the shepherds kept watch over their flock by night, how the angel appeared and said, "Fear not, for behold, I bring you good tidings of great joy, which will be to all people." I, too, longed for a shepherd to tenderly care for me in my loneliness.

Then I realized that I did have earthly shepherds. My friend Marlene had decorated my house for Christmas. We'd spent days sharing and working on greeting cards. Kate called daily; Marilyn prayed with me and for me; Jean let me use her computer for my articles; Mary Beth invited me over for supper. These dear friends helped me, watched over me, hugged me in their arms . . . God's arms with skin on them.

On December 27, I decided I'd change Christmas down into Christmas up. These actions helped me.

1. I began a gratitude journal. I wrote down how I'd been blessed by my friends, concentrating on what I did have instead of what I didn't have. I jotted down special things I could do to repay kindness shown me.
2. I took a daily brisk walk. Breathing fresh air and increasing my heart rate released hormones that dispelled my depression. When the weather was inclement, I exercised by walking in a local mall.
3. I set apart a day a week to be with the Lord. I fasted from television, the telephone, the newspaper. I spent a day or afternoon in prayer, Bible study, praising the Lord and journaling my thoughts. As I "fasted" from the world, I "feasted" with the Lord.

Many times, December does become depressing. However, I realized that this didn't mean my faith was weak . . . only that I needed to be especially close to my Shepherd. He is the One who lifted me up from Christmas down.

The LORD is my shepherd, I shall not be in want.
Psalms 23:1

Send old Christmas card fronts to: St. Jude's Ranch for Children, Box 985, Boulder City, NV 89005.

Perseverance

LYNDA HUNTER

Inspiration without perspiration leads to frustration and stagnation.

Bill Bright

I've always liked to run. In every race, all the runners start out of the chutes similarly, but then the contest becomes an individual thing. Each race offers a clearly marked course, though the route becomes apparent only as we move ahead. I'm not sure where I'm going, but I know that if I just keep putting one foot in front of the other, I'll eventually reach my goal.

One especially memorable race took place on a rainy Saturday morning in June. Determination marked my hobbled steps as I made my way to pick up my number. A throbbing strained ankle and nausea from my pregnancy were not enough to keep me home.

The gun sounded. My ankle throbbed some more. Rain plastered my hair against my cheeks and eyes. Gnawing pain in my tummy constantly reminded me I would be a mother in a few months.

None of those things held me back. I followed the course one aching, nauseated, drenched step at a time. At the top of a hill just past the halfway point, I caught a glimpse of the sun breaking through the clouds. I couldn't help but notice the early summer smells of redwoods and other plants.

The finish line ribbon warmed my heart as I felt it fall to my side. I had finished 157th out of 175, but I had finished—in spite of the obstacles.

Hebrews 12:1 tells us to throw aside everything that hinders us and persevere in the race. Though we can't see the finish line, we know we'll successfully reach it if we keep running with God.

One evening I took Courtney to the emergency room after she broke the growth plate in her ankle during a soccer game. She received bad news from the doctor: "No track, basketball, or soccer for six weeks—maybe longer."

Silently she hobbled to the car. On the way home she said, "Mom, I can't believe how quickly something can be gone that I counted on so much. The only thing we can count on and keep working toward is God."

Small words, big truth. Our kids each have an individual race to run that is different from our own. Let's not hold them back or shield them from injury or confine them to a race that's not what God designed. Instead, let's help them lay aside every weight that hinders them. And then let's help them hear what God is teaching them.

> *Perseverance must finish its work so that you may be mature and complete, not lacking anything.*
>
> James 1:4

To find a discounted hotel room, call a consolidator like Express Reservations at (800) 356-1123.

Winter

Even as Winter cold swirls around us, the New Year begins, and with it the anticipation of new resolve to live abundantly with Jesus at the center of our lives. Winter can seem discouraging at times, but with the right perspective we can rejoice—regardless of the weather. Instead of grumbling, we can humbly accept God's gift of a white wonderland or rain as an investment in future flowers.

It's all a matter of focus. And through these selections for this season, we are reminded that God's provision of love and protection is abundantly available.

The Value Of A Thank-You Note

MARITA LITTAUER

For any gesture of kindness shown to us—a visit, a gift, or anything that made us feel good—we should try to send a thank-you note as soon as possible.

Hermine Hartley

Once I had the opportunity to go to the home of Bob and Emilie Barnes for a meal. Emilie's home is warm and lovely. She is an excellent cook and a gracious hostess. I left thinking I must send her a thank-you note.

However, the next day brought its own set of crises and the thank-you note did not get written. I was still thinking about it when I received a note of thanks from Emilie! While I do not recall the exact wording of the note, I know it made me feel so special and went something like, "Thank you for coming to our home last night for dinner. It was great to see you and Chuck again and we enjoyed catching up on your lives. We'll have to do it again soon!"

I was so touched by Emilie's thoughtfulness, I decided that I wanted to do the same for my guests. Unfortunately, I am not quite as organized as Emilie. While I intended to send my guests a note the next day, it didn't happen. Nor did it happen in the days or weeks that followed. Before long it was too late to bother with it.

Then I stumbled onto this plan, which I have shared with thousands of people in my seminars and which has been used successfully by many.

I like to take pictures. I almost always have a pack of recently developed prints with me that chronicle my recent escapades. When I have guests over and I have done an especially nice job of setting the table, I like to take a picture of it before the guests come. Once everyone is there, seated, and having a good time, I get the camera out again. Using what I call a Ph.D. camera ("Push here, Dummy"), I simply tell everyone to look my way, push the button, and know that I have captured the moment and the memory. Sometimes that shot was the last on the roll and I have the picture the next day. Other times it may be weeks or months before I finish that roll and get it developed. When I get the photos back, or when I organize them into an album, which may be months later, I send a copy of the print to the guests with a note. The fact that I am sending the picture seems to excuse the tardiness, as everyone knows that it may take months to use up the roll. I send a note with the print that starts out with: "I just got my pictures developed" or "I have finally had time to get my pictures organized and into the photo album." Then I continue:

"When I saw this picture of our dinner together, it made me smile. What a great time we had that night. Your presence made it so special You really know how to keep the conversation lively! I hope looking at this picture brings back the wonderful memories of that night for you, as it did for me. We must do it again soon!"

Always give thanks for everything.
Ephesians 5:20a

Always have film ready in your camera.

Ordinary Ceremonies
MARY BAHR FRITTS

The only time I find peace is when I stop looking for it.
Vern McLellan

Two years ago I underwent some serious back surgery. I attended a six-week Pain program where doctors and therapists agreed that stretching my muscles every day for the rest of my life would be more important for me than most.

I'd have trouble walking if I didn't. I continued the stretches faithfully for weeks after the program was over. Then one day, I stopped. A doubting Thomas? Maybe; more probably, just a millennium woman without forty-five minutes a day to "waste."

"Sorry, Cheyenne," I said to my cat who "purr-rrred" beside me every morning from her spot in the sun. Although she stretched, I countered, "I don't have time for this like you do."

It wasn't long before I was walking "oddly" again. "No matter how long you've been away," my therapist reminded me, "it's never too late to come back." So, after two months' abstinence from something that was good for me, I began my stretches again.

As I finished up my first workout, I lay on the carpet by my friend who "purr-rrred." "Somehow I've got to make this forty-five minutes special . . . ," I said to her, "special enough to want to do it day after day."

Cheyenne stretched in the sunlight, letting it spread over her body like butter on toast. And so did my answer.

Isn't that what children and pets do best—remind us there are simple answers to our complicated questions? I moved over to the patch of sun. I stretched. I felt Cheyenne's body rumble with soft noises. I took my time. I felt the sun on my skin. I felt the sun in my heart. Slow and simple doesn't mean "wasted."

How about you? Stretch! Yawn, if you must. But *purrrrr* when the sun hits your face—giving thanks to Him who made it.

Every good and perfect gift is from above . . .
James 1:17

Create your own ceremony utilizing one of God's simple pleasures (prayer, silence, sunshine, etc.) as you perform a not-so-favorite task.

Every Problem Has A Limited Life Span

Robert H. Schuller

Problems are only opportunities in work clothes.

Henry J. Kaiser

Every mountain has a peak. Every valley has its low point. Life has its ups and downs, its peaks and its valleys. No one is up all the time, nor are they down all the time. Problems do end. They do go away. They are all resolved in time.

This principle is evident when you look carefully at history, for the history of humanity is a study in peaks and valleys. Humanity peaks at times when societies rise from decadence to a highly sophisticated state of civilization. Eventually, however, most cultures allow decay to set in. Rather than rooting out the negative influences, the human institutions adjust to the downward movement. The decline continues and accelerates until it reaches a low ebb, at which point it begins the long, slow ascent once more.

History teaches us that every problem has a life span. No problem is permanent. Do you have problems? They will pass; they will not last. Your problem will not live forever, but you will! Storms always give way to the sun. Winter always thaws into springtime. Your storm will pass. Your winter will thaw. Your problem will be resolved.

Therefore, among God's churches we boast about your perseverance and faith in all the persecutions and trials you are enduring.

II Thessalonians 1:4

Cut down on your grocery bill by seeing how long you can live on food you've already bought.

No Regrets

AUDREY McINTOSH

There is no joy in life like the joy of sharing.
Billy Graham

"Keep in touch," Mom whispered as she hugged me good-bye and choked back tears. She enjoyed the children so much and the feeling was certainly mutual. A military transfer required our family to move several states away from Grandma and Grandpa. We knew it would be a long time before we could visit again.

While in Mom's embrace, I remembered as a teen reading a story about a man who made sure his mom heard from him often. At her death, he remarked, "I have no regrets. I frequently called or wrote my mom, no matter how far away I was." At that moment, I resolved to follow his example.

As soon as we were settled in our new location, I began my weekly routine of writing. I shared cute things the children said or did, even sent pictures they drew and colored. When I called, Mom told me how she laughed over some of their art work.

Little did I know, like the man whose story I had read, that my mother was also dying. Though she had been ill for quite some time, she chose not to tell us of her terminal condition.

Two years passed and one day when the phone rang, it was Dad. "Mom's been taken to the hospital and it doesn't look good," he said. "If you want to see her, you should hurry home." With heavy hearts, we started our journey of several days.

Weary from the long trip, I stood in her hospital room. Mom looked up and smiled.

She motioned for me to come closer so she could tell me something. "Thanks for keeping in touch," she whispered. " I eagerly waited for your letters to come every week."

Within a month, Mom slipped quietly and peacefully into Heaven while she slept.

Though I knew my life would forever have a void, deep in my heart I had no regrets.

Would you have regrets if someone you love died? What steps can you take to make sure you won't have regrets?

Be devoted to one another in brotherly love.
Honor one another above yourselves.
Romans 12:10

Just a brief phone call or short note means a lot
to aging parents.

Pull Away To God
GWEN SHAMBLIN

Once a man is united with God how could he not live forever?
Once a man is separated from God, what can he do
but wither and die?
C. S. Lewis

The Spirit of Christ is not just a vapor or mist. The Spirit of God and Christ that is referred to has deep meaning, and part of that is reflected in the individual's mind-set. In other words, you need to have the same focus as Christ. What was the mind-set of Christ? To please the Father and to do His will. That attitude, although just a part of the make-up of the "Spirit of Christ," is still a part. If that is the case, then you are talking about the power that raised Christ Jesus from the dead. This power will give life to our mortal bodies!

The sun, being much larger than the earth, has a much stronger gravitational pull. We are not conscious of it because we are so close to the earth and so far from the sun. However, if a spaceship were to be launched out of earth's orbit, it would begin moving toward the sun's gravitational pull. The farther it traveled, the less earth's gravity would affect it and the greater the sun's attraction would become.

We want you to pull away from the world and turn your path toward God. As your spaceship draws nearer to God, you will discover that He will draw near to you; He and His ways will become increasingly attractive to you. You will become unable to resist His will because His powerful, magnetic, wonderful force is much, much stronger than the world's pull.

You, however, are controlled not by the sinful nature but by the Spirit, if the Spirit of God lives in you. And if anyone does not have the Spirit of Christ, he does not belong to Christ.

Romans 8:9

If you receive a prayer request through e-mail, keep it in your active file so that you'll be reminded to pray.

Slaying Dragons

CATHY MESSECAR

Prayer does not equip us for the greater works—prayer is the greater work.

Oswald Chambers

Rubber boots on and lunch pail in hand, he was leaving for work. After a goodbye kiss, he headed for his vehicle—a tricycle. My four-year-old son, Russell, was going to work, just like his daddy. Within ten seconds the back door flew open, and I looked into his ashen face. Coiled on the sidewalk by our whitewashed gate lay a three-foot snake. Like most country moms, I kept a hoe or shovel handy for such emergencies. The reptile was slain, but my son's fear of snakes increased that day.

Much later, when Russell was eleven, he gave me a handmade Mother's Day card. On the front it read, "HAPPY MAMA'S DAY." The inside message declared: "Dear Mom, Thank You For Killing The Snake When I Was Four Years Old! Happy Mother's Day." In the lower left corner he had drawn a huge star and labeled me a "GOLD STAR SPORT." The construction paper heart is one of my treasures.

Just as I slayed that snake, you and I as mothers slay the enemy of our children through prayer for all their lives. Little boys and girls will grow up and leave home, but it's a lifetime work to keep after their enemy, "the great dragon . . . that ancient serpent called the devil" (Revelation 12:9). Remember how you sometimes got up in the middle of a cold night and tiptoed into your child's room to make sure he hadn't kicked off his blanket? You may still be making those night checks, or your children may not have lived at home for many years, but every child, grown-up or infant, needs to be covered by their mother's prayers. You may be thousands of miles from your child, physically or in your relationship, but you can touch their world through the hands of our omnipresent Father. You can be the prayer warrior that prompts God to move mountains, calm storms, and bring about peace.

Several years ago, on my grandmother's very last visit to my mother's house, their physical roles were reversed. One evening, after Mom helped her into her nightclothes, my father then lifted my grandmother into bed. My grandmother apologized for the inconvenience as my mother tucked her in and kissed her good night. A little later, my mom walked through the dark hall and heard my grandmother saying something. Mom peeked into my grandmother's room to see if she was okay. Grandmother wasn't talking to herself. She was speaking to our Father, praying for her grown-up children by name. Feeble in body, but with a mother's spirit…she was slaying dragons.

No matter how old or young your children are, you are still slaying dragons through prayer.

Save your people and bless your inheritance;
be their shepherd and carry them forever.
Psalm 28:9

In a folder with brads, place a few sheets of notebook paper.
Title three columns: Date, Requests, and
Thanksgiving/Answers. Record your prayers—
especially those for your children.

Bless His Heart
LIZ CURTIS HIGGS

Praise from a wife is praise indeed.
Ernest R. Punshon

A group of my friends gathered with me to study Proverbs 31 and one week I gave them a homework assignment. "Ask your husband, 'What speaks love to you?' Don't worry, he'll know what you mean." They came back with their research, and we found the answers to be very different than we expected. One husband said he sensed her love for him by "the look in your eyes when I enter the room"; another said, "the way you address me in conversation"; a third answered, "the sacrifices you are willing to make on our behalf." With answers like that, it's a question worth asking.

In our marriage, there is a question that Bill poses several times a week. He knows just when I need to hear it, just when my to-do list is on tilt, and I'm feeling overwhelmed. He simply says, "What can I do to bless you tonight?" And he means specific tasks, something he could do to make my life easier—the dishes, the laundry, the groceries, whatever. Do I deserve a man this good? Absolutely not. But I don't deserve grace either, and I'm grateful to have that poured over me daily.

Grace and peace to you from God our Father and the Lord Jesus Christ,
I Corinthians 1:3

> Perfumes have a shelf life of about two years.
> If you're not using yours up within that time,
> buy smaller bottles.

Cut Out The Lump!

TONY EVANS

To a person with a toothache, even if the world is tottering, there is nothing more important than a visit to a dentist.
George Bernard Shaw

Several years ago, my family and I had a scare. I had a growth on my body that my doctor thought was cancer. He told me and my wife, "We need to operate very quickly."

As I lay in bed the night before the operation, I can assure you I wasn't thinking, "I hate for them to cut on me. I'll have a scar. It will hurt. I'll be sore for a week." No! I thought I might have cancer. I couldn't wait for the doctor to perform surgery.

They cut out the lump. I opened my eyes in recovery and said, "What's the verdict, Doc?"

"I've got good news for you. Your lump was benign, but it's good we took it out when we did, because they have been known to become malignant."

Do you know what? That doctor did me a favor that day. If he had played around and said, "I got lumps. You got lumps. All God's children got lumps," I could be in trouble today. But even if a lump is malignant and has spread, chemotherapy and radiation can address it so that it regresses.

You may not be able to get rid of your alcoholic urging all at one time. But the church can help to "chemo" it back. You may not be able to cut out the malignancy of your temper all at once, but we can radiate it back. You may not be able to eradicate all your immoral passions with one treatment, but for your sake, the sake of the rest of the body of Christ, and for His sake, let us put the medication to it!

As you know, we consider blessed those who have persevered. You have heard of Job's perseverance and have seen what the Lord finally brought about. The Lord is full of compassion and mercy.

James 5:11

If your family members are fighting over the toothpaste tube being squeezed in the middle, buy the pump kind.

An Adversary To Abundance

KAREN HAYSE

What discord we should bring to the universe if our prayers were all answered? Then we should govern the universe and not God.

Henry Wadsworth Longfellow

Why? A dangerous question. Not in an inquisitive sense; not when one is seeking wisdom. Without the *why* of life, progress cannot be made. However, when trust is central, *why* rarely benefits anyone.

225

At age twenty-seven, I began a troublesome journey with a chronic health problem. The illness invaded every aspect of my life from my family to my job to my emotional stability. Several times, close friends prayed specifically for my healing. But the illness didn't seem to listen. And by appearances, neither did God.

The most agonizing periods of my illness came during my pleas of, "Why won't you heal me? You have the power. You love me. I don't understand . . . Why?" More painful silence followed, leaving a black cloud of bitterness hovering over my days. Until I got past the little question, its shadow continued to oppress me, perhaps even more than my health problem.

I finally uncovered the destructive tactics of that three-letter word, "why?" It had the power to lead me backward when I needed to move on. It demanded a cause or a reason. And even if God were to grant me its answer, chances were that I would *still* not feel satisfied. *Why* provided no hope for anything better in the future.

Or for the here and now.

That nagging question prevents us from finding peace in the present. We rationalize, *If I am given a reason for life's situations, perhaps I can control them or fix them.* But only a surrender of our human strength leads to a kind of peace that allows God to handle the details.

"*Why* is a fighting word. It says, 'I don't trust you. I might know better than you do if you give me your reason.'" I've explained this to my daughter on occasion when she questions my decisions for her. I expect her to trust that I have her best interests at heart. When God asks us to rest in Him, must we know all the reasons? If so, what does that accomplish but a focus on our own inadequate reasoning when God knows everything?

If you struggle with disappointment or grief, if you grapple with life's unexpected turns, or if you resist the small voice that whispers His will, find strength to leave the *whys* where they belong in the past. Instead, look ahead and ask, "*What now, God?*" And though pain or uncertainty may continue to try to taint your life, Christ's peace and hope will have license to overcome their ill effects.

Trust in the LORD with all your heart and lean not on your own understanding.

Proverbs 3:5

> Always carry a sports nutrition bar in your purse in case you don't have time for breakfast or lunch.

A Ministry Lifestyle

GAYLE CLOUD

The first prong of contemporary feminism's offensive has been to convince society that a woman's full-time commitment to cultivating her marriage and rearing her children is an unworthy endeavor.

F. Carolyn Graglia

As a full-time mother and homemaker, I periodically wrestled with feelings of inadequacy. In my heart I made a commitment to raise my family and nurture them to the best of my ability, something I truly enjoy doing. But my mind didn't always cooperate. I have a college degree and I reasoned, *I could be using it to teach a class full of eager students and be bringing in some much needed financial support.* But we have six children who needed a lot of parental guidance and oversight. After the whirlwind rush to get them ready for school in the morning and my brief perusal of the morning paper, I was busy for two hours doing laundry, sweeping, tidying up, checking phone messages, etc., etc. Then there were the errands to do—banking, appointments, grocery shopping and taking care of the apartments we manage. Thursday mornings were Bible Study respites and Fridays I visited my mother-in-law and I quilt. Then, nearly once a week, one or more of my children would have a day off from school. Whew! There wasn't nearly enough time to keep up with it all.

And yet, there was the nagging thought that perhaps I should get a paying job. I'd surely be accomplishing something of worth then! It seemed like just doing those daily chores had little lasting value. The kids barely appreciated all the work I did for them. And they felt put upon when they were required to pitch in. Surely, someone out in the workforce would appreciate my talents!

And so my feelings went. My husband, who often comes up with real gems of wisdom, approached me carefully one afternoon after again hearing my lament. He broached this sensitive subject by telling me that the Lord had showed him he was getting the prophet's reward.

"What?" I asked.

"You're a full-time minister," he answered. "You share the gospel with our kids. You visit the sick in our neighborhood. You volunteer your time. You're a minister. And I get the blessing of supporting you financially. So I get the prophet's reward."

Wow! I had never looked at my life that way. Perhaps he was right. Finances and personal portfolios had never been my goal. Yet I was being influenced by the world's view of their worth. I hadn't been listening to what the Lord was telling me. He's always been more interested in people than affluence . . . I knew that. Sure, our finances are lean—we have six children! But my investment has been in them and that really has been a full-time job. The satisfaction of being around to instill godly virtues in my gang when they would just as soon please their flesh has been immeasurable. And I'm doubly blessed to have a husband who has a "higher" perspective.

If you're discouraged because you feel like you're not using all your talents and skills, just remember God's perspective. And let whoever is supporting you to receive their prophet's reward.

Anyone who receives a prophet because he is a prophet
will receive a prophet's reward . . .
Matthew 10:41a

Look around your neighborhood for an opportunity
to minister God's love.

Let Me Be Aware

DORIS C. CRANDALL

The art of awareness is, among other things, striving to stretch the range of eye and ear. It is taking time to look, listen, and comprehend.

Wildred A. Patterson

Usually, I don't shop for groceries on Wednesdays because the store is too crowded. It's double-stamp day, and some items are on special for nine cents and a page of stamps. I'd rather forgo the extra stamps and the stamp bargains than be jostled about.

However, because I was out of so many items, I did face the throngs one Wednesday. I hurried down the aisles, zigging and zagging around the shoppers, but not really seeing them. I just wanted to get my groceries and get out of there.

Luckily, I was third in the checkout line behind two ladies. One was frail and stooped with age and didn't have much in her basket. *Good, she won't take long.* But the one ahead of her was a young mother with two toddlers and an overflowing grocery cart. I glanced around at the other lines. They were even more crowded, so I stayed where I was.

While I waited impatiently, the younger woman gently scolded her children as they grabbed at the bread, cheese, and other goodies. Finally, the clerk rang up the total then punched a few buttons, sending several feet of trading stamps snaking out of the dispenser. She folded them neatly (taking a lot of time) before passing them to her customer.

Now that's unusual, I thought, *what's that young mother doing?* Without saying anything, she had unobtrusively slipped the stamps into the elderly customer's hand, acknowledged her surprised look with a quick nod, and left the store.

It was a tender, compassionate drama with an audience of one. My heart was touched; my impatience vanished. I wished the thoughtful mother had stayed for the last act. If she had, she would have seen the elderly lady go back for one of the nine-cent specials, a quart of milk. Also, she would have seen her moisten and glue some of the stamps on a page, then pay for her meager supply of groceries with the sheet of stamps and a few coins. I wanted to clap and shout, "Bravo!"

That young mom thoughtfully shared her abundance and another woman benefited. How can you share your abundance today, even if it's in trading stamps?

> *He who is kind to the poor lends to the LORD, and He will reward him for what he has done.*
> Proverbs 19:17

Wash down the shower doors or bathtub immediately after finishing; that way it's easy to keep it clean.

Let Your Light Shine
PAMELA ENDERBY

You who have received so much love—share it with others. Love others the way that God has loved you, with tenderness.
Mother Teresa

Young children are a natural when it comes to reaching out to others with God's love. They possess time, talents, and resources that accomplish two purposes: lost souls are touched and the giver gains a boost in self-esteem. Consider helping your pre-schooler or elementary age child with these ideas:

- *A Tisket A Tasket.* Collect wicker baskets from thrift stores or garage sales. After decorating them with colorful tissue paper, add homemade cookies and attach a tag that says, "Jesus loves you." Your child drops a basket on your neighbor's doorstep, rings the doorbell, and runs. The suspense of not "getting caught" fuels this activity while practicing the principle of giving in secret.

- *Give to the poor.* When allowances are doled out, teach your child the importance of giving. After a few months, combine his savings with your contributions and go grocery shopping together. Surprise a needy family from your church by anonymously leaving the groceries on their doorstep.

- *Write a prisoner.* Our compassionate five-year-old dictates letters to our church member's incarcerated son and adds personal touches of glittery pictures. The prisoner's response? "Your letters bring a lot of happiness to my heart."

- *Pick a bouquet of wildflowers.* Your elderly neighbors especially welcome the smiles and charm of children. Even dandelions sprinkle God's love in their hearts.

- *Pray for others.* Collect pictures of unsaved family members and friends. Post them in an album, one to a page. At bedtime, peruse the book with your child, guiding him to pray for one person of his choice.

- *Help at a downtown soup kitchen*; set up tables, clean the dining room, and serve meals.

- *Plan a party. Jesus' Christmas Party* by Nicholas Allan (Random House)is a simple skit of Jesus' birth from the innkeeper's viewpoint. After practicing the skit with your neighbor kids, invite their parents to view it. Celebrate with a birthday cake for Jesus, sing traditional Christmas songs, and end with a prayer blessing your neighbors.

Be devoted to one another in brotherly love.
Honor one another above yourselves.
Romans 12:10

Keep a master Daytimer accessible for family members
to record every doctor appointment, sports event,
church activity, etc. Each person may color-code his
or her obligations for quick identification.

Tell A Friend

DAWN RICHERSON

*...that is our vocation: . . . to create the free and fearless space
where brotherhood and sisterhood can be formed
and fully experienced.*

Henri Nouwen

"Mommy, I told my friend about Jesus, just like Paul!" Luke exclaimed one
day. He was bursting with excitement and had a look of pure joy written on
his tiny face. I caught a taste of his joy and smiled with him.

My mind flashed back to when I was 14. Overcome with the vastness of
God's love and deeply grateful that God had allowed Jesus to die for me, I
was eager to "tell a friend."

Back then it was easier, I thought. Immediately I questioned my reasoning,
which, even as a passing thought, seemed more an excuse than a reason. It's so
easy to neglect sharing our faith with others. We rationalize by thinking things
like, "After all, life is hard. Things happen that remain difficult, if not impossible, to explain. They won't listen. They already know. They're too busy right
now. I'll tell them later."

But Jesus didn't do it that way. He hung on the cross precisely for a world
too busy to care. He gave His life in spite of the fact that no one had listened.
He didn't wait for the easy time, the easy way. He steadfastly pursued the
mission of telling sinners and righteous leaders, Pharisees and ordinary folk,
friend and foe of God's love for them.

Tell a friend today. It'll bring a smile to your face. It may even rekindle hope down deep in somebody else's soul.

Andrew, Simon Peter's brother, was one of the two who heard what John had said and who had followed Jesus. The first thing Andrew did was to find his brother Simon and tell him, "We have found the Messiah" (that is the Christ). And he brought him to Jesus . . .
John 1:40–42

To help with witnessing, carry with you gospel tracks.

A Simple Walk Calms The Spirit
SUSAN KIMMEL WRIGHT

The little cares that fretted me,
I lost them yesterday,
Among the fields above the sea,
Among the winds at play;
Out in the fields with God.

Unknown

A couple years ago, I'd gotten myself into a worrisome tangle. It deprived me of sleep and so paralyzed me that I couldn't focus on my work, even though I knew I needed to do several things to resolve the problem.

One rainy morning, after my devotional time, I felt overwhelmed by the crushing load of undone tasks. Like too many other mornings, my mind wandered to avenues of escape, but the strongest attraction lay outside the window. Somehow, I wanted to walk in the rain. I felt such a strong pull that I soon found myself buckling on my child's red slicker.

My dog waited expectantly beside the door, but I shook my head.

"It's too wet," I told him, and went out.

Trudging downhill, I emerged in the field above the creek. I walked slowly, stopping often to look and listen. The rain hit my face and soaked my pant legs and beat-up old canvas shoes. Windfall apple-plunks and the chirp of a cricket punctuated the constant patter of drops hitting leaves.

The grass and bug-eaten leaves were just past their peak, yellowing and drooping gently under the rain. But there, along the rusted barbed wire fence, burst a bright spray of orange rosehips. Coming into an overgrown section, I was surprised by a sudden crabapple with its vivid load of round red fruits dragging at faded branches. Crystal raindrops reflected the world like mirrored beads.

God's hand was everywhere.

At last, I climbed back up and sat on my porch, getting wetter. My mind was empty of all but the feel and smell of rain, and the pleasant tingle of relaxed limbs.

When I came back inside, my dog greeted me with wags and kisses. Tea, dry clothes, and a warm fire were welcome pleasures.

My life with its small problems no longer loomed so large. Like the rain-washed world outside, I rested in the palm of God's hand. With a calmer spirit, I tackled my work. Knowing I was facing it, at last, brought satisfaction, too.

I wrote myself a prescription that day that I could refer to in the future when things became tense: "God first, then exercise and fresh air, and my creative work." It has served me well.

What seemingly unusual thing could you do today to make life simple, yet abundant?

. . . speak to the earth, and it will teach you, or let the fish of the sea inform you. Which of these does not know that the hand of the Lord has done this? In His hand is the life of every creature and the breath of all mankind.

Job 12:8–10

Take a walk outside, in any weather or season, and see God's power and love everywhere.

Listen With Your Face

CATHY W. LOTT

*There is only one way to love God: to take not a single step without
him, and to follow with a brave heart wherever he leads.*

Francois Fenelon

When my son, Ryan, was about two or three years old, he had trouble listening to my instructions. Like most toddlers, he was a very busy boy! He had toys to play with, *Sesame Street* to watch on television, tricycles to ride, friends to see, and so on. He was usually so busy that he simply did not have time to listen to me. I began to notice that he also didn't bother to look at me when I spoke to him. He became distracted by whatever he was busy doing at the time. In order to get his attention, I began bending down to get on his level, placing my hands on each side of his face and saying, "Look at my eyes." Only when he made eye contact did I know that he was really listening. After several months of using this technique, I was busily working in the kitchen one afternoon, preparing dinner, when Ryan walked in and began telling me about his day. Seeing that I was busy, he climbed up on the kitchen counter, took my face in his chubby little hands and said, "No, Mommy—*listen with your face!*"

Don't you think that God sometimes wants to tell us to listen to Him with our face? He longs to have a relationship with us. And we're so busy with work, school, our kids' activities, our church activities, keeping up with the housework, and spending "quality" time with our family, that we often miss out on what God is trying to communicate to us.

God uses a number of different ways to speak to His children. He uses His Word, the Holy Spirit, people we come in contact with, and our circumstances. However, Satan can also use people and circumstances to persuade us to do his bidding. So, how do we identify the true voice of God? God never tells us to do anything that is inconsistent with His Word. So before you act on any suggestion or instruction you may have "heard," check it out by studying Scripture first.

In order to "hear" what God has to say to us, we must listen:

- with anticipation—We must believe God has something to say to us.
- with quiet attentiveness—God's voice is gentle and we will miss it if our lives are filled with constant distractions like television, gossip, and radios.
- with patience—While we wait, God is preparing us to receive His answers.
- with an open heart and mind—Sometimes, we don't want to hear what God says, especially when He corrects us. But remember, God sees the "Big Picture" even when we can't!

Take time to "listen with your face" and find out what God has to communicate to you. In doing so, you will be able to achieve the intimacy with God that you desire.

I will listen to what God the LORD will say . . .
Psalm 85:8a

> To improve communication with your spouse,
> try sitting "knee to knee." Look directly into his eyes
> and say what you mean.

Inhale, Exhale

AUDREY McINTOSH

Freely have you received, freely give.
Unknown

Open a book. A really good book. One that has been read over and over. What do you see? Pages filled with exciting stories. Some with love, some with battles fought and won, and some with miracles so unbelievable that you wrestle with their reality. What book could possibly hold such treasures? The Holy Bible.

Inhale it deeply by reading about the power of God's promises to people who lived long ago. This book is so interesting, it is almost impossible to put down. You continue to absorb each facet of this story of a Heavenly Father who cared so much about the world He created that He would send a flood to destroy it rather than allow Satan to take over.

As you read on, you see a girl barely in her teens willing to be scorned and shamed by her neighbors for becoming pregnant before marriage so that she could bring a Savior into the world. A world He made. And before He came, He caused to grow the particular tree on which He would be crucified. Still He didn't hesitate to rescue this world from the clutches of its worst enemy, sin. This was the only way. Even though His disciples didn't understand when He shared with them his approaching crucifixion and resurrection, His plans didn't change. Consequently, He proved to the religious leaders that He really was God's son in the form of man.

As you inhale the wonders of this glorious book, you breathe deeply and the Holy Spirit makes it a part of your spirit. But you must not stop there. You have a job to do, even as Jesus did. You must exhale. All around you each day are people who haven't a clue of the unspeakable truths contained in this won-drous book. They don't know the contents of its pages can solve their prob-lems. As you exhale the magnificent power of the Holy Spirit to them, words come from your mouth that make you wonder, "Why did I say that?" The solutions they need pour from your heart. The Holy Spirit provides you with answers you have never considered and backs them up with Scripture after Scripture. You can truthfully say, "These are not my words, but God's. I'm only exhaling His Spirit for the healing of your body, mind, and spirit."

The blessings you share replace worry, fear, anxiety, and grief. This greatly pleases your Heavenly Father. You have been obedient. Strangely enough, the more you have inhaled from his Word and his Spirit, the better you can exhale healing and blessing to a hurting, dying world.

Are you ready for the challenge? God is looking for willing servants to inhale from Him, then exhale to others.

*Let the word of Christ dwell in you richly as you teach
and admonish one another . . .*
Colossians 3:16a

> If you find a nylon stocking that you really like, cut
> or tear off the label and put it with the rest of your nylons.
> That will help you remember its brand, color, and style.

Shop Vigorously . . . Trade Profitably
JAN McNAUGHT

If you are tired of shopping you are going to the wrong shops.
Wallis, Duchess of Windsor

"But I want to shop at the mall," my teen daughter whined. "I don't want to shop at an old thrift store. What if my friends saw me?" Horrified, she stomped to her room.

That was the extent of our conversation those years I tried to clothe and guide my fashion-conscious, peer-pleasing, normal daughter. She desperately wanted to be "in" and wanted me to never run "out" of money. Repeated efforts on my part only brought repeated tears and pleas on her part. Then one spring I suggested a slightly revised idea.

"Let's stop by the thrift store on the way to the mall today," I said. "You can see what they have, and then when we get to the mall you can compare." My junior higher rolled her eyes and sighed, but she tried it. Soon she changed her requests.

"Can we run over to the thrift store this afternoon?" she'd ask. "I'd like to try on a cute blouse I saw there. I saw one in the mall almost exactly like it, but they wanted at least twice as much."

My daughter and I enjoyed thrifting together several times after that, finding dresses, shoes, jewelry and more. I came to prefer the leather bag with a patina made possible only after years of loving use and shoes comfortably broken in. My daughter began bumping into her friends at the local thrift shop too . . . after she shared her shopping secret.

We offer these suggestions:

- Keep a list and head for those things first.
- Check zippers, sizes, labels; search for stains, cracks, smells, etc.
- Shop the men's section for loafers, vests, sweaters, hats.
- Put 50%-off days on the calendar
- Shop alone; it's easier to concentrate.
- Recycle your items; donate them to a thrift store
- Hold a style show with models wearing only thrift finds . . . and a price tag!
- Plan a Thrifting Party for your friends at a local thrift store. Spending Limit: $3.00. Time Limit: 30 Minutes. Follow with lunch. The group treats for lunch the one who made the best deal.
- Be patient. You can find almost anything you want at a thrift store over time.

An equally enthusiastic thrifter challenged me that she could make the best shopping discovery and bargain. My friend won the day she came to work and, holding up a bit of the beautiful wool skirt she wore, said simply: "Quarter! Quarter! Quarter!"

She sets about her work vigorously . . . She sees that her trading is profitable . . .
Proverbs 31:17a, 18a

Did you know you can barter even in antique stores? Learn the value of what you have, then offer a trade for what you want.

The Birthday Box
CATHY MESSECAR

If, instead of a jewel, or even a flower, we could cast up the gift of a lovely thought into the heart of another, that would be giving as the angels give.
Anonymous

My grown daughter, Sheryle, handed me a medium-sized box covered in pink floral paper. It was my birthday! Hastily pulling off the lid, I discovered several small packages with folded notes attached and a much smaller box filled with folded strips of paper.

Sheryle began to explain. "Mom, since you're busy and always doing things for other people, I just wanted you to spend a little time enjoying life's pleasures. Each day for the next three weeks, open a package or read one of the folded notes and follow the advice. If you don't have time for the suggested activity, then drop it back in the box and keep choosing until you find one that fits your schedule for that day."

The present proved to be one of the most thoughtful I ever received. The "instructions" helped restore balance and joy to my chaotic life. Some of her simple but creative suggestions calmed my spirit, some prompted thoughts toward others:

- Sit on your porch and drink your afternoon coffee or tea.
- Read a book for enjoyment (at least one hour).
- Phone a "long distance" friend.
- Put on perfume.
- Paint your fingernails and toenails.
- Cook your favorite meal for dinner; don't worry about fat content.
- Pick a bouquet of flowers.
- Write for three hours.
- Drink your morning coffee out of a teacup.
- Go for a stroll—not for exercise but to enjoy nature's beauty.
- Take a bubble bath.
- Turn off phones for an entire afternoon.
- Phone your grandmother.
- Light a candle.
- Eat on your china.

The soothing gifts included shower gel and nylon scrubber, hand lotion, plant sticks, a pinwheel, tea, and a box of chocolates. All of the tiny treasures had an "instruction" note, as well.

Nourishing inner peace is a worthwhile project. My daughter's gift caused me to reflect on the busy schedule I keep. It seems that every time a friend asks, "How are you doing?" I find myself replying, "Busy, too busy."

Since receiving the birthday box and enjoying its suggestions, I have a new answer. When asked how I'm doing, I now reply, "I'm learning to relax more and finding that the joy is being restored in my life."

Thank you, my dear daughter.

But let all who take refuge in you be glad; let them ever sing for joy. Spread your protection over them, that those who love your name may rejoice in you.

Psalm 5:11

Customize a gift box of relaxing suggestions for yourself, a busy friend, or a relative.

God's Love Letters

Lynn D. Morrissey

I am a little pencil in the hand of a writing God
Who is sending a love letter to the world.

Mother Teresa

One of the simplest ways to share the abundant love of God with friends, family, and those who don't know Him is through personal correspondence. I write an average of over three thousand letters annually, sharing God's comfort and love. People often tell me how touched they are by my letters. The greatest compliment I've ever received is from those who say they keep "Lynn files" in which to store my correspondence.

Unfortunately, letter-writing is becoming a lost art; but God considers it extremely important. The Bible is filled with letters. Paul wrote to Philemon for his instruction, John to believers to complete their joy, Jude to warn them of false prophets, and Peter to "stir up" their faith. How would you, as a Christian, have felt to receive a letter like that? Our letters can have tremendous purpose. We can lift a pen and lift a burden.

Once you understand the importance of writing letters, and how easy it is to do, it will become one of the greatest pleasures of your life, opening up a whole world of adventure.

There are no prerequisites for writing; you need not be a professional to write. All you need is a love for God and people, and a willingness to share your heart on paper. Avoid these pitfalls and adopt these simple principles, and you will soon experience the abundant richness that letters provide.

Pitfalls:

- Intimidation: You may fear you can't write well and people will reject you. The opposite is true. People will be thrilled to receive your letters, because no one takes the time to write.
- Procrastination: My motto is "write right now"—write while the inspiration is fresh (as soon as you receive a gift, whenever you experience something you want to share). Be brief and you won't tend to procrastinate.
- (Lack of) Preparation: This is the biggest reason for procrastination. Stock your desk in advance with pretty stamps, greeting cards, lovely stationery, an address book, and "letter stuffers" (like postcards, photos, bookmarks, hand-written poetry or quotations, etc.). It will be easy to write when the Spirit moves you.

Principles:

- Write passionately: Write about things in which you believe and that excite you—like your love for Jesus or causes you support. Express your emotions.
- Write purposefully: Make a bullet-point outline, and know what you want to write before beginning.
- Write personally: Use everyday language and have a conversation on paper. Share daily experiences and interests; draw your reader into your world.
- Write picturesquely: Paint vivid word-pictures to make your letters more enjoyable for you and the reader.
- Write pleasantly: Create an attractive ambiance or rituals that "lure" you to your desk (surround yourself with pretty paperweights, photographs, inspirational books, others' letters, etc. Make a cup of tea, light a fire, and play classical music.)

John Donne's observation rings true: "Letters mingle souls." And if you write to others sharing the Good News of salvation, your letters just might mingle souls for eternity!

You yourselves are our letter, written on our hearts,
known and read by everybody.
II Corinthians 3:2

You don't even need to leave the comfort of your home to stock your writing desk. Call *Victorian Papers* (1-800-800-6647) for a catalog featuring an entire "wardrobe" of gorgeous greeting cards, stationery, and assorted writing accoutrements.

Don't Work The Night Shift
DELORES ELAINE BIUS

If you have trouble sleeping, don't count sheep—talk with the shepherd.
Unknown

Do you work the night shift? I don't mean actually working a night job, but rather, stay awake all night worrying?

Not long ago, I discovered that one reason I was always tired was because I was lying awake at night worrying about problems instead of committing them to the Lord. My restless nights often had me exhausted during the day.

Then one day in my devotional time, I was reading Psalm 121. The writer was pointing out that *He who watches over you will not slumber nor sleep* (verse 4).

That night I decided that since God was awake all night and watching over all my concerns, it was a bit presumptuous of me to think He needed my help. So in my bedtime prayers, I listed all my cares to God and then left them with Him. I followed the example of the Psalmist, who also proclaimed, *I will lie down and sleep in peace, for you alone, O Lord, make me dwell in safety* (Psalm 4:8).

You don't need to work the night shift, either. God is your Night Watchman, too.

In vain you rise early and stay up late, toiling for food to eat—
for He grants sleep to those He loves.
Psalm 127:2

Do the things that are most unattractive during the times of your day or evening in which you have the most energy and enthusiasm. Save the desirable tasks as a reward for doing the others.

A God For All Seasons
SANDRA PALMER CARR

There shall be seasons refreshing,
Sent from the Savior above.
Daniel W. Whittle

One day when the sky was filling with dark rain clouds, my mind filled with early memories of my mother and her marvelous gift for dramatization. She used it to great advantage on rainy days when my three younger sisters and I had to stay indoors. We were quite a quartet, lined up on the old, purple couch, hearts pounding with anticipation of the characters Mom would portray. The kitchen provided whatever props her impromptu stories required, from colander hats to dishtowel handkerchiefs and spatula scepters. There seemed to be no end to Mom's imagination and our giggling laughter, begging for encores, between bites of warm cookies and sips of hot chocolate. I am thankful for those happy times.

I have a good friend who often feels depressed in rainy weather. She usually calls and we talk about the good side of rain—the cleansing of the earth, the fresh-scented air, and the sounds that speak of God's peace and power.

We recount God's faithfulness to us and the blessings of our friendship. Sometimes we exchange a recipe and make plans to bake something for our families. We always conclude that there is joy in Jesus no matter the weather.

If your memories of rainy days past are tainted with sadness, try planning something new and wonderful! Begin by thanking God for the gift of rain. Then call a friend to share your new perspective. And don't forget to scan the skies for God's beautiful rainbows (sometimes there are several) to remind you of His love and faithfulness.

I will send you rain in its season . . .
Leviticus 26:4

Plan a rainy day potluck with friends. Remind everyone that rainy days can be "up" days if we look up.

Fasten Your Seat Belts

JANET E. PRATT

Don't bother to give God instructions; just report for duty.

Corrie ten Boom

After eleven years in the Marine Corps, my husband came up for reenlistment, but we felt God was telling us it was time to leave. Even though we knew it was God's leading, I struggled with worry and doubt. I wanted to know what we were going to do, where we were going to live, and what kind of job my husband would get. Since he felt called into ministry, I wanted to know what kind of ministry, where he would get his training, and how would we afford Bible college.

For several months prior to his discharge, these thoughts whirled around in my brain. One afternoon as my children and I piled into the car to run errands, my son interrupted my buzzing thoughts with his usual string of questions.

"Where are we going? How long will it take? How come we're going this way? When will we get home?"

Finally, I sighed, "Jacob, just sit down, buckle your seat belt, and trust me to get us where we need to go."

Then the significance of what I'd just said hit me. "O-o-h, I get it!"

As I pulled away from the curb, that still, small voice of my Father whispered, "Buckle up." I know it was said with a smile.

Are you trying to have all your questions answered about your future? God knows exactly where He's guiding you. Just sit down, buckle up, and trust Him to get you where He wants you to go.

In you our fathers put their trust; they trusted and you delivered them. They cried to you and were saved; in you they trusted and were not disappointed.

Psalm 22:4, 5

Sort your mail as you walk from the mailbox to the trash can.
Unwanted items go immediately in the trash, then file bills
in folders or manila envelopes marked 1, 2, 3, or 4 depending
on the week of the month you intend to pay them.

Sunday Morning Rush

ALICE KING GREENWOOD

Even a bee can be too busy making honey to savor the taste.

God's Tender Promises For Mothers

Sunday is the most beautiful day of the week. I love walking into the church sanctuary with calmness, my heart in tune with God, ready to worship Him. It was not always so. When my children were small and needed lots of help in getting ready for Sunday School, I usually arrived at the church harried and out of sorts, definitely not in a spiritual attitude of worship. Something had to change.

The biggest hassle was getting the children bathed and dressed. Often they got only "a lick and a promise" of a bath. There were arguments about clothes—getting Tommy to wear his clean shirt instead of the wrinkled sweat he'd been playing in; convincing Kathy that an orange hair ribbon wouldn't look good with her pink dress; frantically searching for matching socks. And how did their shoes get so scuffed? A polishing job was in order. Hair must be combed or curled, and more time elapsed in finding lost Bibles. Then we jumped into the car and rushed down the street, hoping lights would stay green (or at least yellow) until we got through the intersections. Surely this weekly process could be simplified!

In His Word, God had already given the formula I needed, if only I would apply it. The instructions to His people traveling across the wilderness were simple: complete the work during the first six days of the week, keep the seventh day as a sabbath of rest and worship. Sounded easy enough. Could I do that?

I resolved to try God's plan. On Saturday night after baths and bedtime rituals, I laid out clothes from underwear to accessories, checking each article for rips, spots, and wrinkles. I made whatever repairs were needed, matched socks, polished shoes, and set out Bibles. In the morning our household was amazingly serene.

The next obstacle was the family's dinner. God had given the Israelites some instructions for this problem, also: prepare food on the day before the Sabbath. For persons like me, who never planned meals too far in advance, that would be a challenge. I usually started cooking the meal when we got home from church, and after an hour's wait, the children were fussy and hungry. Wouldn't it be great to have everything ready to eat when we walked in the door?

Again, the simple answer lay in adequate preparation on Saturday. For the main dish, I fixed a roast, meat loaf, or casserole which could bake while we were at church. My oven's automatic timer worked beautifully. Heavenly aromas greeted us when we got home. Canned vegetables were heated by the time the table was set, and preprepared desserts such as ice cream and cookies topped off the meal in style.

The long, restful afternoon that followed was exactly what I needed to complete the transformation of a hectic rush to a quiet time of reflection.

Could your Sunday morning rush benefit from some Saturday preparations? Why not try it?

Commit to the LORD whatever you do, and your plans will succeed.
Proverbs 16:3

Make a Sunday afternoon visit to residents of a nursing home. Share your talents of reading, singing, playing an instrument, or being a good listener.

Tradition

SHERRIE WARD MURPHREE

Without a Psalm, life would be grim.

Sherrie Murphree

Fifteen years ago my sister, Beverly, introduced to me a treasured tradition we observe in our immediate and extended family. Every year on a person's birthday, we read the Psalm from the Bible that corresponds to the age of that person. That Psalm becomes ours, and there are enough to cover us up to age 150! No one gets left out. I shared this tradition with an acquaintance and she responded, "I'd be reading the thirty-ninth Psalm every year."

Sometimes we read their Psalm with and sometimes to the person. When away from family members, we read the scripture in *honor* of them. In the situation of our Marlon, who has already gone to be with the Lord, we read the Psalm of how old he would be, in *memory* of him.

I mention a special verse from "their" Psalm and include it in a birthday card. Or I remind my siblings, "Be sure to read your Psalm today." If it's a short Psalm, I type out the entire chapter—letting it speak for itself, and put it on beautiful paper. When I'm lacking for words, God's words for birthday greetings can't be beat.

Look what Psalm 71:9 had to say for my mom's 71st: *Do not cast me away when I am old; do not forsake me when my strength is gone.*

For Valerie, who turned nineteen, we read Psalm 19:14: *May the words of my mouth and the meditation of my heart, be pleasing in your sight, O Lord, my rock and my redeemer.*

For David, who hits forty this year, chapter 40 will be read. I'll highlight verse 3: *He put a new song in my mouth, a hymn of praise to our God.*

And for my four-year-old nephew, Christian, look at how the fourth Psalm, verse 8, was so apropos: *I will lie down and sleep in peace, for you alone, O Lord, make me dwell in safety.*

Our tradition tightens our family bond, and we'll continue it until we're all in heaven where none will have birthdays and the family reunion of forever begins. I'm glad that our abundance of life doesn't depend on how long we live on earth.

Teach us to number our days aright, that we may gain a heart of wisdom.
Psalm 90:12.

If you live to be an average age of 70, figure up exactly how many more days you have to live and write that number in pencil above Psalm 90 every year. Maybe you're living on borrowed time. Make every day count, whichever side of 70 you are on.

In His Name
BETTY C. STEVENS

Do what you can, with what you have, where you are.
Theodore Roosevelt

Do you ever wish you had just the right card to send to a friend in need? I've found that sending a scripture card is a welcome gift to a friend. Years ago I would type out a certain Bible verse on a 3 by 5 card, and send it on to a friend in need or to a loved one.

I sent one of those cards to a dear Christian friend who was home-bound because of a bad heart. She hand-drew a pretty flower in the upper left corner of the card and sent it back to me. It was beautiful!

For a number of years we joined together. I would get the scripture cards printed, and my friend Grace would hand-draw a beautiful little flower in that upper left corner of each card. She was so happy to have a part in that work. That dear friend went home to be with the Lord several years ago.

But Grace had started something I wanted to continue. I now have the cards printed reasonably at a Kinko's store. (Let your printer know you are going to have art work on that upper left corner, otherwise they may try to center your scripture verse.)

On one 8½ by 11 inch master sheet I have lined off five 3 by 5 card spaces. And I've typed in the Scriptures the way I want them, according to the space shape. I ask them to print that master sheet on ten copies each of five different light colors of card stock: for instance, yellow, pink, cream, orchid, and green. Then I ask them to cut them for me. This gives me a total of 50 scripture cards.

Some people can possibly paint something in that upper left corner as my friend Grace did. I use a little rubber stamp, labeled "Bl666 Violet Corner," for that upper left corner. Some people could possibly color that in, but I'm not able to. I think it is pretty just as it is.

They will still bear fruit in old age; they will stay fresh and green.
Psalm 92:14

> Carry some scripture cards in your purse at all times. You never know when you may be able to lift a needy heart!

Forever Friends

VIVIAN LEE BANIAK

Friendship improves happiness, and abates misery,
by doubling our joy, and dividing our grief.

Joseph Addison

Four months into my most recent re-location, I sat leisurely sipping my Sunday morning coffee and glancing through the USA Weekend magazine. An article by Laura Zigman entitled "The Latest Ailment: Best Friend Replacement Anxiety" grabbed my attention.

The article told how the author phoned her best friend who had recently moved only to find out that her best friend was having no difficulty making new friends in her new location. She was making new friends with people who had more in common now with her new place in life. Friend jealousy, also known as friend-replacement panic disorder, happens when a close friend has other close friends or suddenly makes a new friend who becomes a close friend.

Building close friendships is a part of God's design for relationships. Knowing that I'll have all eternity to spend with my sisters in Christ certainly takes much of the anxiety out of separating from them for a time. Having moved away from dear and close friends a number of times, I've learned that I can do some things to maintain our intimacy over the miles and through the years.

Several of my long distance friends have set up a telephone date with me for a specified day and time monthly or bi-weekly. We take turns calling one another to share the cost of the phone calls. We've calculated that we are not spending any more per month at our dime-a-minute long distance rate than we would if we lived in the same city and went out to lunch together regularly. On the off-weeks when we are not visiting by phone, we will sometimes drop each other a note, a clever or sentimental card, or some article or tape we know the other would enjoy. I once bought two identical coffee mugs and sent one to my friend so that while we chatted together we could drink our coffee from matching mugs.

Friendships are extremely important to women and time-tested close friendships are a rarity to be treasured and nurtured. Once God sovereignly moved me right back to the town where a close friend lives. Because of our mutual efforts over the three and a half years I was away, we were still current on what was important to each of us at this new time in our lives. Lasting friendships take time, effort, and commitment but they're a gift of God's abundance to you.

I no longer call you servants . . . Instead, I have called you friends . . .
John 15:15

Save time by making one trip to the card store
to buy all the birthday, anniversary, and note cards
you will need for the year.

Singing Therapy
MARTHA B. YODER

Let God perform His own music on the strings of your heart.
Raymond P. Brunk

That evening I was so tired. Eight hours as nurse in the nearby nursing home greatly taxed my strength. My husband had enjoyed his time with our two little sons. Susie came to keep them the hour between his going to work and my coming home.

Though laundry waited to be done in the basement by the wringer washer, I wanted to spend a loving evening meeting the boys' needs. Now it was bedtime for the boys. How I wished it were mine also.

After baths, I tucked their sweet-smelling bodies into cozy beds with prayers and kisses.

"That's enough for tonight, boys. Mama needs to go wash clothes," I said as I flipped off the light and started for the door. I was anxious to get the washing completed so I could go to my own bed.

"No, Mama, sing," requested four-year-old Mark.

I hesitated, fighting the desire to get on with my work. Slowly I turned back to the chair where I nightly sat in the dimness of the night-light and sang choruses and hymns. Could it mean that much to our four- and two-year olds?

First I sang their favorites. Then I sang as the Spirit brought songs to my memory. The words ministered to my fretful spirit and fatigued body. I sensed the tiredness falling away as my spirit became refreshed. On and on I sang softly. No longer was time important. The boys were breathing deeply in sleep. The preciousness of those moments filled me with peace and rest.

As I quietly left the sleepers to go do laundry I was thrilled with the singing therapy God had given me.

The next time you find yourself tired or discouraged, try some of the same singing therapy.

For You make me glad by Your deeds, O LORD;
I sing for joy at the works of Your hands.
Psalm 92:4

During your busy day, take a fifteen-minute break to sit near the phone. Prop up your legs. Then phone an elderly friend who lives alone. Limit your call to fifteen minutes. You will be refreshed and you have brightened a lonely day for another.

Taste And See

MARJORIE K. EVANS

When we read God's Word, it provides light for life's pathway.

John Hash

It was wintertime. The Kansas wheat harvest had been very poor, and the farmers were unable to pay my Daddy for repairing their machinery. He and Mama struggled to provide for my sister, brother, and me.

One evening the only food Mama had to prepare for supper was potatoes, onions, and milk. So she made a big pot of potato soup. As she lifted the lid and added the milk, I peered into the pot. The soup was white and un-appetizing-looking. "I don't want any of that soup. It doesn't look good," I said.

Little sister Mary spoke up, "But Ma-do-we, maybe it tastes good. When I taste it, I'll see."

Later Mama added browned onions, salt, pepper, and butter to the soup. When she ladled it into our bowls it looked good. We tasted it, and it was delicious.

Isn't that sometimes the way we are as we begin to read certain portions of the Bible? We think, "That doesn't look interesting," or "That doesn't apply to me." But when we really taste God's Word—study and meditate upon it— we find it is "delicious." It nourishes us and enables us to grow as Christians.

My prayer is that the Lord Jesus Christ will help me each day not just to look at, but to truly "taste" His Word. Then it will strengthen me in faith and love regardless of the circumstances of my life.

How are your spiritual taste buds lately?

Taste and see that the LORD is good; blessed is the man
who takes refuge in him.

Psalm 34:8

Read *My Utmost for His Highest* by Oswald Chambers.

Faith Tucked In A Pocketbook

LISA L. KECK

Honesty is the first chapter of the book of wisdom.

Thomas Jefferson

God is still in the business of supplying our needs in spite of or perhaps due to our shortcomings. Just before Easter I had to go out to buy my son a pair of socks. I already had his outfit and shoes, but even little boys have to be properly accessorized. My favorite store is only ten minutes away, but with construction in the area it was now more like thirty. After I'd bought the outfit at my second favorite store I ventured over to my third favorite store which is only five minutes from my home. I found the almost perfect socks (on an unorganized rack) and other things I needed and proceeded to the cashier. As I left the store, there was an unwelcome chill in the air and the beginnings of hunger pangs in our stomachs. After putting the children in the car, I reached for the bag and noticed the socks in the cart, apparently hidden by my purse while I was in the store.

"Oh, no, the socks!" I exclaimed.

"What's wrong?" my daughter asked.

"I didn't pay for the socks."

I contemplated taking them anyway and coming back the next day to pay for them. But I wasn't sure Kellee would understand that. I certainly didn't want my daughter to think I would steal anything, so after I put my purse and the children back into the cart, I again trudged into the store. Thankfully, I was able to cut in line and pay for the socks.

When I arrived home, I pulled into the garage and was about to take the children out of the car when I realized that my pocketbook was missing. I hurriedly told Kellee to pray and drove back to the store.

"Oh, Lord, please! I hope I left it at the cashier's desk," I pleaded. I couldn't imagine it staying safe if I'd left it in the cart. But once I arrived back in the parking lot, I knew I'd done exactly that. Because sitting in the cart, illuminated by a nearby lamppost, was my purse!

"Kellee, isn't God good?" I exclaimed.

I was so excited for the opportunity to show Kellee that God answers prayer. He even protects purses that are left unattended for ten minutes while would-be thieves lurk in the shadows. Then again, maybe my purse wasn't unattended. Maybe there's a wee angel in charge of guarding purses as well as a child's (and mother's) faith.

The next time you make a mistake, make it right. And the next time you lose something, pray! It just may be the Lord's will for an angel to look after it.

*Are not all angels ministering spirits sent to serve those
who will inherit salvation?*
Hebrews 1:14

Write the date and brief answer to prayer on a garden stone.

Fruits Outdo What Flowers Promise
DORIS HAYS NORTHSTROM

*You may break, you may shatter the vase, if you will,
But the scent of the roses will hang round it still.*
Thomas Moore

I didn't count the roses and they're gone. The divorce and move from the family home of forty years to the apartment is a blur and I can't remember what happened to the quilt Char (Charlene), my daughter-in-law, crocheted for me. It had thick, red roses on an innocent-white background.

But I do remember that Christmas so long ago when she and our son, Bob, lived up north a thousand miles away. Char worked marvels with their budget and young children while he finished advanced courses.

During that winter she squeezed in needle time and made the queen-sized quilt for me. They traveled through the snow and ice to spend Christmas week with us. What joy to share in making gingerbread boys, reading old favorite stories, and sipping hot chocolate from Minnie Mouse mugs. Christmas morning I caught my breath as I opened that huge package, pulled back the tissue, then buried my arms in the soft yarn.

Amidst squeals of the children, a crackling fire, and the sweetness of warm cinnamon rolls permeating every corner of the house, I noticed Bob and Char didn't have a gift for each other. "Our trip down and your quilt are our gifts this year," Bob said with a boyish grin. "Char was like a little kid each payday, buying more yarn so she could have your gift ready by Christmas."

Through the years, I cherished that heirloom. But in the confusion of moving, I lost track of it as I stored things with each of the four children and scaled down my possessions. I had to box up parts of my life and make a new one. Eventually, I checked with everyone, but the quilt was gone.

"Lord," I prayed, "that quilt is a symbol to me. Please help me find it." We all looked again, pawed through each closet, but came up empty. *How could I have been so careless?* I wondered. My mind continued to drift back to Char and my feelings on that special Christmas. In those lean years our greatest gifts were time for each other.

Life changes and years pass quickly, yet the sun still warmed the kitchen and me in my small apartment. And I realized my prayer had been answered after all. Though the quilt was never found, Char's efforts and caring will stay with me forever. And I feel her love, tucked around me like rose petals, rolled carefully each night at the foot of my bed.

If God hasn't answered one of your prayers for something precious to be found, don't fret. Instead, remember the specialness of receiving it and let the memories of the love it represents renew your spirit.

For where your treasure is, there your heart will be also.
Matthew 6:21

Mentally list your memory heirlooms daily, storing them like blankets for the soul.

The Melody Of The Golden Years

LEEANN S. YAMAKAWA

Life isn't always what you want . . . but it's what you've got.

Barbara Johnson

If you have reached your golden years, have you grown "grumpier by the minute" or "sweeter as the years go by"? Is your heart full of anger and bitterness or full of melodies of praise to the Lord? Do you constantly complain about your miserable life or refuse to give an "organ recital" of your difficulties?

Life may have dealt you some serious blows, but God hasn't forsaken you. He's always been there and He's still there now. You are not alone, but you have a choice. You can either learn to accept the experiences you've had during your lifetime or grow bitter. If you choose to move toward the Lord, He will sweep you up into His lap where you can experience peace and comfort. But if you choose to push away from God and turn your face from Him, you will be a miserable, lonely individual.

It may help to draw you closer to Him if you reflect on the good things that have come from all your heartaches—like having wisdom to share with others. Perhaps there is another woman experiencing the same pain you've experienced during your lifetime. God may be calling you to minister to her. You may be the answer to her aching heart's prayer for help. You may be the only one who understands her pain enough to know just what to say and do that will bring peace and comfort.

Why not look around today and see how you might be a healing blessing in another woman's life?

Praise be to the God and Father of our Lord Jesus Christ . . . who comforts us in all our troubles, so that we can comfort those in any trouble with the comfort we ourselves have received from God.

II Corinthians 1:3, 4

Sit down today and begin a list of the wisdom you've obtained because of your life experiences. Then make another list of those who might benefit by you sharing it with them.

How's Your A.Q.?

MATHEW J. BOWYER

I carry the sun in a golden cup,
The moon in a silver bag.

William Butler Yeats

One of the most remarkable ladies of modern times was the blind woman, Helen Keller. She became literate by having a teacher trace the alphabet on her hand. She wrote: "Once I knew the depth where no hope was, and darkness lay on the face of all things. My life was without past or future. I fretted and beat myself against the wall that shut me in. But a little word from the fingers of another fell into my hand and my heart leaped to the rapture of living. Night fled before the day of thought, and love and joy came up in a passion of obedience to knowledge."

There's one thing more important than your I.Q. It's your A.Q.—*Adaptability Quotient*. When the chips are down, when it seems as if you don't have a friend in the world, when you are standing alone on the stage of life, will you panic or persevere? What you do depends upon your A.Q. Though you may have the unfailing support of a husband, family, and friends as you journey through life, your ultimate action is decided as you stand alone.

Many individuals have very high I.Q.s but are dismal failures when it comes to adapting to the foibles of life's changes. Though a person may be shackled by a low I.Q., he or she can rise above those smarter by developing a high A.Q. Many things may contribute to this upgrading. They range from formal education to a simple pursuit of perfecting interpersonal relationships.

Study the success stories of great people throughout history. They all, in their various ways, are but triumphs of an ability to change. Increasingly today, living in this modern era of fast-changing morals and technology, one needs to be open to considering new ideas and adjust expectations. Though one's I.Q. may be constant, the A.Q is unstable. Like a barometer, it mirrors our emotions and makes problems manageable or unmanageable. Our A.Q. travels with us daily, allowing us to cope with the demands of the day. As certain as the sun rises and the sun sets, God causes things to change. Nothing is forever. Do you have the power within you to properly accept the foibles of this uncertain world? God's Word offers the secrets of how to develop an A.Q.—an "Adaptability Quotient"—that surpasses the highest I.Q.

He changes times and seasons; He sets up kings and deposes them. He gives wisdom to the wise and knowledge to the discerning.

Daniel 2:21

When you receive an unsoliticed, unwanted telemarketing call, tell them, "Please put me on your 'Do Not Call List.'" By law they must not call you within twelve months.

Gifts Of Love

RUTH E. McDANIEL

Love is, above all, the gift of oneself.

Jean Anouilh

When I opened my front door on Saturday morning, there was no note, no card, just a beautiful store-bought bouquet of flowers in a water-filled mug, along with a fresh cantaloupe. I looked up and down the empty street wondering who left these gifts for us. Faces flashed in my mind, but I dismissed them one by one. Immediate family or close friend would have presented these offerings in person.

I brought the gifts into the house and placed the flowers in a vase, then sampled the cantaloupe, all the while trying to identify the gift-giver.

"Maybe it's from our walker-friend," my husband suggested. A woman had been fast-walking past our house, daily, for over two years, and she would stop to chat with us as we sat on our front porch. Over time, we became good friends. She had given us gifts on various holidays, so it was possible she could be our unknown benefactor. However, when I called her, she said, "No, but I wish I'd thought of it. It's a lovely idea."

"Maybe it's our neighbor across the street," Ken said. Ruth had been a dear and generous friend for twenty years. Although she'd never done anything like this before, there's always a first time. Her response was, "Sorry, I'm not the mystery person, either."

I phoned a devoted Christian acquaintance, but she also denied leaving the gifts. Finally, it dawned on me. Obviously, the giver wanted to remain anonymous. These presents were given in love, no strings attached, no recognition required.

So, Ken and I stopped trying to identify our secret admirer. Instead, we gave thanks for the unexpected treats and settled down to enjoy them, filled to the brim with love and gratitude. It continues to be a wonderful lesson to us knowing that, whoever it was, followed the example of the greatest gift-giver of all time. God showers us, daily, with extraordinary gifts, all given in love: *Every good and perfect gift is from above* (James 1:17). His most perfect gift was His only Son, Jesus Christ, given so that *whoever believes in Him shall not perish but have eternal life* (John 3:16). God expects His people to follow the law of giving gifts of love.

The flowers soon perished and the melon disappeared, but the love behind those gifts goes on and on. Just like the love of God.

> *Let them give thanks to the LORD for His unfailing love*
> *and His wonderful deeds for men.*
> Psalm 107:21

Leave an anonymous gift of love on the doorsteps of people who need it most. Let them experience God's warm embrace, firsthand.

Just for Today
MARY J. DAVIS

The Bible was never intended to be a book for scholars and specialists only. From the very beginning it was intended to be everybody's book, and that is what it continues to be.

F. F. Bruce

Bible study and prayer are vital to every Christian's life. But, so are our families, jobs, and everything else that creeps in to crowd out our personal time with God. Although we often decide to turn over a new leaf and stick to a daily Bible study and prayer time, it's common to get discouraged after a few days. Other things in our lives just get in the way. Then we feel guilty and defeated, and we stop trying.

Here are some practical suggestions that will help you keep a personal time with God each day.

1. Just for today, plan to pray at least twice and grab five minutes to read your Bible. With this attitude, you will not feel like you failed if you don't stick to a schedule for weeks on end. Also:

- Pray alone by using extra minutes in your schedule to have a cherished conversation with God.
- Pray first thing in the morning, even if you have to pretend to be sleeping.
- Pray while you eat lunch, which is usually the quietest meal of the day.
- Pray while driving to or from work.
- Pray when the family is watching TV.

You might also consider praying with someone. Spend just a couple of minutes in prayer with someone during the day. You will both gain strength from it. Pray with a co-worker. Invite a neighbor over for a morning prayer break. Call someone from your church and pray with them on the phone. Pray with the children before they get on the school bus or leave your car. Pray with your own mother or dad, brother or sister. Stop at the church and pray with your pastor.

2. Just for today, plan to open your Bible and read for five minutes, even if the five minutes are broken into small segments. Consider:

- Use wasted moments, such as during commercials while you watch a favorite program.
- Use private moments, such as during your bath or right after your shower.
- Use the first or last moments of the day, when you get up or just before you go to bed.
- Use the time while you are waiting for a meal to cook. Keep a Bible on the table to read between preparations for the meal.

When you are away from home:

- Use idle time. Carry a small Bible with you to read on your break at work.
- Use waiting time. Study while waiting in doctor's or dentist's office, or while waiting in the car for your spouse or children.
- Use wasted time. Study while waiting for others to arrive at a meeting or gathering.
- Use leisure time. Sit and read at your favorite spot/beach, park/mall/etc.

Bible study and prayer need not be done in strict discipline. In today's world, you will do better to grab a few minutes when you can. God will bless your efforts.

May the Lord direct your hearts into God's love . . .
II Thessalonians 3:5a

When placing catalog orders, make a note on the order form that your name is not to be given out for distribution.

Coping With Stress
GLORIA H. DVORAK

You cannot fix what you will not face.
James Baldwin

Overload! Stress! Most of us have experienced overwork and stress either at the office, at home, or by overextending ourselves. The problem arises when we are unaware of the overload. Others can tell us to slow down, but only we can make it happen. You know you've said it yourself, "as soon as I finish this, I'll stop." Or "I'll cut that out." We stretch ourselves like a rubber band and we know what happens when a rubber band is stretched too far.

Most women hate to say no to someone in need. Even though our schedules are crammed with too many chores, when someone asks us to do something, we usually say yes. "Super Mom" comes to the rescue. But who is taking care of Super Mom?

I often wondered how our Lord Jesus Christ handled stress. What did Jesus do with the wearisome Pharisees and Sadducees and doubting Thomases? Jesus handled each person or crowds of people in simple ways.

1. He talked with His Father-God.
2. He rested in the garden.
3. He went fishing.
4. He went to visit friends like Mary, Martha, and Lazarus.
5. He walked, talked, and ate with His disciples and friends.
6. He was never too pressured or rushed to help someone in need.
7. He had His priorities straight.

I learned a lot from those seven points. I had to change my way of living after suffering from burn-out. I had been using too much energy without replenishing it. I didn't take the time to talk to the Lord in prayer. I had to learn to say "no" nicely and not worry what people would think of me. Obligations had been crowding out what was best for me. I was too much of a perfectionist. I was afraid of failure, which only led to more stress. I had to learn to forget past mistakes.

It has been said that the mark of a successful individual is someone whose mind isn't cluttered with past failures. I needed to dwell more on my successes.

I soon learned to rest on Sundays and to take long walks with my dog. I also took up golf with my husband. Eliminating stress completely is not pos-

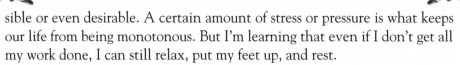

sible or even desirable. A certain amount of stress or pressure is what keeps our life from being monotonous. But I'm learning that even if I don't get all my work done, I can still relax, put my feet up, and rest.

Now that's progress.

But Jesus often withdrew to lonely places and prayed.
Luke 5:16

Don't donate to charity through telemarketing calls. Many illegitimate organizations use names similar to valid charities but don't do the same good work. Contribute to the charity of your choice directly.

Beauty: More Than Skin Deep
WENDY DUNHAM

The most attractive people in the world are the ones who are interested in others—turned outward in cheerfulness, kindness, appreciation, instead of turned inward to be constantly centered on themselves.

P. Boone

As women, most of us strive to maintain our youthful beauty. We color our hair and make appointments for perms. We use blow-dryers, curling irons, and hot rollers. Then, for the extra "lift," we use an assortment of hair sprays, gels, and mousse. We join fitness clubs and enroll in exercise classes. We jog, walk, and even roller blade to "keep our youthful glow." We have bathroom vanities filled with facial creams and cleansers, mud masks, skin toners, foundation, blush, eye-liner, lip-liner; you name it, we've got it. We spend a considerable portion of our time and energy trying to slow, cover up, or even reverse the aging process. We go to extremes and have a face lift. Let's face it—we want to be attractive. We want to be beautiful.

But I wonder. Is it all the extra "stuff" that makes us truly beautiful? Do we value our outward beauty more than the inward?

As I reflect on that question, a close friend of mine comes to mind. My friend is one of the most attractive women I know. Her beauty stems from deep in her soul and radiates outward. She's a woman who smiles, a woman who laughs. She's a woman who loves to talk. She talks to her cats, to herself, and to all kinds of people. Even though she talks a lot, she's the best "listener" I know. She's also a woman with a vast vocabulary, yet she has a tendency to use six words over and over again. Several times a day, I'll hear her voice as she speaks those six words to her co-workers: "What can I do for you?"

Oh, I nearly forgot. You might be wondering. Yes, she's attractive on the outside too! She takes care of herself. She's well-kept. Her smile is bright, and her eyes are filled with the interest of others. Funny, though, I can't recall what clothes she wore yesterday, but I do remember she asked how I was doing. Then she asked about my family. Not with superficial concern, but with deep interest. She's a woman who patterns her beauty after her creator.

As women, I believe it is important to keep our outward appearance as attractive as possible, to make the most of our potential. Unfortunately, some of us have limits to our outward beauty—but with the inward, there is no limit. Here are some ideas for developing your inner beauty:

- Be a listener—tune your ears to the concerns of others.
- Take a genuine interest in the lives of others.
- Make a commitment to volunteer for a worthy cause on a weekly or monthly basis. Your community, church, or extended families offer many opportunities.
- Reach out to someone who could use a friend. Go beyond your normal boundaries of age, race, status, health, or mental well-being.

Ask yourself, "What can I do for someone else?"

. . . The LORD does not look at the things man looks at. Man looks at the outward appearance, but the LORD looks at the heart.
I Samuel 16:7

Pick one of these ideas, or form your own,
and concentrate on that today.

Seize The Day

JANIE LAZO

There are 1,440 minutes in each day. Whatever you do not use or invest in a good purpose is lost forever.
Unknown

What would you do if each morning you were given $1,440.00 to spend in any way you desire? The money is all yours, no strings attached! However, you cannot save any of the money. Any amount that you do not spend before twenty-four hours has passed will be taken back from you. You would spend every last dime, wouldn't you?

Now, consider the fact that at the dawn of each new day we each are given a priceless gift, the gift of time: 1,440 minutes of time, to be exact. Time is a fleeting commodity. Time management has moved to the forefront of our society. Huge corporations invest millions of dollars in "effective time management" training for their employees. There are seminars as well as countless versions of day planners that we can purchase to help us master the art of time management. We are advised to list our short-term and long-term goals and review them constantly. We are told to prioritize our daily activities in such a manner that will enable us to turn our dreams into reality.

We can apply those same principles to our spiritual life. The fourteenth chapter of Luke tells us of Martha and Mary, two sisters who opened their home to Jesus and His disciples. Martha was scurrying about, preparing things for their guests while Mary sat at the feet of Jesus, listening intently to his every word.

Martha became irritated and approached Jesus, "Don't you care that I have been left alone to do all the work myself? Tell my sister to help me!"

The Lord answered, "You are worried about many things, but only one thing is needed. Mary has chosen what is better and it will not be taken from her."

Perhaps you've thought about starting a Bible study group or organizing a home visitation program. Maybe you simply would like to spend more time in prayer and meditation each day. If you, like so many others, feel that you are just too busy to fit anything more into your schedule, I urge you to make a list of your "spiritual" goals. Once you have done this, it will be easier to trade off less important activities for more valuable ones. We'll know God's will more clearly.

God calls us to be good stewards of our time. How will you spend your 1,440 minutes today?

Sow for yourselves righteousness, reap the fruit of unfailing love, and break up your unplowed ground; for it is time to seek the LORD, until He comes and showers righteousness on you.
Hosea 10:12

For one week, keep a log of how you spend your days.
Look for patterns of wasted time that can be exchanged
for spiritually enriching activities.

Blow Me A Blessing, Lord

BETTY HUFF

"To dream the impossible dream . . ."

Man of La Mancha

Spring cleaning always means our church's biggest fund raiser—the rummage sale. Michele, a single mother on disability because of Gran Mal epilepsy, is one of our most faithful workers.

For their week of pricing, sorting, and displaying the mountains of donations, the volunteers get coffee and doughnuts in the morning, a hot lunch at noon, and first choice of any items they wish to buy. On the morning of the sale each worker tallies up their items and pays for them or puts them back.

When Michele's tally was twenty dollars more than she had, she tried to eliminate some purchases, but everything she chose was essential. In desperation she prayed aloud. "Lord, if someone is going to lose twenty dollars today and they don't really need it, will You blow it my way? Amen."

A few minutes later Michele's little daughter came running up. "Mommy," she shouted, "look what I found in the parking lot." It was a crumpled up twenty dollar bill. Thinking someone had dropped it, Michele went looking for the owner. "You're never going to find who lost it," the gardener said. "I saw it just blowing on the ground."

Some of us were surprised, but after all, the wind has always obeyed its Creator.

It became calm on the Sea of Galilee and it blew right through the walls of the Upper Room. To lift a small green piece of paper and deposit it where it was most needed must have been an easy assignment!

If God wants to provide for you in a unique way, He has the power and creativity to do it. Why not trust His love that wants to meet all your true needs?

And my God will meet all your needs according to His glorious riches in Christ Jesus.

Philippians 4:19

For tips for dealing with clutter, order the book *Clutterology* by Nancy Miller on www.roundsmiller.com.

ℛemember 𝒲hen

PATTY STUMP

Because God wants only the best for you, you can hand your problems and frustrations over to His capable hands.

A.W. Thorold

Shortly after we were married, my husband and I began a tradition of ending each day briefly recapping "highlights and hurdles." We jotted these reflections down in a small, colorful notebook, categorizing each entry as either a thanksgiving or a request. We then spent a few moments praying about each item before we set the notebook aside and headed to bed.

Recently we read through a random selection of entries. We exclaimed, "Remember when our dryer broke and we couldn't afford to have it repaired? A couple of days later we found an almost new washer/dryer set for an incredible price at a yard sale!"

"Remember when we couldn't afford a full-sized Christmas tree and you brought home a tiny tree in a bucket! Our two-year-old daughter cried at the sight of it! We rented 'A Charlie Brown Christmas' and afterwards everyone thoroughly enjoyed decorating the little tree. We couldn't believe it when the very next day we received a written invitation to stop by the corner tree lot to pick out any Christmas tree we wanted, compliments of an out-of-town

273

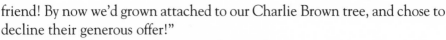

friend! By now we'd grown attached to our Charlie Brown tree, and chose to decline their generous offer!"

Our "remember when's" continued on and on.

It's been ten years since we first began ending each day in prayer. These moments together have been a wonderful way for my husband and I to stay in touch as well as a daily reminder to lay our hopes, needs, and concerns at the feet of the Lord. In doing so we've found ourselves to be more expectant regarding how He will provide for us in the midst of our circumstances.

Our "prayer journal" has become a keepsake containing reminders of God's abundant faithfulness in seeing us through times of thanksgiving and times of need. It's easy to get caught up in the pace of life and miss the movement of the Lord in our midst. Yet as we've taken the time to record both high-lights and hurdles, we've been able to see His creativity in providing for our needs and His partnership each step of the way.

I sought the LORD and He answered me…

Psalm 34:4a

Consider purchasing a brightly colored notebook to record your highlights and hurdles as well as God's provisions. You'll discover His abundance in ways you might have otherwise missed!

Love Through Shaving Cream

Jan Brunette

Peace is seeing a sunset and knowing Who to thank.
Unknown

Splat! Shaving cream sprayed onto paneling, the floor, and into the hair of those surrounding her. Laughter radiated around the table like electricity through a light bulb.

Again Trina lifted her hand, smacked the table laden with shaving cream and relished the explosion of foam bubbles. Giggles of glee exuded from the three other cherubs sitting around her.

As I reclined in my favorite chair, I loved the frolicking of my four children. Thanking God for their importance to me, I took comfort in the simple forms of play they managed to think of. A can of shaving cream and a safe location for making messes allowed for hours of fun and laughter.

Yet, only days before, I had punished the two boys for jumping off the roof and spent hours cleaning "the messiest room in town." Homework wasn't always done on time and sibling arguments needed settling. But today those memories were overshadowed by the inner desire to love the best side of them.

During those years of raising four young children alone, I struggled at times, but today, only the refreshing blessings they brought into my life touch my heart. When we get together today, little is said of messy rooms and incomplete homework. The times we remember the most are the pudding fights, making snowmen, and spraying shaving cream everywhere.

In my own personal memories, the children stand out as avenues of strength for me. No greater gift could have been given to me from my loving, heavenly Father than that of my four precious gifts from His throne above.

As you regard your children, do you focus more on the problems they bring or the joy? Do you allow them to be children and make messes, or do

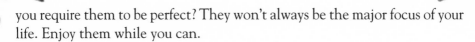
you require them to be perfect? They won't always be the major focus of your life. Enjoy them while you can.

The LORD has done great things for us, and we are filled with joy.
Psalm 126:3

> When having your devotional time, write down the things you need to do later as they pop into your mind—rather than trying to remember them and be distracted from focusing on the Lord.

Contentment
D. HARRISON

How many times have I rested tired eyes on her graceful little body, curled up in a ball and wrapped around with her tail like a parcel . . .
If they are content, their contentment is absolute; and our jaded wearied spirits find a natural relief in the sight of creatures whose little cups of happiness can be so easily filled to the brim.
Agnes Repplier

I own the cutest cat in the whole world. She is a tabby, and she is as much my child as your children are to you. As I have observed her over the past eleven years, I have found her to be very content. They say a purring cat is a contented cat. Well BingoKitty purrs like a chainsaw. I believe she's very content. The other day I stopped to ponder what it is that makes her so content and here are my findings.

I realized that she knows she is loved. She is stroked, hugged, and told, "Mommy loves you." Plus, she knows that all her needs will be met. I protect her from the other cat and a dog that live at our house. I feed her, and take care of her health needs. And she knows that she is always welcome in my lap. No matter what I'm doing, I always have time for her because she has priority over all other tasks.

I think there is a lesson to be learned from BingoKitty. How content are you? God the Father loves you. Do you feel His strokes, His hugs, do you hear Him say, "I love you?" He is meeting your needs. He is your protection. His lap is always open to you. You are His priority.

> . . . *for I have learned to be content whatever the circumstances.*
> Philippians 4:11

Everyone, even "domestic engineers," should have a business card. It prevents trying to find a scrap piece of paper to write down your telephone number.

Helping Hands
KAYLEEN J. REUSSER

If you can take today and put a little sunshine and sparkle into it,
you will have truly blessed a life—even if it is only your own.
Dr. Robert Schuller

You can perform a valuable service to your church and meet the needs of everyone in it, without ever teaching a class or singing in the choir. How? By organizing a "Helping Hands" ministry. "Helping Hands" consists of groups of women who volunteer to take meals to members who are unable to provide their own, such as new mothers, shut-ins with long-term illnesses, families of women in the hospital, and singles home from the hospital.

Each group consists of four members with one of the ladies designated as the leader. The groups are then divided up between four additional women who act as chairladies.

This is how the groups work:

1. Someone in the congregation contacts a chairlady when they know of a need.
2. The chairlady relays the call to one of the leaders under her.
3. The group leader assigns each member of her group a certain dish: meat loaf, vegetable, salad, or dessert.
4. The prepared dishes are brought to the group leader's home.
5. The group leader delivers the meal.

It is a good idea for the group leader to call the individual receiving the meal to make arrangements for delivery. She should also find out if there are special dietary restrictions and how many the meal will be expected to serve.

All volunteers are encouraged whenever possible to use disposable dishes. Otherwise, the dishes should be clearly marked with first and last names.

Funeral dinners are also organized through the "Helping Hands." All of the groups under one chairlady participate, either preparing food, serving, or cleaning up. Each group brings one two-pound meatloaf, potatoes or other vegetable, salad and relish tray, and dessert.

The groups are restructured every two years and every effort is made to keep the volunteers living in an area in the same group. Instruction sheets printed with names, telephone numbers, and the newly organized groups are handed out to the congregation.

Our "Helping Hands" groups had the opportunity to minister to a single mother who was dying of cancer. The volunteers who brought in meals sometimes stayed a few minutes to chat, thus brightening her day.

The "Helping Hands" ministry has brought the people of our church together in times of need. Couldn't your church use a "Helping Hands"?

Serve wholeheartedly, as if you were serving the Lord, not men.
Ephesians 6:7

Purchase disposable aluminum pans before you are called
to help with meals.

Give Until It Tickles
LAURA SABIN RILEY

A person completely wrapped up in himself makes a small package.
Harry Emerson Fosdick

One of the simplest ways I have discovered to live abundantly in love at
all times is to do something positive for someone when I am feeling negative
about them. When someone I love has hurt me, it can be difficult for me to
act kindly toward that person—my husband in particular. However, through
our twelve years of marriage, one secret of abundant love is found in one
simple precept: "giving until it tickles."

The phrase "give until it hurts" is commonly heard. But who wants to quit
giving when they have reached the point of pain? Not me! Then, the only
feeling I would associate giving with is "ouch!" I want to feel good when I
give. Giving past the point of pain results in giving until it tickles!

I can remember a specific time early in my marriage when my husband had
done something that deeply hurt my feelings. Rather than wallowing in my
misery, however, I decided to do something nice for him. His favorite treat is
brownies, so I began pulling ingredients from the cupboard, all the while reflecting on the unkind things he had said to me earlier. An amazing thing
happened, though, as I mixed, stirred, and poured. My thoughts began to change
from negative to positive. I began dwelling on the things I love most about my

279

husband, instead of the things I like least. By the time the brownies were finished baking, I was finished being angry! I was ready to forgive.

My husband was touched by my gesture and quickly apologized for his unkindness. We laughed and talked about how we could better communicate over a pan of warm brownies.

Next time someone you care about hurts you, don't stop giving your love to them. That's only giving until it hurts. Instead, demonstrate a simple act of kindness to them. Then you'll be giving until it tickles!

Be kind and compassionate to one another, forgiving each other,
just as in Christ God forgave you.
Ephesians 4:32

> Evaluate whether you use frequently enough all of the
> items on the top of your desk or by the telephone.
> Put away those items not used every day.

God Yearns To Talk With Us

JOY ANNA ROSENDALE

Prayer is a sincere, sensible, affectionate pouring out
of the soul to God.

John Bunyan

"I miss my son! I wish he'd talk to me. I don't know why he's staying away from me." Pain dragged down the corners of Mary's mouth, and deep lines wrinkled her forehead.

I stroked her shoulder for a moment. "You must love your son an awful lot!"

"Oh, I do! He's very special to me. We used to be so close—on the phone with each other almost every day. I loved hearing him tell me about the kids and his work. I don't know why he doesn't call me any more. If I phone him, he briefly says hi and then hands the phone to my grandkids. He doesn't seem interested in me."

Tears glistened in her gray-green eyes and spilled over. How could I comfort her? "Mary, this must be so hard!" I said.

"It is! Sometimes the pain in my heart hurts so much it almost chokes me. I want to be part of his life! I want him to share with me what he's doing."

Something clicked inside me. "Mary, I wonder if this is how God feels! I think you're reflecting the heart of God! Maybe He feels just as much pain as you do when we get too busy to talk with Him."

Her face softened. "I know you're right, Joy. When somebody loves someone, they want to be close to them. God probably yearns to talk with us even more than I want to with my son. That's a lot!"

Hungry to discover more about God's feelings, I meditated on several Bible verses that invite us to pray: "Come unto me, all you who are weary and burdened" . . . "Come boldly to the throne of grace" . . . "Cast all your cares" . . . "Pour out your hearts" . . . "Come and pray to me, and I will listen to you." . . . I had always thought that these verses meant that any time we feel like praying, we are welcome to come to the Lord. But now I could see that God isn't just inviting us: He's urging us—for His benefit as well as ours. Connecting with us satisfies and delights Him.

He says in His Word that He thinks about us constantly. He guards and shields us intently as the apple (or pupil) of His eye. He sees everything that happens to us, understands our inner concerns and needs, and feels every emotion we feel. He is with us every moment and will never abandon us. Because He expends so much attention and interest on us, it must hurt Him when we forget He's there.

We can make prayer so complicated that we don't have enough time to do it. Prayer is something simple: it is sharing our life with the Lord. As we talk with Him frequently throughout the day about whatever we're doing or feeling, we form a love-bond together. He rejoices because He has access to us to help us. And our lives are filled with the comfort and sweetness of His presence.

Trust in Him at all times, O people; pour out your hearts to Him, for God is our refuge.

Psalm 62:8

Write out a Bible verse on prayer and attach it
to your bathroom mirror.

Keeping In Touch

DORIS SCHUCHARD

God evidently does not intend us all to be rich, or powerful or
great, but He does intend us all to be friends.

Ralph Waldo Emerson

Often in the midst of caring for our families, homes, and careers, we neglect to nurture our friendships, especially if miles separate us. Here's an easy way to maintain those connections, be it a pal around the corner or around the world. Include a small gift with each handwritten Bible verse and simply drop into the mail. Or gather them all together in a pretty basket for a special occasion. Remembering a friend in this way provides a double blessing—not only an encouragement for her, but each of these verses are God's promises for you, too. So keep those cards and letters going!

January Beginnings

. . . keep my commands in your heart, for they will prolong your life many years . . . Proverbs 3:1b–2a. Send a pocket calendar.

Friendship February

A friend loves at all times, and a brother is born for adversity. Proverbs 17:17. Send some heart candy.

March Planting

But grow in the grace and knowledge of our Lord and Savior Jesus Christ . . . II Peter 3:18a. Send a seed package.

April's New Life

. . . just as Christ was raised from the dead through the glory of the Father, we too may live a new life. Romans 6:4. Send a chocolate egg, butterfly sticker, or cross pin.

May Flowers

Flowers appear on the earth; the season of singing has come . . . Song of Songs 2:12a. Send a homemade pressed flower bookmark or flower-scented perfume sample.

Love and Marriage in June

. . . as a bridegroom rejoices over his bride, so will your God rejoice over you. Isaiah 62:5. Send a toy ring.

July Heat

The LORD watches over you—the Lord is your shade at your right hand; the sun will not harm you. Psalm 121:5–6. Send a paper fan or inexpensive sunglasses.

Restful August

Find rest, O my soul, in God alone; my hope comes from him. Psalm 62:5. Send a postcard of a beach, woods, mountain, or other peaceful vacation spot.

Back to School in September

. . . I pray that you, being rooted and established in love, may . . . grasp how wide and long and high and deep is the love of Christ . . . that you may be filled to the measure of all the fullness of God. Ephesians 3:17–19. Send a ruler.

October Harvest

He . . . will enlarge the harvest of your righteousness. You will be made rich in every way so that you can be generous on every occasion . . . II Corinthians 9:10–11. Send a wheat stalk or decorative gourd.

November Thanksgiving

Give thanks to the LORD, for he is good . . . who gives food to every creature. Psalm 136:1, 25. Send a teabag, soup or popcorn packet, small candy.

December Celebration

My lips will shout for joy when I sing praise to you—I, whom you have re-deemed. Psalm 71:23. Send a jingle bell, sheet music of a favorite hymn, or Christmas music tape.

Birthday Wishes

With long life will I satisfy him and show him my salvation. Psalm 91:16. Send a birthday candle or balloon.

Baptismal Birthday

. . . But you were washed, you were sanctified, you were justified in the name of the Lord Jesus Christ and by the Spirit of our God. I Corinthians 6:11. Send a small decorative soap or bath beads.

Anniversary

Two are better than one . . . If one falls down, his friend can help him up . . . Ecclesiastes 4:9a–10a. Send a newspaper front page of the anniversary date, small framed picture of the couple, or gift certificate for dinner or movie rental.

Get Well

He heals the brokenhearted and binds up their wounds. Psalm 147:3. Send a colorful bandage.

I have called you friends . . . Love each other.
John 15:15b,17b

Stay in touch! If corresponding at Christmas is too hectic, send a New Year's letter or Easter cards instead. And include not only news of your family, but also a special memory you have of your friend.

You're Not My Mother
CATHERINE DUERR

Actually most of what I am today I learned from the older women in my life.

Emilie Barnes

I measured sugar and dumped it into the mixing bowl. Then I started pressing the brown sugar into the cup. My mother-in-law, Lynda, finished unloading the dishwasher and got out the cookie sheets. After depositing the brown sugar into the bowl, I went to the refrigerator to get out the margarine and eggs.

Lynda looked in my direction and with a casual tone said, "When my mom was teaching me to cook, she told me to get everything out first and then put it away after I used it. That way it was all put away when I was done."

"Oh, really?" I said. But I thought, *If you want to make all those trips back and forth to the pantry just so you won't have to clean up afterwards, great. But I just want to get these cookies in the oven and I can clean up while they are baking.*

I put the margarine in the microwave so it would soften a little. Lynda picked up the two sugar containers. "Are you done with these?" she asked.

"I was going to sprinkle a little sugar on top of the cookies before I bake them, like my mom does." I answered, feeling a little like my new mother-in-law was trying too hard to be my mother.

She took the brown sugar and put it in the pantry. I thought, *If she wants to do that, it's okay with me.* And I started to cream the sugar.

I was a young newlywed wanting to prove myself. I resented my mother-in-law trying to tell me how to do things, as if I didn't know how to make cookies.

Years have gone by, and it would be hard to say how many times I had to run to the store to get an ingredient in the middle of a recipe, or how many times I forgot something because I skipped over it in the cookbook. Finally I realized that Lynda did have some good ideas. By getting everything out first I would know if I was missing anything before I started.

I also understood that learning from her and tapping into her wisdom would not be dishonoring to my mother, it would actually be prudent for me. Now when I make cookies, I get all the ingredients out first and put them away as I use them. And I sprinkle a little sugar on top before I bake them. This way I end up with cookies that have all the ingredients and have that special little touch at the end.

If you are feeling disgruntled about someone who seems to be telling you how to live your life, could it be that you might learn something from them if you had a teachable spirit? They may not be trying to control you like you think. They may just be thinking they are sharing wisdom.

Listen to advice and accept instruction, and in the end you will be wise.
Proverbs 19:20

Write the page number of frequently used recipes
in the front of the cookbook. Then you can check
the page number and turn right to the directions
without having to search the index.

Those Darn Socks

IRENE CARLONI

*Children are an invaluable gift from God, a treasure
of which we must be careful stewards.*

Charles Stanley

I was at our local woman's club at a monthly meeting and several of us were standing in a group talking. As usual, the topic of conversation centered on our children. We talked about our children from the ages of the terrible two's to teenagers. I popped up with my favorite complaint, doing laundry for my three children. I hated separating and mating socks. Separating clothes didn't seem as bad as matching those darn socks. When you do laundry every four days for three children, you end up with twenty-four socks looking for their mates in three different sizes.

As I finished my complaint, one of the women asked me, "How old are your children?"

"I have two girls, twelve and fourteen, and my son is nine years old." I replied.

The same woman asked me, "You mean you are still doing laundry for the girls?"

"Yes," I said.

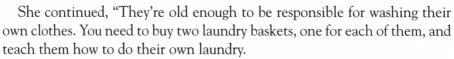
She continued, "They're old enough to be responsible for washing their own clothes. You need to buy two laundry baskets, one for each of them, and teach them how to do their own laundry.

I really had to take time to think this over. If I had the girls do their own laundry, I would have to present it in such a way that the girls would think it was fun, and "grownup." I did buy two laundry baskets and introduced "laundry" to their weekly chores. We spent several weeks learning the different laundry cycles until they understood you don't wash jeans with your best blouse. I had my blessing when I didn't have to separate those darn socks again.

I had a learning experience as well. As I gradually released control of the laundry to the girls, they gained a sense of individuality and responsibility. The Bible is very clear when it tells us to train up a child in the way they should go. Training means giving them responsibility according to their abilities.

Maybe you're doing things for your children that they could be doing. Oh sure, you may have to put up with their complaints in the beginning, but they'll actually feel like you trust them with new responsibilities. And when they're ready to get married, you will have prepared a competent bride for some happy groom, or a helpful husband for some thankful wife.

Train a child in the way he should go,
and when he is old he will not turn from it.
Proverbs 22:6

Baking powder will remove tea or coffee stains
from china pots or cups.

Baby & Everyday-ism

CHRISTINE EUROPA LISTER

To me, every hour of the day and night is an unspeakably perfect miracle.

Walt Whitman

I suffer from everyday-ism. Every day I wake up, take a shower, eat breakfast, take care of the baby, get some work done, maybe run some errands, have some alone time, and wind down for bed. Every day, I launch into a routine that I used to long for during the first few chaotic weeks of my baby's life. I yearned for a sense of order and routine when things wouldn't be so out of control, but now I bemoan the monotony of everyday life. Am I ever satisfied?

I want to look at every day with a sense of freshness, a sense of newness. Yet when I get up in the morning and see that this day looks suspiciously like the one before, I waver in my resolve to embrace the day with thankfulness. I believe God gives us each new day as an opportunity, and yet here I am grumbling that it looks like I'll yet again be going through the motions just to get to the end of the day.

So what can I do to put a twist in my day that shakes me out of the mundane? I can concentrate on the small things I cherish. Like when my baby looks up at me and cracks a wide smile that travels all the way up to her blue-gray eyes. Or when I flirt with her and she belts out baby giggles that warm my heart. And I can allow myself to be fascinated watching this little one develop an awareness of what's around her.

My daughter's sense of discovery reminds me how even the simple things are intriguing. I watch as my infant stares transfixed at her hand as if it were some amazing, mystical thing. I have also learned the value of quality baby time. I chat with her, sing to her, take walks with her, flirt with her and help her develop her muscles with simple exercises.

It comes down to my attitude and how I view each day. I must enjoy these days as my baby's mom. For now, I need to see my everyday-ism as a blessing from God. I can choose to be thankful for that, even if things do get a little redundant sometimes.

Are you thankful for your everyday-isms? Even if it's wrapped in a fog of stress and pressures? Push the fog aside and focus on the joy of simple things, even the mundane. You can live abundantly in the midst of them.

Whatever you do, work at it with all your heart, as working for the Lord, not for men.
Colossians 3:23

Look for something that is a regular occurrence in your day, and open your eyes to how God can use it to bless you unexpectedly.

Notes on Prayer
ELISABETH ELLIOT

Oh, that we would turn eye and heart from everything else and fix them upon this God who hears prayer until the magnificence of His promises and His power and His purpose of love overwhelm us.
Andrew Murray

People who ski, I suppose, are people who happen to like skiing, who have time for skiing, who can afford to ski, and who are good at skiing. Recently I found that I often treat prayer as though it were a sport like skiing—something you do if you like it, something you do in your spare time, something you do if you can afford the trouble, something you do if you're good at it.

Otherwise you do without it most of the time.

But prayer isn't a sport. It's work. As soon as I've said that I'm in trouble because so many sports have become professional and as such are almost wholly indistinguishable from work. I could say that work is something you have to decide to do, you have to allow time for, you have to go at with energy, skill, and concentration. But all those things could be said of the big business which is sports. Competition is deadly, equipment highly technical and expensive, salaries absurdly high.

But prayer is no game. Even if you are part of a "team," as when others join you in prayer, you are not cheered on by spectators or coached by any experts. You won't get any trophies—not on this side of the Jordan, anyway. It's not likely you'll get any credit at all. For some people prayer might fall into the category of "fun," but that's not usually the reason we pray. It's a matter of need and responsibility.

Prayer is work because a Christian simply can't "make a living" without it. He can't live a Christian life at all if he doesn't pray.

For our struggle is not against flesh and blood, but against the rulers, against the authorities, against the powers of this dark world and against the spiritual forces of evil in the heavenly realms.

Ephesians 6:12

To keep track of all your credit cards, place all of them face down on a photocopier and take a picture.

Choosing The Right Rock

JOAN RAWLINS BIGGAR

"Stand strong in God . . .
for after winter, summer comes;
after night, the day returns;
and after a storm, calm is restored."

Thomas á Kempis

A winter storm tossed huge logs high on the beach and left them as a reminder of its fury. Caught in the roots of one log, I found a curiosity which stands now like a wrought-iron sculpture on my window sill. It's a small kelp plant, sinuous stalk and rippling leaves dried black and hard by the sun. It stands erect because its roots are still glued to the same flat rock where it grew, swaying in the currents, until the storm came. The kelp plant had chosen a rock that wasn't solid enough. Though the roots held their grasp, the rock itself was picked up and flung ashore.

Near my home is another rock. Years ago, a sapling took root in a crack in this great glacial boulder. Its roots found nourishment in the soil caught there and descended until they reached the deep soil beneath. Today, a gnarled maple stands firmly on that massive rock. Who knows what storms have tried to destroy it? It picked the right rock to grow on.

We sing, " . . . anchored in the Rock that shall not move." Have we picked the right rock? Friendships fail. Fame is fickle. Fortunes don't satisfy. We can grasp these rocks with all our might, but they will not hold steady in the storms of life. Only one Rock will not move.

The LORD is my rock, my fortress and my deliverer;
my God is my rock, in whom I take refuge . . .

Psalm 18:2a

Next time you're near the water, take time to look closely at the stones and pebbles. Let their beauty and variety remind you of the permanence of God's love for you.

Apple Pie In A Bag

GAYLE CLOUD

Who practices hospitality entertains God himself.
Unknown

You might call my apple pie the chicken soup of desserts. This apple pie, baked in a paper bag (or cooking bag for modern chefs), has a reputation in my family for being "good for what ails you." We've delivered it to neighbors who've been ill and friends in need of cheer. My children, while not happy that others are in need, are happy I'm baking because I seldom bake just one pie. And we've all learned the joy of sharing treasured gifts with others.

PIE CRUST

Cut together:

3 cups flour
1 teaspoon salt
1 heaping cup of Crisco

Mix together:

1 slightly beaten egg
1 tablespoon vinegar
5 tablespoons cold water

Add the liquid to the dry mixture and cut together until dough is easy to handle. Roll out two pie crusts on well-floured board and place in two pie pans.

Paper Bag Apple Pie (1 Pie)

8 MacIntosh apples, cored, peeled, and sliced
2 tablespoons lemon juice
1 teaspoon cinnamon
½ cup granulated sugar

Stir ingredients together.

Crumb Topping
½ cup granulated sugar
½ cup flour
½ cup butter or margarine, softened but not melted

Cut together.

Place apple mixture in crust. Top with crumb mixture. Place pie in a grocery-weight paper bag (or commercial baking bag) inside oven, ensuring the bag does *not* touch the oven walls. Close bag by folding ends together. Bake at 425 for 50–60 minutes—until apples are soft. Remove *carefully* making sure the pie is held securely. The pie is very juicy!

Share with God's people who are in need.
Romans 12:13

Replace the battery in your watch every year
on your birthday. That way you'll always remember.

WINTER segment?

The Lovely, Lowly Lentil

Heather Harlan Bacus

Do what you can, with what you have, where you are.

Theodore Roosevelt

Soup bubbling on the stove holds in its hands an elegant solace. On occasions, hunger pangs may drive me to my cutting board and stock pot, but more often some small child in me demands the steamy comfort of smelling and stirring soup as its cooks. When a chapping winter blast laughs at drifting snow and plummeting wind chills or the budget cries, "No more grocery shopping until pay day," I construct a tasty lentil soup with humble ingredients I'm sure to have on hand.

The lentil is a quicker cooking member of the bean family; it is about the size of a split pea. The lentil comes in a variety of colors with slightly varying tastes, among them are red, brown, and yellow. The red lentil, as you might remember, caused a family rift of biblical proportions, as recorded in the Old Testament.

"Once when Jacob was cooking some stew, Esau came in from the open country, famished. He said to Jacob, 'Quick, let me have some of that red stew! I'm famished!' Jacob replied, 'First sell me your birthright.' 'Look, I am about to die,' Esau said. 'What good is the birthright to me?' But Jacob said, 'Swear to me first.' So he swore an oath to him, selling his birthright to Jacob. Then Jacob gave Esau some bread and some lentil stew. He ate and drank, and then got up and left" (Genesis 25:29–35).

I can't say my variation of a lentil soup recipe my mother gave me is delicious enough to tempt you to sell your birthright. I can say, however, that it is an economical, filling, and healthful dish you can simmer up in about sixty minutes. It can announce to that small child in you (and a hungry family), "Soup's on!"

Smoky Lentil Stew

1 cup lentils
½ cup chopped onions
2 small garlic cloves, minced (or garlic powder)
¼ cup uncooked brown rice (may substitute white rice)
¼ teaspoon oregano
2 or 3 chopped carrots
2 stalks of celery chopped
¼ teaspoon black pepper
4 cups of water
One 8oz. can tomato sauce
One 8oz. can mushrooms, drained (optional)
½ teaspoon liquid smoke (or more to taste)
2 beef bouillon cubes (or use canned beef broth, and decrease water
   accordingly)

If you first soak the lentils, they will cook faster, but that's not necessary.
Bring all ingredients to a boil. Simmer until done—about one hour. Serve
with grated cheese, which is optional.

The combination of legumes, rice, and cheese makes this nutritionally fit
as a main dish.

When it snows, she has no fear for her household . . .
Proverbs 31:21a

Stock your spiritual pantry abundantly with God's Truth
to enable you to survive those inevitable winters of the heart.

Credits

Get Rid Of That Chaff *from* Drumbeat of Love *by Lloyd John Ogilvie, Word, TX,* 1976. [47]

Parents Need to Change, Too! *From* Parents & Teenagers, *edited by Jay Kesler, Victor Books, IL, 1988. Used by permission.* [15]

Groceries and Grace *from* When God Whispers Your Name *by Max Lucado, Word Books, TN, 1994. Used by permission.* [60]

Bless His Heart *from* Only Angels Can Wing It *by Liz Curtis Higgs, Thomas Nelson, TN, 1995. Used by permission.* [223]

Changing Your Mindset, *adapted from* Marriage in the Whirlwind, *by Bill & Pam Farrel, IVP, IL, 1996. Used by permission.* [155]

HMD Labels *from* Who Put the Pizza In the VCR? *By Martha Bolton, Vine (Servant), MI, 1996.* [20]

A Few Well-Chosen Words *from* Promises and Priorities *by H. Norman Wright, Vine Books, MI, 1997.* [83]

Cut Out the Lump! *from* Returning to Your First Love *by Tony Evans, Moody, IL,* 1995. *Used by permission.* [224]

Choosing Who We Are *from* The Gift of Family, *Naomi Rhode, Thomas Nelson, TN, 1991. Used by permission.* [84]

Notes on Prayer, *adapted from* Love Has A Price Tag *by Elisabeth Elliot, Vine Books, MI, 1979.* [290]

Accepting Others *from* Porcupine People, *Lee Ezell, Servant, MI, 1998.* [71]

The Upward Climb *from* A Confident, Dynamic You *by Marie Chapian, Servant,* 1997. [137]

Listening With Your Heart *from* A View From The Porch Swing *by Becky Freeman, Broadman & Holman, TN, 1998. Used by permission.* [141]

Welcome, New Day! *From* It's About Home *by Patsy Clairmont, Vine (Servant), MI, 1998. Used by permission.* [12]

Serenade *adapted from* It's About Home *by Patsy Clairmont, Vine (Servant), MI,* 1998. *Used by permission.* [94]

The Value of A Thank-You Note *adapted from* Talking So People Will Listen, *Florence and Marita Littauer, Vine (Servant), MI, 1998. Used by permission.* [215]

Get Ready For Exciting Prayer *from* How to Pray For Your Children *by Quin Sherrer with Ruthanne Garlock, Regal, CA, 1998).* [144]

Know Your Heavenly Father's Nature *from* I'm Listening, Lord *by Marilyn Willett Heavilin, Thomas Nelson, TN, 1993.* [7]

Dream Big *from* Living Above the Level of Mediocrity *by Charles R. Swindoll, Word, 1987.* [75]

Every Problem Has A Limited Life Span *from* Tough Times Never Last, But Tough People Do *by Robert H. Schuller, Thomas Nelson, TN, 1983.* [218]

Capsules of Marriage Joy *from* Marriage Moments *by David and Claudia Arp, Vine, MI, 1998.* [153]

Find Something To Laugh About *from* Laugh Again *by Charles R. Swindoll, Word, TX, 1991.* [9]

Shake Those Guilty Feelings *from* Mama, Get The Hammer! There's A Fly On Papa's Head! *by Barbara Johnson, Word, 1994. Used by permission.* [77]

Time Wasters *from* Quiet Moments for Working Women, *Mary Whelchel, Vine (Servant), MI, 1999. Used by permission.* [80]

Pull Away To God *from* The Weigh Down Diet *by Gwen Shamlin, Doubleday, 1997, NY.* [220]

Wonderwoman Wannabe *from* Shop, Save and Share *by Ellie Kay, Bethany House Publishers, MN, 1998. Used by permission.* [89]

Tell a Friend *from* From the Heart of a Child, *Dawn Richerson, New Hope Publishers, Birmingham, AL, 1999. Used by permission.* [232]

Perseverance *from* You Hold the Keys to Your Child's Character, *by Lynda Hunter, Servant, 1998. Used by permission.* [211]

Contributors

Nora Lacie Abell lives on and writes from the Colville Confederated Tribes' Reservation in eastern Washington State. Her experiences as health care professional, wife, mother, and tree farmer give her a unique perspective on rural America. Contact: Long Rifle Ranch, Inchelium, WA 99138. [164]

Donna J. Adee, a homemaker from Minneapolis, Kansas, has with her husband, Ellis, written the true story of their son, *God's Special Child—Lessons from Nathan and Other Special Needs Children*. Donna wrote *Miriam's Dilemma* and *The Courtship of Miriam* and the one in process: *Miriam and Timothy Face Life*. [76]

Barbara J. Anson, wife, mother, grandmother, and former dental hygienist speaks and writes with a passion for the practical application of biblical truths as she encourages women in their Christian walk. Contact: 1415 Tom Fowler Dr., Tracy, CA 95376. oanson@pacbell.net. [198]

Marie Asner is a journalist, poet, workshop clinician, church musician and won the Grand Prize in Writing at the 1998 Kansas City Christian Writers Conference. Contact: P.O. Box 4343, Overland Park, KS 66204-0343. Fax: (913) 385-5369. [54]

Heather Harlan Bacus is a professional singer/songwriter, storyteller, and speaker. A mother of two, she has one recording project of mostly original songs for children, "I Want More Balloons." Contact: 1005 W. Lafayette, Jacksonville, IL 62650. (217) 243-4585; bacuslup@csj.net. [295]

Cindy Bailey writes abundant features and columns for the Pittsburgh/Greensburg Tribune-Review and Waynesburg (PA) College. Her devotionals, songs, and photos have appeared in various publications, including *Why Fret That God Stuff?* Contact: R.D.#1, Box 191-B, Waynesburg, PA 15370. (724) 852-2563; cinswind@greeenepa.net. [24, 62]

Esther M. Bailey and her husband Ray keep abundance in their marriage with fun dates on Thursday and Saturday of each week. Contact: 4631 E. Solano Dr. Phoenix, AZ 85018. (602) 840-3143. baileywick@juno.com. [55, 124]

Myrna L. Baldwin is an Education Therapist and Resource Consultant. Her hobbies are poetry, graphic/card design, watercolor painting, and collage. She attended Wesley Theological Seminary's (Washington DC) graduate program in the Arts and Religion. Contact: 64 Belvedere Court, Napa, CA 94559-4141. (707) 257-1676. [110]

Vivian Lee Baniak is a freelance writer and speaker with strong Bible emphasis for Christian women's events. Contact: 7914 Teak Way, Rancho Cucamonga, CA 91730. mmviviandy@integrityonline7.com. [253]

Mildred L. Barger, wife, mother and grandmother, is the author of several books including the novel, *Like Abigail*. She speaks in churches and at Christian Women's Clubs in Arizona. Contact: (602) 863-2231; lbarger@juno.com. [145, 195]

Kacy Barnett-Gramckow also uses the pen name Elizabeth Larson. Some of her writings have appeared in *A Moment A Day* and *The Women's Devotional Bible*. She is married to Jerry and has two sons. Contact: grrjk@pacifier.com. [149]

Margarita Garza de Beck is a freelance writer and also pastors Cristo la Roca, an Hispanic outreach of the church where she and her husband are members. Contact: 58 Denwood Dr., Jackson, TN 38305. margaritabeck@msn.com. [142]

Janie Jerman Bennett is the wife of Crane and mother of six. She teaches a Sunday school class at the Arnold, Missouri, Corps of The Salvation Army. Contact: 2410 Alcarol Drive, Fenton, MO 63026-2225. (314) 861-1201. [150]

Ellen Bergh leads the High Desert Christian Writers Guild, where writers realize their God given dreams. Contact: 3600 Brabham Avenue, Rosamond, CA 93560-689. mastermedia@hughes.net. [78]

Joan Rawlins Biggar, a former teacher, is the author of two series of adventure-mystery books for young people set in the Pacific Northwest. She enjoys nature, kids, and indulging her curiosity through writing. Contact: 4425 Meridian Ave. N, #3 Marysville, WA 98271. [57, 292]

Delores Elaine Bius has sold over 1900 articles and stories in 27 years of writing. She is a widow and speaks at writer's conferences and women's meetings. Contact: 6400 S. Narragansett Ave, Chicago, IL 60638. (773) 586-4384. [238, 244]

Mathew J. Bowyer was initially published in 1972. His first four books are hardbound, non-fiction trade regarding history, mysticism, collecting and investing. He also has three historical novels published electronically (thebookden.com). Contact: 5397 Summit Dr., Fairfax, VA 22030. [261]

Ina Mae Brooks is retired after working as a church secretary and as a program manager for an Independent Living Center. Volunteer work, freelance writing, bird watching, and enjoying her grandchildren occupy most of her time. Contact: imbrooks@talleytech.com. [158]

Jan Brunette is the mother of four, stepmother of seven, and grandmother of twenty. Besides freelance writing, she conducts retreats and remains active in her church with children's and women's ministries. Contact: 2711 Bayview, Eustis, FL 32726. (352) 357-7097. brunette@cde.com. [275]

Jacqueline Cain lives with her husband Tom in Bainbridge Island, Washington. She enjoys writing for children as well as adults, and has been published in a number of religious publications. Contact: Tazpuddpat@aol.com. [97]

Irene Carloni writes short stories, devotionals, newsletters, poems, lyrics, and leads a Bible study. Irene enjoys writing, photography, and crafts. The Carlonis have three children. Contact: 6 Cambridge, Manhattan Beach, CA 90266. aicarloni@earthlink.net. [287]

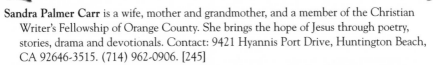

Sandra Palmer Carr is a wife, mother and grandmother, and a member of the Christian Writer's Fellowship of Orange County. She brings the hope of Jesus through poetry, stories, drama and devotionals. Contact: 9421 Hyannis Port Drive, Huntington Beach, CA 92646-3515. (714) 962-0906. [245]

Laraine E. Centineo is a wife, mother, and grandmother. She enjoys writing, painting, reading, and taking walks along the ocean. Her husband recently retired. They thank God for the opportunity to spend more time together. Contact: 2417 Riverside Terrace, Manasquan, NJ 08736. (732) 223-2858. WriterL@aol.com. [165]

Biswita Chaudhuri Mozumdar is an Indian woman writer who has published non-fiction, medical fiction, and travel articles. She is also a magazine columnist. [42]

Jeri Chrysong, a poet and humorist, resides in Huntington Beach, California, with teenaged sons, Luc and Sam. Her work has been featured in newspapers, devotionals, and the *God's Vitamin "C" for the Spirit* series. Jeri enjoys watching her kids participate in sports, and her Pug puppy, "Puddy." [21]

Cathy S. Clark, together with her husband Duane Clark, ministers in music around the world. She is a freelance writer, songwriter, and homeschool teacher to her two children. Contact: P.O. Box 461, Lancaster, CA 93584. duaneclark@qnet.com. [26]

Joan Clayton's sixth book has just been released. She's the Religion Columnist for her local newspaper. Joan and her husband, Emmitt, reside in Portales, New Mexico. Contact: joan@yucca.net. [51]

Doris C. Crandall, an inspirational writer, lives in Amarillo, Texas. She is the co-founder of the Amarillo Chapter of Inspirational Writers Alive!, a group dedicated to Christian writing, Doris devotes much of her time to helping beginning writers hone their skills. [229]

Linda Cutrell is inspired to write on her day set apart with the Lord, where she fasts from the world. Linda has sold articles to *Decision, Joyful Woman, Celebrating Life, Purpose,* and *Expressions.* Contact: 5370 East Forster Ave. Columbus, IN 47201. [209]

Christine R. Davis is mother to 3 sons, writer, full-time secretary and teaches garden/craft classes at Powell Botanical Gardens in Kansas City. She enjoys crafts and tending her flower, herb, and gourd gardens. Contact: crdavis113@aol.com. [13]

Mary J. Davis is an author specializing in Christian Education topics. She has sold many books, including 5 children's journals, now on the market. Mary and her husband Larry reside in Montrose, Iowa, where Mary is a busy housewife, mother, grandmother, writer, and volunteer. [264]

Celeste Duckworth is a CLASS Speaker, author, business woman, wife, mom, and she loves her new grandbaby, Hannah Celese! Contact: 630 N. Brierwood, Rialto, CA 92376. (909) 820-6306. [119]

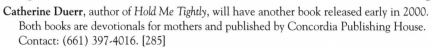

CONTRIBUTORS

Catherine Duerr, author of *Hold Me Tightly*, will have another book released early in 2000. Both books are devotionals for mothers and published by Concordia Publishing House. Contact: (661) 397-4016. [285]

Sylvia Duncan spent half her life as a librarian at St. Louis Public Library. She now teaches, reviews books for *The St. Louis Post Dispatch*, and is a professional storyteller. Contact (314) 353-5815. sylvied@juno.com. [50]

Wendy Dunham is a wife, a "Mom", and a registered therapist for differently-abled children. When she's not playing with her children, gardening, or doing laundry, she can be found at her computer, writing! Contact: 3148 Lake Rd., Brockport, NY 14420. [52, 268]

Gloria H. Dvorak, is a wife and mother of three grown children and grandmom of 6. She has been a religious freelance writer for 10 years and resides in Illinois. [266]

Pamela Enderby, mother of five, teaches Bible studies, mentors women, and leads an evangelistic prayer group. She has been published in books by Kathy Collard Miller (*Why Fret That God Stuff?*) and Lynn Morrissey (*Seasons of a Woman's Heart.*) Contact: enderbyhome@compuserve.com. [230]

Marjorie K. Evans, former school teacher, is a freelance writer of many published articles. She enjoys grandparenting, reading, church work, her Welsh corgi, and orchids. She and Edgar have 2 sons and 5 grandchildren. Contact: 4162 Fireside Cir., Irvine, CA 92604-2216. (949) 551-5296. [256]

Eva Marie Everson is a wife and mother living in Orlando, Florida, where she writes for several ministries and publications. She is the co-author of *Pinches of Salt, Prisms of Light*, and is an active speaker and teacher. Contact: (407) 695-9366. PenNhnd@aol.com. [16, 197]

Jill L. Ferguson, editor, writer, speaker, and businesswoman, lives with her husband and two dogs. Contact: 1615 152nd Avenue SE, Bellevue, WA 98007. (425) 643-0660. jlferg@yahoo.com. [23]

Mary Bahr Fritts, author of *The Memory Box*, *If Nathan Were Here* and 150+ articles, won her 12th award—The Anna Cross Giblin Research Grant from SCBWI. She lives in Colorado Springs with husband, sons, and too many cats. Contact: (719) 630-8244. mmfwriter@aol.com. [216]

Freda Fullerton and husband Jim have three children and four grandchildren. Besides devotionals and poetry, she writes children's stories and adult senior romance. She also likes to read, cook, paint, travel, and teach Sunday school where she has attended church for forty years. [5]

Kimn Swenson Gollnick is a wife, homeschooling mother, and award-winning writer seeking to serve God in real life as well as through words. She's a popular teacher at writers' conferences. Contact: 6314 - 53rd Place N.E., Marysville, WA 98270-9011. http://home1.gte.net/gollnick/. gollnick@gte.net. [121]

Donna Clark Goodrich, freelance writer, editor, and proofreader, is a wife, mother of three, and grandmother of two. She teaches at Christian writers seminars across the U.S. Contact: 648 S. Pima, Mesa, AZ 85210. email:dgood648@aol.com. [123]

Alice King Greenwood is a Bible teacher, poet, song writer, and pianist. She and her husband Morris, retired school teachers, are parents of five children and grandparents of twelve. Contact: 4022 Candy Lane, Odessa, TX 79762. (915) 366-9281. greenwoodsr@earthlink.net. [108, 248]

Suzanne J. Grenier is a freelance writer and an administrative assistant. Contact: 11 Proctor Circle, Peabody, MA. 01960. (978) 531-4150. [105]

Karen Gronvall Larson enjoys life punctuated with smiles. Her inspirational essays have appeared in various publications. Contact: KEGLARS@aol.com. [154]

Linda Harman is Executive Director for the International Pelvic Pain Society and Director of Personnel for OB/GYN South. She holds a Masters Degree in Health Administration. She lives with her husband, Chuck. Contact: 2517 Matzek Road; Birmingham, AL 35226. (205) 979-4501. CHarman888@aol.com. [28]

D. Harrison lives in California with her beloved cat BingoKitty. She has two published poetry books, *Shared Journey* (self published) and *North of the Sky* released April, 1999, Wings of Dawn Publishing Company. Contact: http://members.aol.com/kimilee/DAR/mapdex.htm; HarisonDar@aol.com. [276]

Marilyn J. Hathaway is a retired R.N., community volunteer, and freelance writer of devotionals conveying the message, "Look what God is doing; see what He can do in your life." Contact: 2101 Mariyana Ave., Gallup, MN 87301. (505) 722-9795. [103]

Karen Hayse learns more secrets of God's abundance every day—even amid the stress of balancing her many roles. She loves being a mother, foster mother, pastor's wife, fifth grade teacher, fitness buff, and freelance writer. Contact: KatyKaren@aol.com. [225]

Sarah Healton, Ed.D. is retired. She co-authored *Anytime Craft Series* with her daughter and has articles in *God's Abundance* and *God's Vitamin "C" for the Spirit of Women*. She loves writing, sewing, and gardening. Contact: 6669 Belinda Dr., Riverside, CA 92504. [203]

Sheryl L. Hill has been married nineteen years and is the mother of two teenage daughters. Her writing and speaking career began when friends and family encouraged her to write devotionals from her journals. "The Swing" was written in memory of her grandparents. [128]

Betty Huff writes short devotionals, poems, and true inspirational stories. She has been published in *Angels on Earth*, *Catholic Digest*, and three *God's Vitamin "C" for the Spirit* books. Contact: 10025 El Camino #25, Atascadero, CA. 93422. (805) 461-5619. Bjhuff@thegrid.net. [272]

Dee Hyatt shares her life with her husband, Ted. They are parents of three dogs and two cats. She is currently working on her first novel for children. Contact: 619 Curve Circle, Lancaster, CA 93535. (661) 942-8858; teddee@hughes.net. [162]

Kathy Ide lives in Brea, California, with her husband Rick and two sons, Tom and Mike. She has written magazine articles, Sunday school curriculum, and church playscripts. Kathy has also acted in, directed, and coordinated adult and teen church drama groups. [206]

Pauline Rael Jaramillo is a journalist and freelance writer. Her published works include: research, political issues, profiles and personal experience articles, short stories, one-act plays, and poetry. She is bicultural and bilingual (Spanish/English). Contact: P.O. Box 225, Rimforest, CA 92378. mija100@earthlink.net. [29]

Marilyn Jaskulke is a freelance writer with publications of children's stories and devotionals. Contact: 254 Avenida Madrid, San Clemente, CA 92672. (949) 361-8428. mar68jask@aol.com. [31]

Vickie Jenkins lives with her husband and three children and works as a Medical Assistant for an orthopedic surgeon. Her stories have appeared in *The Daily Oklahoman, The Tribune, Baptist Messenger,* and *Walking Through Open Doors.* Contact: 7921 Duane Drive, Oklahoma City, OK 73132. (405) 728-0706. [32]

Sandra Jensen is a writer and editor as well as co-editor of *Beanie Baby Stories* (Starburst). She also writes for Christian broadcasting, missionary periodicals, and inspirational publications. Contact: 1411 Richman Knoll, Fullerton, CA 92835. RSJensen@earthlink.net. [147, 200]

Jane Tod Jimenez lives with husband, Victor, and two teenagers in Tempe, Arizona. Appreciating life's variety, she has had careers in real estate, accounting, and teaching. When not working, she's either quilting, cooking, or gardening. Contact: jvjimenez@yahoo.com. [67]

Nelda Jones is a grandmother and writer with poetry, devotionals, and articles in several publications, including Starburst books. She is also desktop publisher and editor of her church newsletter. Contact: Rt.1, Box 81, Edgewood, TX 75117. (903) 896-4885. nfjones@vzinet.com. [88]

Veda Boyd Jones is the author of twenty-one books including eight inspirational romances. She and her husband, Jimmie, have three sons and live in the Ozarks of Missouri. [34]

Karen Gronvall Larson enjoys life punctuated with smiles. Her inspirational essays have appeared in various publications. Contact: KEGLARS@aol.com. [154]

Ellie Kay, author of *Shop, Save and Share*, is an international speaker, radio & television veteran, humorist, mother of five, and wife of an Air Force fighter pilot. Contact: Shop, Save & Share Seminars, PO Box 229, Ft. Drum, NY 13603. halfwit5@juno.com. [89]

Lisa L. Keck is a native Californian who resides with her husband and 2 story-starters Kellee, age 6, and Billy, almost 3. She mainly writes for her church devotional. Contact: 920 S. Nutwood #48, Anaheim, CA 92804. [166, 257]

Wilma Kennedy, a polio survivor, has lived in Oregon most of her life and studied at the University of Oregon and Northwest College of the Bible. She and her husband George have four children and four grandchildren. [115]

Helen E. Kesinger is a freelance writer who shares her life experiences through inspirational stories, ideas, and photography. She has written several inspirational romance novels. Contact: 221 Brookside Drive, Paola, KS 66071. (913) 294-2937. kesinger@micoks.net. [91]

Lettie J. Kirkpatrick currently mothers four sons. She also writes and speaks about family, parenting, holidays, and Christian Living. Contact: 373 Charles Circle; Cleveland, TN 37323. Phone and Fax: (423) 479-2063. [132, 175, 176]

Karen Kosman is a wife, mother, grandma, CLASS graduate, and freelance writer. She writes a women's ministry newsletter, articles, devotionals, and Lynn Morrissey's *Seasons of a Women's Heart*. Contact: P.O. Box 1507 La Mirada, CA. 90698. (714) 670-8103 or 991-2855. ComKosman@aol.com. [168]

Tina Krause is a wife, mother of two adult sons, grandmother of Ian James, award-winning newspaper columnist, freelance writer of over 700 columns and magazines articles, and public speaker. Contact: 223 Abington St., Valparaiso, IN 46385. tinak@netnitco.net. [113]

Erma Landis is a wife of 48 years, mother of 6, grandmother of 17, and becoming a first-time great-grandmother in the Fall. Her interests include bird-watching, travelling, photography, and reading. Address: 690 E. Oregon Rd., Lititz, PA 17543. [180]

Faye Landrum is a retired nurse and freelance writer. She has published three books and over a hundred articles in children and adult publications. Contact: 7871 Beecher Road SW, Pataskala, OH 43062-8587. (740) 927-2790; fax: 740-927-2795. FAYELAND@aol.com. [48]

Dr. Muriel Larson, author of 17 books and thousands of published writings and songs, is a professional Christian writer, counselor, and speaker, and has taught at writer's conferences across the nation. Contact: 10 Vanderbilt Circle, Greenville SC 29609. MKLJOY@aol.com. [10, 157]

Janie Lazo is a busy working mom who also homeschools, writes, and assists with her church's music ministry. Contact: 21241 S. Santa Fe Ave., Apt. #3, Long Beach, CA. 90810. [270]

Georgia Curtis Ling is a mom, wife, author and speaker. She lives with her husband, Phil, their son Philip, and his cat, Alice. Contact: 3610 Shore Avenue, Everett, WA 98203. [92]

Christine Europa Lister lives with her husband John and baby daughter, Evniki, in Placentia, California. She has had a passion for writing since childhood and hopes to inspire and encourage her readers. Contact: JCL814@pacbell.net. [289]

Cathy W. Lott, a freelance writer and speaker/singer for women's conferences, is currently working on her third album. She is married and the mother of two fantastic kids. Contact: P.O. Box 72062, Bossier City, LA 71172. (318) 746-2234. [235]

Helen Luecke is an inspirational writer of short stories, articles, and devotionals. She helped organize Inspirational Writers Alive!/Amarillo Chapter. Contact: 2921 S. Dallas, Amarillo, TX 79103. (806) 376-9671. [35, 85]

Marty Magee is a medical transcriptionist who has written for a take-home paper to fill in her empty nest. She and her husband David live miles from their two daughters. Contact: 3051 East Sierra Avenue, Fresno, CA 93710. (559) 325-0456. redwr10104@aol.com. [81]

Ruth E. McDaniel is a Christian writer (published nearly 1,000 items in eight years), full-time caregiver, mother (3), grandmother (8), and co-leader of St. Louis Christian Writer's Group. Contact: 15233 Country Ridge Dr., Chesterfield, MO 63017. [263]

Audrey McIntosh, a retired grandmother, has been deeply involved in children's ministries for many years. In addition to volunteer work, her writing career is a new passion she pursues. She claims she is not retired, just re-fired. [219, 237]

Cathy Messecar freelances and teaches women's Bible classes and retreats. Contact: 20945 FM 2854, Montgomery, TX 77316. (409) 597-4141 or (409) 449-4396. writecat@lcc.net. [240]

Jan McNaught is a minister's wife, grama, and friend. Jan likes home decorating, bargain hunting, crafting, and calligraphy. She enjoys writing and speaking about God's Word, and especially discipling new believers. Contact: P.O. Box 330, Cheney, WA 99004. (509) 235-5572. ejmcnaught@juno.com. [238]

Cathy Messecar freelances and teaches womens' Bible classes and retreats. Contact: 20945 FM 2854, Montgomery, TX 77316. (409) 597-4141 or (409) 449-4396. writecat@lcc.net. [221]

Kathy Collard Miller is a mother, wife, speaker and author of forty books including *Through His Eyes*. She speaks nationally and internationally on viewing life through God's perspective. Contact: PO Box 1058, Placentia, CA 92871. (714) 993-2654. Kathyspeak@aol.com. [36]

Lynn D. Morrissey is the author of *Seasons of a Woman's Heart*, *Treasures of a Woman's Heart*, and a contributing author to numerous bestsellers; CLASSpeaker (specializing in prayer-journaling; women's topics); and vocalist. Contact: PO Box 50101, St. Louis, MO 63105. http://members.primary.net/~lynnswords/. [242]

A. Jeanne Mott, mother and grandmother, works full time as an ESL teacher. She's also a freelance writer of devotionals and inspirational articles. Contact: P.O. Box 550183 Gastonia, NC 28055. ajwrite@ibm.net. [41]

Sherrie Ward Murphree is a Bible teacher, church musician, and freelance writer of inspirational articles and devotionals. Her bachelor's degree is in English and speech. She loves to encourage others. Contact: 1302 E. 52nd, Odessa, TX. 79762. [250]

Elaine F. Navarro is a happy wife, mother and grandmother living in Ventura, California. She graduated with honors from Ventura College last year at the age of 58. Her stories have appeared in other Starburst books. Contact: eldorado@jetlink.net. [44]

Amberly Neese is passionate about Christ. Her humor and enthusiasm have encouraged thousands at various retreats and camps. She ministers in Southern California with her husband of seven years, Scott. Amberly recently received her Master's Degree from Biola University. Contact: (714) 847-3573. [46]

Deborah Nell is a writer, artist and counselor. She lives with her husband Craig and six year-old daughter Sophia. Contact: 735 McAllister St., Hanover, PA 17331. craignell@hotmail.com. [117]

Joy L. Newswanger is a writer, musician, and speaker. She enjoys creatively encouraging women, families, and children. She is a member of the Philadelphia Christian Writer's Fellowship and Toastmasters International. Contact: 4131 Rhoads Road, Kempton, PA 19529. (610) 285-2075. geneandjoy@juno.com. [69]

Doris Hays Northstrom writes for national publications, teaches Creative Writing, and is an inspirational speaker. Other passions are juggling the joys of two families with her new husband Ron, biking, hiking, gardening, and tennis. Contact: 1308 N. Cascade, Tacoma, WA. 98406. (253) 759-9829. [171, 258]

Betty Chapman Plude is a freelance writer and speaker. She is the author of *A Romance With North San Diego County Restaurants*, numerous magazine and newspaper articles, and two newsletters. Contact: 834 Cessna St., Independence, OR 97351. (503) 838-4039. Fax: (503) 838-3239. pludeea@open.org. [99]

Karen Poland is a homemaker and minister's wife living in Corpus Christi, Texas. She and her husband Hugh have 3 daughters, Kayse, Jayme, and Ally. She enjoys reading, writing, and encouraging others. Contact: Kpoland@aol.com. [101]

Janet E. Pratt is a full-time mother, home school educator, and freelance writer. She lives with her husband Ramie and two children, Jacob and Rianne. Contact: 11625 Chesapeake Drive, Reno, NV 89506. (775) 677-2061. JanetPratt@aol.com. [247]

Kathryn Thompson Presley, retired English Professor, has published *Milking Time*, a chapbook of poetry, and numerous short stories. She speaks to women's groups and Elderhostel. Contact: Route 1, Box 312, Somerville, TX 77879. kpresley@myriad.net. [158]

Margaret Primrose is a retired employee of Nazarene Publishing House who was office editor of *Come Ye Apart* magazine. She has authored two children's books, numerous devotionals, poems, and other pieces. [131]

Darren Prince, 24, is part of InnerCHANGE, a missionary community communicating and "incarnating" the Gospel to homeless youth in San Francisco. He enjoys writing poetry, composing songs, and drinking coffee. Contact: 764 Treat Ave., San Francisco, CA 94110. (415) 824-2510. dprince@crmnet.org. [204]

Kendra Prince has been writing Christian drama for ten years. She is very thankful for a Heavenly Father who is the first and foremost Author of creativity. Contact: KPrince697@aol.com. [201]

Lou Ann Prosack is an early retiree from a major corporation and currently writes for a non-profit community newspaper. Contact: 8336 Darkwood Court, Jessup, MD 20794. Fax: (301) 725-5318. louannp@aol.com. [170]

Sharon Raivo Remmen is an author and speaker for Stonecroft Ministries. A former social worker, she also enjoys gardening, music, reading and animals. Contact: 324 Casitas Bulevar, Los Gatos, CA 95032. [126]

Kayleen J. Reusser has published a variety of articles in *Decision, Today's Christian Woman, The Christian Reader, Grit,* and *Business People.* She is married to John and has three children. Contact: 1524 N. Sutton Cir., Bluffton IN 46714. (219) 824-8573. kyreusser@juno.com. [127, 277]

Dawn Richerson is an Atlanta-based writer and author of *From the Heart of a Child: Meditations for Everyday Living,* a collection of devotions based on conversations with her son Luke, available from New Hope Publishers, (www.newhopepubl.com.) Contact (770) 381-7058. dbixrich@aol.com. [232]

Laura Sabin Riley is a wife, mother, author, and passionate speaker. She is the author of *All Mothers Are Working Mothers,* a devotional book for stay-at-home moms (Horizon Books), and numerous short stories. Contact: PO Box 1150, Yuma, AZ 85366. RileysRanch@juno.com. [279]

Joy Anna Rosendale is an executive secretary, the leader of the Single Ladies' Fellowship at her church, and a student at Biola University where she is earning a degree in Organizational Leadership. Contact: joyfullyjoy@earthlink.net. [183, 280]

Suzy Ryan lives in Southern California with her husband and three small children. Her articles have appeared in *Today's Christian Woman, Woman's World, The American Enterprise, Bounce Back Too, Seasons of a Woman's Heart,* and various newspapers. Contact: KenSuzyR@aol.com. [160]

Doris Schuchard is a wife and mother of two children. She enjoys writing children's stories and parenting articles. She recently moved from the Midwest to Atlanta, where she remembers to take the time to keep in touch with friends and family back home.

Camille Schuler lives in Medford, Oregon, with her husband Fritz and their two children, Isabelle and Daniel. Contact: fritzcam@cdsnet.net. [185, 282]

Andi Smith is a freelance writer, worship leader, song writer, piano instructor, and has a teaching degree in music. She desires to inspire others to develop an intimate relationship with the Lord. Contact: 2285 Jasmine Ave. Medford, OR. 97501. (541) 776-3341. [186]

Betty C. Stevens is a freelance writer of devotions. She writes monthly prayer letters for ones praying for a Christian Childcare in Mars, Pennyslvania; and bi-monthly prayer letters for ones in her church praying for a sister church in Pittsburgh. [251]

Ronica Stromberg's work has appeared in five books and several newspapers, corporate newsletters, and magazines. She enjoys writing fiction as well as nonfiction and is active in the Kansas City Christian Writers' Network. [40, 181]

Patty Stump is a wife, mother of two, popular speaker for retreats and special events, writer, Bible study teacher, and Christian counselor. She communicates Biblical truth with humor, insights, and practical application. Contact: P.O. Box 5003, Glendale, AZ 85312. (602) 979-3544. [178, 273]

Lynn Thigpen, formerly a clinical laboratory scientist, is a Christian educator, speaker, and writer residing in Singapore. Her work has been accepted by more than a dozen publications. Lynn has Master's degrees from Southeastern Baptist Theological Seminary and Regent University. [188]

Anita L. van der Elst lives with her husband and four teen to adult children in Orange, California. She contributes to the monthly devotional and directs a drama ministry at her church. She enjoys reading, listening to country music, and emailing her sister. [96]

Marcia Van't Land writes from her wheelchair and is the author of *Living Well With Chronic Illness*. She is available for speaking at women's retreats. Contact: 12648 Ramona, Chino, CA. 91710. (909) 627-2024. [86]

Pat Verbal speaks and writes on behalf of today's kids. She is the founder of "Ministry To Today's Child" and co-authors the *My Family's Prayer Calendar* with Shirley Dobson. Contact: 2836 Summer Brooke Way, Casselburry, FL 32707. (800) 406-1011. MTTC@aol.com. [189]

C. Ellen Watts writes for Christian markets. Author of four books, with two more in progress, this mom to 5 and grandmother to 16 also serves through workshops and as an encourager to fledgling writers. Contact: 702 Alderwood Ln, Nampa, ID 83651-2477. (208) 466-0813. [135]

Mildred Wenger has written many children's stories, and has contributed to several women's devotional books. She gives piano and organ lessons. She and her husband, Daniel, have five grown children. Contact: 1325 Furnace Hill Road, Stevens, PA 17578. [194]

Leslie Whitworth lives on a ranch in the Texas Hill Country. She is a bilingual kindergarten teacher and enjoys kayaking, gardening, and being with her children, Sophie and Ned. Contact: HC16, Box 14, Castell, TX 76831. lesw64@ctesc.net. [191]

Naomi Wiederkehr has had one book published and over 160 articles, devotionals, and book reviews. Her special interest is teaching little children. She worked in libraries for 30 years. Contact: 705 Stucky, Apt. 212, Berne, IN 46711. (210) 589-2445. [173]

Lois A. Witmer is a retired school teacher. She taught for 29 years in elementary, high school, and junior high. She is a member of Willow Street Mennonite Church, a ladies Sunday School teacher, and editor of the quarterly newsletter. [18]

Mary Ellen Wright is a wife, mother of 3 adult children, and grandmother of 4, author, inspirational writer and teacher of how to live the Christian life. Contact: 13605 Scott Avenue, Kearney, MO 64060. (816) 628-5780. Yiya44@aol.com. [129]

Susan Kimmel Wright shares her space with a husband, 3 teenagers, and assorted animals. She's published many articles and a children's mystery series (Herald Press), as well as previous *God's Abundance* contributions. Contact: 221 Fawcett Church Rd, Bridgeville PA 15017. wereallwright@icubed.com. [192, 223]

Leeann S. Yamakawa, devotional writer, poet, vocalist, and avid reader, is involved in discipling hurting women. She lives with her husband Glenn and two daughters, Jeannie and Annie. Contact: 3439 Cambridge Ave., Jackson, MI 49203. (517) 782-6270. [196, 260]

Martha B. Yoder, forced from nursing by post-polio problems, writes for Christian Light Publications, Starburst Publishers, and has nine children's story tapes for Gospel Sunrise, Inc. Contact: 1501 Virginia Avenue, Apt. 159, Harrisonburg, VA 22802. (540) 564-6560. [254]

Denise E. Young belongs to a Christian writers group where she enjoys learning from and encouraging others. "Writing is a wonderful way to glorify God." Contact: 3328 W. Morris Ave., Fresno, CA 93711. Nonnie7260@aol.com. [63]

Doris Sterner Young, retired RN, member of American Christian Writers, who has been published in numerous devotional books, has also facilitated bereavement groups for survivors. Contact 2060 East Cairo Drive, Tempe, AZ 85282. (480) 838-9063. DandGYoung@aol.com. [111]

Karen Johnson Zurheide, MBA-turned-writer, is the author of *Learning with Molly* (Spectacle Lane Press), about lessons of life from a child. She shares about "Upside-Down Parenting" and makes available "7 Suggestions for Surviving the Preschool Years—and Beyond." Contact: (405) 715-0860. Zurheides@aol.com. [65]

Other Books by Starburst Publishers®
(partial listing – full list available upon request)

God's Abundance for Women—*Compiled by Kathy Collard Miller*

Subtitled: Devotions for a More Meaningful Life. Following the success of *God's Abundance*, this book will touch women of all ages as they seek a more meaningful life. Essays from our most beloved Christian authors exemplify how to gain the abundant life that Jesus promised through trusting Him to fulfill our every need. Each story is enhanced with Scripture, quotes, and practical tips providing brief, yet deeply spiritual reading.
(cloth)   ISBN 1892016141   **$19.95**

More God's Abundance—*Compiled by Kathy Collard Miller*

Subtitled: Joyful Devotions for Every Season. Editor Kathy Collard Miller responds to the tremendous success of *God's Abundance* with a fresh collection of stories based on God's Word for a simpler life. Includes stories from our most beloved Christian writers such as: Liz Curtis Higgs and Patsy Clairmont that are combined ideas, tips, quotes, and scripture.
(cloth)   ISBN 1892016133   **$19.95**

God's Abundance—*Edited by Kathy Collard Miller*

Over 100,000 sold! This day-by-day inspirational is a collection of thoughts by leading Christian writers such as Patsy Clairmont, Jill Briscoe, Liz Curtis Higgs, and Naomi Rhode. *God's Abundance* is based on God's Word for a simpler, yet more abundant life. Learn to make all aspects of your life—personal, business, financial, relationships, even housework a "spiritual abundance of simplicity."
(cloth)   ISBN 0914984977   **$19.95**

Promises of God's Abundance—*Edited by Kathy Collard Miller*

Subtitled: *For a More Meaningful Life.* The Bible is filled with God's promises for an abundant life. *Promises of God's Abundance* is written in the same way as the best-selling *God's Abundance*. It will help you discover these promises and show you how simple obedience is the key to an abundant life. Scripture, questions for growth, and a simple thought for the day will guide you to a more meaningful life.
(trade paper) ISBN 0914984-098 **$9.95**

Stories of God's Abundance—*Compiled by Kathy Collard Miller*

Subtitled: for a More Joyful Life . Following the success of *God's Abundance* (100,000 sold), this book is filled with beautiful, inspirational, real life stories of God, Scriptures, and insights that any reader can apply to their daily lives. Renew your faith in life's small miracles and challenge yourself to allow God to lead the way as you find the source of abundant living for all your relationships.
(trade paper)   ISBN 1892016060   **$12.95**

God's Unexpected Blessings—*Edited by Kathy Collard Miller*

Over 50,000 sold! Learn to see the unexpected blessings in life. These individual essays describe experiences that seem negative on the surface but are something God has used for good in our lives or to benefit others. Witness God at work in our lives. Learn to trust God in action. Realize that we always have a choice to learn and benefit from these experiences by letting God prove His promise of turning all things for our good.
(cloth)   ISBN 0914984071   **$18.95**

Why Fret That God Stuff?—*Edited by Kathy Collard Miller*

Subtitled: *Stories of Encouragement to Help You Let Go and Let God Take Control of All Things in Your Life.* Occasionally, we all become overwhelmed by the everyday challenges of our lives: hectic schedules, our loved ones' needs, unexpected expenses, a sagging devotional life. *Why Fret That God Stuff* is the perfect beginning to finding joy and peace for the real world!
(trade paper)   ISBN 0914984-500   **$12.95**

Seasons of a Woman's Heart—*Compiled by Lynn D. Morrissey*

Subtitled: *A Daybook of Stories and Inspiration.* A woman's heart is complex. This daybook of stories, quotes, Scriptures, and daily reflections will inspire and refresh. Christian women share their heart-felt thoughts on Seasons of Faith, Growth, Guidance, Nurturing, and Victory. Including Christian women's writers such as Kay Arthur, Emilie Barnes, Luci Swindoll, Jill Briscoe, Florence Littauer, and Gigi Graham Tchividjian.
(cloth)   ISBN 1892016036   **$18.95**

The *God's Word for the Biblically-Inept*™ series is already a best-seller with over 100,000 books sold! Designed to make reading the Bible easy, educational, and fun! This series of verse-by-verse Bible studies, Topical Studies, and Overviews mixes scholarly information from experts with helpful icons, illustrations, sidebars, and time lines. It's the Bible made easy!

The Bible—God's Word for the Biblically-Inept™

An excellent book to start leaning the entire Bible. Get the basics or the in-depth information you are seeking with this user-friendly overview. From Creation to Christ to the Millenium, learning the Bible has never been easier.
(trade paper) ISBN 0914984551 **$16.95**

Revelation—God's Word for the Biblically-Inept™—*Daymond R. Duck*

End-time Bible Prophecy, expert Daymond Duck leads us verse-by-verse through one of the Bible's most confusing books. Follow the experts as they forge their way through the captivating prophecies of Revelation!
(trade paper)   ISBN 0914984985   **$16.95**

Daniel—God's Word for the Biblically-Inept™—*Daymond R. Duck*

Daniel is a book of prophecy and the key to understanding the mysteries of the Tribulation and End-Time events. This verse-by-verse commentary combines humor and scholasticism to get at the essentials of Scripture. Perfect for those who want to know the truth about the Antichrist.
(trade paper) ISBN 0914984489 **$16.95**

Health and Nutrition—God's Word for the Biblically-Inept™—*Kathleen O'Bannon Baldinger*

The Bible is full of God's rules for good health! Kathleen Baldinger reveals scientific evidence that proves the diet and health principles outlined in the Bible are the best for total health. Learn about the Bible Diet, the food pyramid and fruits and vegetables from the Bible! Experts include: Pamela Smith, Julian Whitaker, Kenneth Cooper, and TD Jakes.
(trade paper) ISBN 0914984055 **$16.95**

Men of the Bible—God's Word for the Biblically-Inept™—*D. Larry Miller*

Benefit from the life experiences of the powerful men of the Bible! Learn how the inspirational struggles of men such as Moses, Daniel, Paul, and David parallel the struggles of today's man. It will inspire and build Christian character for any reader.
(trade paper)   ISBN 1892016079   **$16.95**

Women of the Bible—God's Word for the Biblically-Inept™—*Kathy Collard Miller*

Finally, a Bible perspective just for women! Gain valuable insight from the successes and struggles of such women as Eve, Esther, Mary, Sarah, and Rebekah. Interesting icons like: Get Close to God, Build Your Spirit and Grow Your Marriage will make incorporating God's Word into your daily life easy.
(trade paper)   ISBN 0914984063   **$16.95**

What's in the Bible for™ Women—*Georgia Curtis Ling*

What does the Bible have to say to women? Find out in the second release from the **What's in the Bible for . . .**™ series. Women of all ages will find Biblical insight on the topics that are meaningful to them in six simple sections including: Faith, Family, Friends, Fellowship, Freedom, and Femininity. From the editors of the *God's Word for the Biblically-Inept*™ series, this book also uses illustrations, bullet points, chapter summaries, and icons to make understanding God's Word easier than ever!
(trade paper)   ISBN 1-892016-11-7   **$16.95**

The Weekly Feeder—*Cori Kirkpatrick*

Subtitled: A Revolutionary Shopping, Cooking and Meal Planning System. The Weekly Feeder is a revolutionary meal planning system that will make preparing home-cooked dinners more convenient than ever. At the beginning of each week, simply choose one of the eight pre-planned weekly menus, tear-out the corresponding grocery list, do your shopping and whip up a great meal in less than 45 minutes! The author's household management tips, equipment checklists, and nutrition information make this system a must-have for any busy family. Also included with every recipe is a personal anecdote from the author emphasizing the importance of good food, a healthy family, and a well-balanced life.
(trade paper)   ISBN 1892016095   **$16.95**

God Stories—*Donna I. Douglas*

Subtitled: They're So Amazing, Only God Could Make Them Happen. Famous individuals share their personal, true-life experiences with God in this beautiful new book! Find out how God has touched the lives of top recording artists, professional athletes and other newsmakers such as: Jessi Colter, Deana Carter, Ben Vereen, Stephanie Zimbalist, Cindy Morgan, Sheila E., Joe Jacoby, Cheryl Landon, Brett Butler, Clifton Taulbert, Babbie Mason, Michael Medved, Sandi Patty, Charlie Daniels and more! Their stories are intimate, poignant, and sure to inspire and motivate you as you listen for God's message in your own life!
(cloth)   ISBN 1892016117   **$18.95**

Since Life Isn't A Game, These Are God's Rules—*Kathy Collard Miller*

Subtitled: Finding Joy & Happiness in God's Ten Commandments. We often hear life being referred to as a *game*, but we know this is not really true. In life there is only one set of rules and those are God's. God gave us the Ten Commandments for our good - to protect and guide us. In this book, Kathy Collard Miller explains the meaning of each of the Ten Commandments and illustrates how they are relevant in today's life. Each chapter includes Scripture and quotes from some of our most beloved Christian authors including Billy Graham, Patsy Clairmont, Liz Curtis Higgs, and more! Sure to renew your understanding of God's rules.

(cloth)   ISBN 189201615X $16.95

More of Him, Less of Me—*Jan Christensen*

Subtitled: *A Daybook of My Personal Insights, Inspirations & Meditations on the Weigh Down™ Diet.* The insight shared in this year-long daybook of inspiration will encourage you on your weight-loss journey, bring you to a deeper relationship with God, and help you improve any facet of your life. Each page includes an essay, Scripture, and a tip-of-the-day that will encourage and uplift you as you trust God to help you achieve your proper weight. Perfect companion guide for anyone on the Weigh Down™ diet!

(cloth)   ISBN 1892016001   **$17.95**

Desert Morsels—*Jan Christiansen*

A Journal with Encouraging Tidbits from My Journey on the Weigh Down™ Diet. When Jan Christiansen set out to lose weight on the Weigh Down™ Diet she got more than she bargained for! In addition to *losing* over 35 pounds and *gaining* a closer relationship with God, Jan discovered a gift—her ability to entertain and comfort fellow dieters! Jan's inspiring website led to the release of her best-selling first book, *More of Him, Less of Me.* Now, Jan serves another helping of *her* wit and *His* wisdom in this lovely companion journal. Includes inspiring Scripture, insightful comments, stories from readers, room for the reader's personal reflection and **P**lenty of **Attitude** (p-attitude).

(cloth)   ISBN 1892016214   **$16.95**

Purchasing Information:
www.starburstpublishers.com

Books are available from your favorite bookstore, either from current stock or special order. To assist bookstore in locating your selection be sure to give title, author, and ISBN #. If unable to purchase from the bookstore you may order direct from STARBURST PUBLISHERS. When ordering enclose full payment plus shipping and handling as follows: Post Office (4th Class)—$3.00 (Up to $20.00), $4.00 ($20.01-$50.00), 8% ($50.01 and Up); UPS—$4.50 (Up to $20.00), $6.00 ($20.01-$50.00), 12% ($50.01 and Up); Canada—$5.00 (Up to $35.00), 15% ($35.01 and Up); Overseas (Surface)—$5.00 (Up to $25.00), 20% ($25.01 and Up). Payment in U.S. Funds only. Please allow two to three weeks minimum (longer overseas) for delivery. Make checks payable to and mail to: STARBURST PUBLISHERS, P.O. Box 4123, LANCASTER, PA 17604. Credit card orders may also be placed by calling 1-800-441-1456 (credit card orders only), Mon-Fri, 8:30 a.m. to 5:30 p.m. Eastern Standard Time. Prices subject to change without notice. Catalog available for a 9 x 12 self-addressed envelope with 4 first-class stamps.